Randall Thompson

Randall Thompson, 1949. Photo courtesy of E. C. Schirmer Music Company, Boston.

RANDALL THOMPSON
A Bio-Bibliography

Caroline Cepin Benser
and
David Francis Urrows

Bio-Bibliographies in Music, Number 38
Donald L. Hixon, Series Adviser

GREENWOOD PRESS
New York • Westport, Connecticut • London

Library of Congress Cataloging-in-Publication Data

Benser, Caroline Cepin.
   Randall Thompson : a bio-bibliography / Caroline Cepin Benser and
David Francis Urrows.
     p. cm.—(Bio-bibliographies in music, ISSN 0742-6968 ; no. 38)
   Includes discographies and index.
   ISBN 0-313-25521-0 (alk. paper)
   1. Thompson, Randall, 1899- —Bibliography. 2. Thompson,
Randall, 1899- —Discography. I. Urrows, David Francis.
II. Title. III. Series.
ML134.T42B46 1991
016.78′092—dc20
[B]   90-29279

British Library Cataloguing in Publication Data is available.

91 00004301

Library of Congress Catalog Card Number: 90-29279
ISBN: 0-313-25521-0
ISSN: 0742-6968

First published in 1991

Greenwood Press, 88 Post Road West, Westport, CT 06881
An imprint of Greenwood Publishing Group, Inc.

Printed in the United States of America

∞

The paper used in this book complies with the
Permanent Paper Standard issued by the National
Information Standards Organization (Z39.48-1984).

10 9 8 7 6 5 4 3 2 1

*ML
134
.T42
B46
1991*

Copyright Acknowledgments

The author and publisher gratefully acknowledge permission from the following:
   The Wellesley College Archives and the *Wellesley College News* for quotations from various
items and articles.
   The Oral History Collection (#9800-OH-12), Manuscripts Division, Special Collections
Department, University of Virginia Library, for quotations from the oral history interview of
Randall Thompson.
   Andrew L. Pincus, for quotations that appeared in the *Eagle* and in *Scenes From Tanglewood,*
© 1989 by Northwestern University Press.
   Columbia University, Oral History Research Office, for quotations from interviews with Robert
Lester and Otto Luening.
   Hildegard Stanley and the Southwestern Baptist Theological Seminary, for a quotation from
"The Major Choral Works of Randall Thompson with Particular Emphasis on the Analyses of
the 'Testament' of 'Freedom,'" a master's thesis written in partial fulfillment of the
requirements for the degree of Master of Church Music from Southwestern Baptist Theological
Seminary, School of Church Music, James McKinney, Dean.
   National Public Radio, for excerpts from an NPR news report that aired on October 23, 1983,
during the Morning Edition with Bob Edwards.
   The Houghton Library, Harvard University, for quotations from manuscripts by George
Herbert Palmer and Randall Thompson. By permission of the Houghton Library.
   E. C. Schirmer Music Company, for permission to use a photograph of Randall Thompson.

Contents

Acknowledgments

For granting permission to use materials in the bibliographies, works list, and discography, the following are thanked:

Harvard University: Rodney G. Dennis, Curator of Musical Manuscripts, Houghton Library; Kathleen A. Markees, Curatorial Associate, Harvard University Archives; Robert Strider, President, Harvard Glee Club Foundation; Elliot Forbes, Professor Emeritus of Music

University of Virginia: Diane Parr Walker, Music Librarian; Alderman Library-Michael Plunkett, Curator of Manuscripts/University Archivist; Lynda Fuller Clendenning, Public Services Assistant; Laura A. Endicott, Public Services Assistant

University of California, Berkeley: Steve Repasky, Music Reference Librarian; Keith Stetson, Administrative Assistant/Music Library; William M. Roberts, University Archivist

University of Alabama: Larry Harbin, Acting Head of Reference; Charlene Shorts, Reference Librarian; Interlibrary Loan Staff-Eloise Griffin; Rosetta Royale; Angela Wright; and my friend Charles E. Brewer, Assistant Professor of Music

Wellesley College: Margaret Clapp Library-Wilma R. Slaight, Archivist; Carla Stewart, Archives Assistant

Boston University: Mugar Memorial Library-the late Frank Gramenz, Head of Music Library

Curtis Institute of Music: Kenton T. Meyer, Assistant Librarian

Emory and Henry College: Marianne Grzywacz, Chair of Music
Department

University of Pennsylvania: Maryellen C. Kaminsky, Archival
Specialist

Eastman School of Music: Sibley Music Library-Mary Rame,
Assistant in Rare Books/Special Collections

University of Iowa: Rita Benton Music Library-Elaine B.
Bradshaw, Library Assistant

Brewton-Parker College: Hildegard Jo Stanley, Music
Department

Elizabethtown College: Carl N. Shull, Chair of Department of
Fine and Performing Arts

Southern Methodist University: Library-Robert Skinner

American Academy and Institute of Arts and Letters: Nancy
Johnson, Librarian

Library of Congress: Music Division-Robin Sheets, Music
Specialist

Pierpont Morgan Library: Fredric Woodbridge Wilson

Columbia University in the City of New York: Butler Library-
Oral History Research Office, Mary Marshall Clark

E. C. Schirmer: William Thorpe

Carl Fischer, Inc.: Serious Music Department-Patrick S.
McCarty, Administrative Assistant

King's Chapel, Boston: Daniel Pinkham, Director of Music

Worcester Art Museum: Donna Winant, Library Assistant

Bay Cities Music: Bruce Kimmel; Alain Silver; John Proffitt

National Public Radio: Marion C. Pierce, Paralegal

The Cleveland Orchestra: my long-time friend Charles E.
Calmer, Director of Educational Activities

Jacques Barzun; Alan G. Green; Mai Kelton; Andrew L. Pincus

Caroline Cepin Benser

Preface

When Randall Thompson died in 1984 America lost one of its most distinguished musicians. Apparent was the lack of an assessment of his varied contributions to our musical life in the context of his contemporary generation. In developing a picture of the composer of the world-famous <u>Alleluia</u> and in attempting to formulate the right questions in order to discover the underlying reasons for his being relegated in some sense to the sidelines of mainstream composition, I found an eloquent spokesman for Thompson in his student and amanuensis.

My sincere thanks go to David Francis Urrows: first, for his acceptance of my challenge to write Thompson's biography from his post in Hong Kong, and secondly for the pleasure of our harmonious collaboration. His generous contribution of time and attention to detail are in evidence throughout the volume.

Hopefully, both annotated bibliographies will, along with the biography, bring into focus Thompson's often-obscured, but multi-faceted musical face, and that an exploration of his catalog of compositions will keep alive the admiration long shown toward his choral works and will further spark a renewed interest in those works that have been too long unperformed.

And, finally, I cannot overlook expressing my special thanks to my husband, Jerry Benser, who made the original suggestion for this study and for his continued interest and support.

Caroline Cepin Benser
Tuscaloosa, Alabama

To decide what to include in a monograph of the present length is to encounter an eternal, irresolvable problem that has always confronted authors. Samuel Johnson expressed this dilemma when he wrote: "It is impossible for an expositor not to write too little for some, and too much for others . . . how long soever he may deliberate, [he] will at last explain many lines which the learned will think impossible to be mistaken, and omit many for which the ignorant will want his help. . . ." If anything has simplified my task in formulating a concise biographical sketch of a man who was my friend and mentor for far too brief a space of time, it has been the present dearth of information about him available anywhere in the literature. Randall Thompson is surely the most frequently performed and least written about American composer of the twentieth century, and, in critic Richard Dyer's phrase, a composer more often performed than honored.

A number of people deserve to be thanked for assisting me with this work: First, Caroline Benser, for inviting me to collaborate with her, and for respecting my own continuing work on a larger and more comprehensive volume on Thompson; the faculty Research Committee of Hong Kong Baptist College for underwriting a large part of the cost of the research and granting me time away from the College to prepare the final draft; Debi Osnowitz and Clare McKeown, for extracting my files from storage and sending them from New England to Asia; and many mutual colleagues and friends, among them Elliot Forbes and Mason Hammond (Harvard), Alfred Mann (Eastman), Rodney G. Dennis (Houghton Library), Robert Schunemann and William Thorpe (E. C. Schirmer), Lucilla Marino (American Academy in Rome), E. S. Whitney Thompson and the Thompson family, and "some . . . which have no memorial," whose indulgence I must ask on account of space.

David Francis Urrows
Hong Kong and Cambridge, Massachusetts

Randall Thompson

Biography

Introduction

Randall Thompson was born in New York in the penultimate year
of the nineteenth century, and died in Boston eighty-five
years later. Between those dates, he composed the single
most popular piece of American choral music, Alleluia (1940),
and established himself as the primary American figure in the
world-wide renaissance of choral composition and performance
to which the twentieth century has been witness. This is a
biographical study of the life of the man behind these dates
and these widely performed choral works. It seeks to
emphasize that Thompson's smaller and less well-known body of
instrumental pieces are of equal importance in his oeuvre,
drawn as they are from the same well of imagination.

To the extent that the texts he selected for his vocal
compositions are a part of the literary culture of America,
he can be seen as a Nationalist, a composer in the American
genre. Indeed, to some critics, he so much took on the
coloration of his surroundings, that he was seen, glibly, as
the 'Norman Rockwell of American music.' But while he
occasionally set American texts (and the majority of his
texts were taken from the Bible and British poets) he brought
to his art a background enriched with European sensibilities
and skills. He spoke and read French, German, Italian,
Spanish, and Latin. He spent three crucial, formative years
at the American Academy in Rome. He was twice a Guggenheim
Fellow. Much of his music was composed in Switzerland, and
for a time he planned to become a permanent resident. He was
created 'Cavalieri ufficiale al merito della Repubblica' by
the Italian government. He saw, however, nothing incongruous
in being made an honorary Kentucky Colonel. He was no more
merely an American composer than the author of Hamlet and
Macbeth was merely an English playwright.

While much of his vocal and instrumental music was
inspired or even modeled on traditional or vernacular forms,
he was never a 'folksong' composer. There is not a single

instance of traditional melody in any of his original works.
He was too gifted a melodist to need to resort to the tunes
of others, and he saw the pitfalls of a language based on
adoption rather than invention. Nevertheless, he was deeply
interested in things indigenously (that is, socially rather
than politically) American: the traditional shape-note
hymnody of the southern states, spirituals, dance tunes, and
ragtime and jazz. He was a great Duke Ellington fan. His
gifts did not often call upon him to work in a purely instrumental medium, but at his best he wrote with wit and verve in
works like the Suite for oboe, clarinet, and viola (1940),
and the Second String Quartet (1967). His three symphonies
show what a master orchestrator he could be: the first
(1929), a youthful work combining the post-impressionist
éclat he absorbed from his teachers Bloch and Malipiero with
the clarity of contrapuntal logic which always characterized
his work, the second (1931) a tautly constructed, neo-classic
symphony with strong jazz/ragtime influences, and the much-
neglected third (1947, his finest), an elegiac post-war piece
that ranks with the third symphonies of Harris and Copland in
terms of formal and melodic inspiration. His surprisingly
small output for solo voice accurately reflects the fact that
art-song and piano writing were not his strong points. He
wrote, however, vast amounts of light music for private
productions at his Boston club. This music shows a keen and
unfailing sense of parody, and a polish which 'real' popular
music never achieves.

Despite this full and rewarding creative life, it will
probably be as an academic and educator that Thompson will be
remembered, and this is curious and paradoxical. He had few
students who achieved fame as composers (Leonard Bernstein
nominally studied with him at the Curtis Institute), and he
tended to teach only the 'strict forms,' such as counterpoint, fugue, choral composition, and orchestration. Not
surprisingly, his most successful students were generally
musicologists. After World War Two, the focus of activity in
contemporary music in America shifted from conservatory and
concert hall into universities, partially through major
changes in government funding and policy, and partially
through the work of people like Thompson, who had an
unshakable belief in the supremacy of the liberal arts
education, and an equally negative and dim view of the
conservatories' 'manual training.' Thompson, for example,
spent a disproportionate amount of time and effort trying to
keep merely practical studies, such as instrumental lessons
and membership in performing organizations, from counting as
academic credit for college students. He was, in this,
distancing himself from his one-time friend and later
adjudged enemy, Howard Hanson (this dislike was largely one-
sided and paranoid on Thompson's part), whose Eastman School
of Music was, from Thompson's viewpoint, at the other end of

the spectrum of academic philosophy. What Thompson failed to
realize was that his very own music was appreciated far more
in quarters where music making was a priority than in the
universities of post-War America, where the grip of the
serial and atonal schools was gradually choking to death what
little remained of the audience/composer relationship. Like
many of his colleagues, Thompson the composer was swiftly
felled by the axe wielded by (among others) Pierre Boulez,
who declared in his famous manifesto of the 1950s, all non-
serial composers to be 'superfluous.'

Beginning with his book College Music, which he compiled
in the early 1930s for the Association of American Colleges,
Thompson was influential in creating the basic blueprint for
the way in which music is today integrated into the liberal
arts curriculum of most tertiary institutions in America.
Hanson also served on the committee that published the book,
and disagreed with Thompson's recommendations in printed
rebuttals at the end of each chapter. Like so many other
composers of his years, Hanson included, Thompson the
composer evaporated from the scene after 1945, and never
really knew why. There is something tragic in seeing how his
educational philosophy helped to engineer his own eclipse
after such a brilliant beginning. There was no room in the
hyper-intellectual world of academia that produced the 'Who
cares if you listen?' attitude for the composer of Pueri
Hebraeorum. He was too emotional, and he wrote tonal music.
Had he lived another ten years, he might have seen how a new
generation of composers has broken away from academe, and
taken affairs into its own hands, to change for the better
the lamentable relationship between listeners and composers
that has existed concurrently with the Cold War Era. It
would have heartened Thompson to see the music of his
contemporaries reassessed in light of the changes which have
swept through American serious contemporary music in the past
decade. Capax imperii nisi imperasset. He would have been a
more successful composer if he had not felt he had a mission
to reform music education and thereby ensure that, for many
years, there was no room for his own lyric, romantic voice in
the forum in which he worked, and in which he desperately
wanted to be acclaimed. His music, so widely performed on
the 'community level,' in schools, churches, civic choruses,
and amateur ensembles, suffered in the court of fashionable,
academic opinion just because it was seen as populist and
accessible. This is why he has been compared--unfairly,
carelessly compared--with Norman Rockwell. The story of his
life is tangential to all the major figures and movements of
American music history of the first half of the twentieth
century, and makes an absorbing document to write, and it is
my hope, to read.

Childhood and Youth: 1899-1916

[Ira] Randall Thompson was born in New York City on 21 April 1899, the second of three sons of Daniel Varney Thompson and Grace Brightman Randall. His Christian name, Ira, derived from an uncle on his mother's side of the family. His great-great-grandfather emigrated from Scotland to Antrim, New Hampshire around the time of the Revolutionary War, and from venerable stock of old New England families came Ira Randall.

Daniel Varney Thompson (1867-1932) was an English teacher and an editor of anthologies of poetry for school use. He taught at the Lawrenceville School in New Jersey from 1904 to 1920, and it was in Lawrenceville that Ran or Rannie, as he was variously known, grew up. The Thompsons were house parents at one of the residential dormitories in the school, and a relaxed, intellectual environment in pleasant surroundings suited Ran, a somewhat slight boy with cherubic features and distant blue eyes. Bertrand H. Bronson (1902-1986), who was the son of the German teacher at Lawrenceville, became his friend at an early age. Their friendship with each other lasted through seven decades, although they both moved to very different kinds of musical careers.

His earliest musical training was from an elderly spinster, a certain Miss Harris, who had some functionary role at Lawrenceville. This was perhaps when he was four or five years old. As a reward for practicing his lessons, she would give him a picture of a famous composer. He recounted in his old age that he practiced not because he was interested in the music, but "because I was mad to have that picture each week."[1] The lessons, it seems, went nowhere.

The Thompson family spent the summers of the first decade of the twentieth century in the small village of Vienna, Maine, twenty-five miles north of Augusta, on a subsistence farm on a mountainside four miles from the town center. This farm had been in the Thompson family since the time of the Civil War. Here, in the evening, the family and their frequent guests and relations would gather around an old broken-down melodeon for songs and stories. Especially popular were traditional Scottish songs (though mostly of the ersatz Robert Burns type), sung by Ran's father and which were Ran's first introduction to traditional music of the kind which would be so important to him in later life.

Here in Vienna (pronounced Vy-EN-ee) Ran began to learn to play the organ--actually a so-called 'vestry organ' (reed harmonium)--with help from his affectionately styled 'Aunt'

Marietta Eaton (1856-1946).   In 1909, Ran was left with Mrs.
Eaton for a few weeks, during which time she taught him the
rudiments of music notation.   He practiced playing hymns on
the organ in her parlor, while Aunt Eaton corrected his
mistakes by shouting from the kitchen.   Later that summer,
due to his progress, and the deteriorating condition of the
melodeon,

> One night my father arrived at midnight, having bought
> a piano en route.   We had nothing but a pedal-pump
> organ [i.e., the melodeon] before that, and I was
> thrilled when my father produced this old-fashioned
> square piano. [2]

In the fall of 1911, Ran entered the Lawrenceville School,
where he began to study piano and organ with the school
organist, Francis Cuyler van Dyck, Jr. (1873-1916).   Van Dyck
was also the mathematics teacher at Lawrenceville, but
Thompson remained impressed with his musicianship: in later
life he frequently remarked "I never heard him play a wrong
note."   Van Dyck seems to have given him some lessons in
harmony and counterpoint as well, and gave to his pupil a
transient taste for French music of the Franck-Vierne-
Boellmann-Widor sort.   He was also something of a composer.
Thompson kept one of his anthems, "The Lord Reigneth," for
mixed voices and organ, in his files for his entire life, and
performed more of his music at Wellesley in the 1920s.

In March 1915, van Dyck fell seriously ill with a lung
infection, and Ran filled in as school organist during his
senior year at Lawrenceville, for which he was paid a total
of $150.   His earliest known compositions date from this
time.   During the summer of 1915, Ran was sent to Akron,
Ohio, where he had secured a summer job working for the
Goodyear Rubber Company (probably as a clerk, at $50 a
month).   He had access to a piano in his rooms in Akron, and
as his mother's diaries from the following fall report, he
composed a piano sonata that was performed back in
Lawrencevile the following December, "receiving favorable
criticism."   It has not survived.   In 1915 he also composed a
part-song for Christmas, As of old, for which he also wrote
the words, and had it printed as a Christmas Card at his own
expense.   His mother noted in her diary on New Year's Eve,
"Many kind notes & words re: his carol."   A hymn for the
Lawrenceville Hymnal (Anniversary, # 276) also survives, but
an organ work In Memoriam, F. C. van Dyck, Jr. is lost. [3]

In Akron, Ran seems also to have made friends with a group
of boys who fired his imagination about a career as a
musician, and who convinced him that Harvard was the ideal
place to pursue his studies.   At home his parents were cir-
cumspect: "Ran crazy to go to Harvard," noted his mother in

mid-September of 1915, "and trying to arrange for it." They felt, understandably, that music would be a good avocation, but hardly a profession. Then there was the family loyalty to Williams College, which a son at Harvard would shake. In the end his father told him, "Well, Ran, I think it's entirely up to you." He lost no time in applying, and was accepted.

The Cosmopole: Cambridge and New York: 1916-1922

At the time of Randall's arrival in September of 1916, the Department of Music at Harvard, then under the guidance of Walter Raymond Spalding (1865-1962), had a compact curriculum. This was largely the invention and bequest of John Knowles Paine (1839-1906), and was a fair representative of musical liberal arts training of its time. Requiring study in theory and composition, with literature (history) an elective area, it also had a pronounced French accent. This is not surprising: Spalding had studied with Widor, as had Edward Burlingame Hill (1872-1960), Archibald T. ('Doc') Davison (1883-1961), and William Clifford Heilman (1877-1947), the core of the department faculty. Heilman and Spalding had studied with Joseph Rheinberger (1839-1901). Hill would later write a significant early book on the Modern French School, and did much to promote the music of the Impressionist/Symbolist composers in America. All four men were also active composers at the time. The courses offered covered music from the sixteenth century (Palestrina) to the then-present (Debussy), and differed significantly from conservatory training in that performance was regarded as something between an extra-curricular and leisure activity. It was assumed that all students being musicians, were, de facto, performers. Consequently no credit was offered for performance, a view of music education which stayed with Randall.

Randall auditioned for the Harvard Glee Club, but was turned down by Davison.[4]   He was able to take part in informal singing sessions which Davison organized, and here had undoubtedly an opportunity to sing more interesting repertoire than he would have had in the Glee Club. The seeds of his quickly developed Italophilia may have been sown here, in his singing early modern editions (which in those days were hard to come by) of the works of Palestrina and Monteverdi. He studied Italian and, becoming quite proficient, went so far as to translate for his own amusement and that of his friends the text of Gibbons' madrigal The Silver Swan into Italian, a sort of parody of a parody.

He was not a model student at Harvard, so involved was he

in musical pursuits, and was placed on academic warning for poor marks in his junior year (though this may have been complicated by his naval enlistment). He spent a great deal of his time writing music and practicing the piano, as he began to take piano lessons with Frances L. Grover, a widely traveled and cultured woman, with whom he maintained contact into the 1970s. Under Grover's guidance he developed into a fine performer, and had at least the technical ability to handle a work like César Franck's Symphonic Variations, which he admired considerably even in old age, though perhaps then only for sentimental reasons.

Harvard at this time was especially strong in the area of philosophy; and particularly close to Thompson was George Herbert Palmer (1842-1933), Alford Professor emeritus. Palmer had retired in 1913 but maintained a residence in the Yard, and was a fixture of campus life. His field, ethics and moral reason, and the strength of his views deeply impressed Randall. In part, Palmer held that neither individual conscience nor the pursuit of individuality were in themselves sufficient to validate art, life, or any area of human endeavor. Only the individual working within a society, utilizing his individuality to correct and ensure the harmonious working of the system, was following the correct moral course. "Ally your labor with an institution" was his motto. The course of Randall's life played out Palmer's ethical scenario with remarkable loyalty and precision.[5]

A significant friendship made in these Harvard years was with Leopold Damrosch Mannes (1899-1964). An earthy foil for Thompson's young and patrician outlook, this dark, troubled, and now all-but-forgotten figure in the history of American music became his confidant in all matters that young men must have confessors for. Mannes, better known for the Mannes School of Music, founded by his parents David and Clara Mannes, and known for his significant inventions and patents in the field of color photography, was also a composer and an exceptional pianist as well. Thompson encountered him, when the Harvard Music Club sent him down to audition the younger man for membership. Mannes matriculated in 1917, although he graduated with Thompson in 1920. In early 1918, Thompson and Mannes went to a wartime rally on Boston Common, and happened to hear a band playing one of the popular tunes of the day, the Indianola fox-trot. Later that spring the two of them worked on a set of seven variations on the tune for piano, four-hands, and played it on a concert at Harvard on 18 December 1918 and, after scrutiny by Hill, at a gathering of the Harvard Musical Association on Beacon Hill. The mutual admiration society thus established was needed more by Mannes than by the indefatigable Thompson. With Mannes and their mutual friend, William (Billy) Theodore Richards (1900-1940), who was a violinist, Thompson played chamber music and was especially fond of John Alden Carpenter's Sonata for Violin and Piano (1911).[6]

Randall tired of dormitory life after his freshman year, and a stint of apartment living with Mannes was not satisfactory. In Randall's junior year, Richard Henry Dana, 3rd (1851-1931), suggested that he could provide him with living space in his rambling, 1870 Queen Anne style house on Brattle Street in exchange for his playing 'the old songs' on the piano in the evenings.[7] Although he recognized that his social life suffered a little from this self-imposed hermitage, this began, it may be seen in retrospect, a kind of domestic retreat, a desire for a carefully controlled environment of a kind that he worked hard on developing for his peace of mind and for his work throughout his life. There always remained to the minds of many observers an unreality about it, the impression that he was a nineteenth-century gentleman living slightly out of sync with his times.

America entered the First World War during the end of Thompson's freshman year. During his second semester there, he volunteered and spent his sophomore year and the fall of 1918 in a reserve capacity in the Navy. Attached to the US Naval Unit, 6th Company, at Machias, Maine, he found trips out to sea on the cruisers fairly awful. During his junior year at Harvard, his 'watches' at the Charlestown Naval Yard were at inconvenient times, and he could not catch the last streetcar back to Cambridge when he came off duty; therefore, he rented a small room on the back of Beacon Hill as a pied à terre. After the signing of the Armistice, he was demobilized, and went back to "Old Mr. Dana's," as he called it.

His compositions of these college years reflected a cosmopolitan outlook: songs; a Septet for flute, clarinet, string quartet, and piano; some choral music; piano pieces; and a Quintet for flute, clarinet, viola, cello, and piano (dedicated to Mannes). This last item won the George Arthur Knight Prize at Harvard in 1920. Clearly he was working in as many forms as possible, at the behest of Davison, who taught him counterpoint and the history of choral music and his composition teachers, Spalding, Hill, and Heilman. His setting of Longfellow's The Light of Stars won the Francis Boott Prize in 1919. It was a natural text for him to set: Dana's house, where he was then living, was adjacent to Longfellow's, and the poem describes the moon as seen rising from but a few steps away from Thompson's front door. There were, of course, some disappointments. He submitted another work, Night, for the Boott Prize in 1920, and was incensed when it was rejected in favor of Listen to the Lambs, the perennial favorite then newly composed by R. Nathaniel Dett

(1882-1943), who had been studying with Arthur Foote at Harvard during the 1919-1920 academic year. In his senior year, Kenneth Raisbeck (1899-1931), who had written a play, Torches, which was to be performed at Sanders Theatre, asked Thompson to compose the incidental music. This consisted of a setting of one solo song, and a Prelude for viola and piano (which incorporated the song). Published in 1920 by Brentano in New York, this was Randall's first music publication.[8]

Upon graduation, he moved to New York, probably (and understandably) in search of a life which would allow him a measure of independence from his family, who moved to Boston that fall. Once in New York, he became acquainted with other composers who were also trying to eke out a living. One of these was the young Roger Sessions (1896-1985) who had been studying privately with Ernest Bloch (1880-1959).[9] Sessions convinced Thompson that Bloch was the man to work with, an antidote to the severe and dusty kinds of composition encouraged at Harvard. It was neither an easy nor an economical proposition. Bloch came from Cleveland every other week to give lessons in New York, and charged the exorbitant fee of twenty dollars for each hour's lesson. He worked with Thompson on the small traditional forms, at the same time integrating into his style the trenchant, chromatic, Post-Romantic harmony which Bloch himself had employed (although Bloch's own music at this point was becoming contrapuntally streamlined and Neo-Classical). Thompson initially produced for Bloch a Scherzino for flageolet, violin, and viola, written on 14 December 1920. At Bloch's, Leopold Mannes played the flageolet (tin whistle) for the first performance, complete with his perfected loopy glissando, which Thompson used at the final cadence. Bloch also worked with him on fugue and sonata form (a page of fugue subjects written for Bloch surfaced in Thompson's study in 1983), but little music from this period survives, except for two more Scherzi for piano, written early in 1921. The Bloch influence would make itself felt in Rome.

Returning to Cambridge in September of 1921, Thompson rematriculated at Harvard for a Master's degree, which was then a one-year course requiring little more than composition lessons and an orchestration seminar. By this point he had tentatively found his feet as a composer, and while living at his parents' house in Roxbury (his father had quit his job at Lawrenceville in August of 1920, and was appointed Headmaster of Roxbury Latin School that fall), he wrote two of his important early works: The Last Invocation for six-part unaccompanied chorus, to words by Walt Whitman, and the orchestral work Pierrot and Cothurnus, a kind of valse-fantasie which he called a "Prelude for Orchestra," suggested by a play by Edna St. Vincent Millay.

That fall, he was made aware of an important development at the American Academy in Rome. In 1921, a series of three rotating three-year fellowships (effectively two years in residence at the Academy; a third year was to be spent traveling), bearing the names of Horatio Parker, Frederick Juilliard, and Walter Damrosch, were established along with a Department of Musical Composition. Although the original intention of the Academy's trustees had been to forbid instruction or classes at the Academy, they nevertheless apppointed Felix Lamond (1863-1940) as the first Professor in Charge of the Department of Music.

Leo Sowerby was summarily awarded the Parker Fellowship, without a competition being held, on 23 October 1921, by a committee headed by Walter Damrosch and John Alden Carpenter.[10] The result of the first competition, for the Juilliard Fellowship, was announced on 16 November 1921: Howard Hanson was the recipient. The deadline for the Damrosch Fellowship, 1 February 1922, was announced at this same time. It was extended to 1 March, and ultimately to 1 May. Thompson was tardy in applying. He tried to get Bloch to write a letter of recommendation for him, but Bloch felt that Thompson had not shown sufficient achievement, and indicated that he could not write the kind of letter which Thompson wanted.[11] Thompson turned to Palmer, thinking that a character reference might be more successful. Palmer wrote:

> Since he entered Harvard I have known him intimately, and . . . have seen no young man whom I could place above him in either intellectual or moral power. . . . While enthusiastically devoted to his art and showing genuine originality in it, he is no bohemian but a well rounded man. Music is his natural mode of expression . . . . His success can be counted on with some assurance, for his general good judgement and breadth of intelligence are no less remarkable than his musical genius.[12]

The works he submitted are not all known. For the competition he would have had to submit an orchestral work. Pierrot and Cothurnus, according to the surviving manuscripts, was not begun until 22 March 1922, after the first extension of the deadline. The Last Invocation, finished on 19 February, is known to be one of the three works sent in. Since the announcement of his winning the prize was not made until 24 May 1922, he may have sent in Pierrot and Cothurnus, finished on 2 May 1922, after the actual ultimate 1 May deadline. An early version of his song for soprano and orchestra, The Ship Starting, may also have been submitted, but this was only begun on 22 May according to the manuscripts. It may have been a spontaneous expression upon learning of his winning the Prix de Rome.

The American Academy in Rome: 1922-1925

When Thompson arrived in Rome in mid-October of 1922 Italy was in political and social turmoil. Mussolini staged his so-called march on Rome (he came by train) within a week of Thompson's arrival. Giacomo Puccini wrote in his diary for 28 October: "Italy! Italy! Fascists. . . . Taxes, high prices, filth, disorder, bad taste, an Eldorado of horrors, all in all." [13]

Ensconced in its neo-Classic Charles-McKim-designed fortress high up on the Janiculum Hill, the American Academy, a self-contained, very American community, went about its business as though nothing was happening. Thompson was given rooms in an outbuilding on the other side of the road from the main building of the Academy, close to the Villa Aurelia, where Felix Lamond and his wife had taken up residence.

Felix Frederick Lamond is a mysterious figure, about whom little is known. [14] He was a British citizen, an organist who had studied in London with William Henry Monk (1823-1889) and Ernst Pauer (1826-1905), who seems to have immigrated to the United States in 1886, and who became a naturalized American in 1892. After teaching jobs in Baltimore and Michigan, he came to New York in 1897 as organist of Trinity Chapel,[15] was music critic of the New York Herald, and taught at Columbia from 1909 to 1920. With his American wife, Margaret, he seemed the ideal person to take up the job of managing a fledgling department, and keeping a weather eye on three young men in their early twenties. Mrs. Lamond, a natural mother figure who endeared herself to Randall, especially seems to have helped here. [16] Whatever Lamond's training, and compositional musical taste, he must have been astonishingly broadminded to scrutinze in a professional and fairly non-judgemental way the works of Sowerby, Hanson, and Thompson. His experiences at Columbia, in a department still bearing the stamp of Edward MacDowell (1860-1908), must have brought him in contact with the latest works of the Modern Schools, as they were then called, but organists have never been known for espousing the avant-garde of their day. He seems to have had high expectations of his unofficial pupils, combined with a light touch, and his students seem to have kept him informed of their progress while away from the Academy to an extent that exceeded the requirements of the Fellowship.

One of the first friends Thompson made in Rome was a fellow American, Huntington Brown, a linguist studying Latin in preparation for the exams for a B.Litt. degree at Oxford:

> He and Randall had a game in Rome, calling each other
> up and trying to stump each other with some new Italian
> phrase they had learned. If the other was stumped he
> would immediately complain that the traffic was so
> noisy that he had not heard what was said. . . . [17]

More important than their game was Hunt Brown's
observation about Randall's reading matter. Randall had been
reading the Renaissance Italian poets Cecco Angiolieri and
Petrarch since Harvard days, but Brown urged him to read the
Latin poet on whom they based their works, Quintus Horatius
Flaccus, better known as Horace. He responded enthusiastically to this new discovery. Horace's farm, in the Sabine
Hills near Rome, had been excavated, and together with the
alleged site of the Fountain of Bandusia, these made for
interesting expeditions for the two.

Another of his new friends here was Fernando Remacha (b.
1898), who was then studying composition at the Spanish
Academy in a situation similar to Randall. He had won the
Spanish Prix de Rome. Remacha was also an enthusiast for
classical art and literature, and urged "Tommy," as he called
Randall, to visit Spain with the purpose of seeing the Roman,
classical influences on the Iberian peninsula. Remacha also
dedicated several of his piano works to Thompson. Most
importantly, he had come to Rome to study with Gian Francesco
Malipiero (1882-1964), a prominent member of the so-called
'compositori degli anni ottanta' ('composers of the
eighties'). Malipiero was at that time professor of
composition at the Parma Conservatory, and somehow Thompson
and Malipiero were introduced in late 1922 or early 1923. It
was a fortuitous meeting. If Thompson had met Malipiero a
year later, it is quite possible that Thompson's music might
have developed quite differently. The fire of enthusiasm for
the Renaissance (what Thompson later termed 'Classical art')
which had gripped the volatile Malipiero, was caught by
Thompson, who was very much his protegé. Malipiero, emerging
from years of psychic torment during and after the First
World War, had in 1922 been married for the second time,
purchased a house in Asolo, near Venice, and begun his
massive edition of the works of Monteverdi. In Thompson,
Malipiero found a youthful devoted disciple, such as
Malipiero himself had been to Antonio Smareglia (1854-1929),
the principal Italian follower of Wagner, whose amanuensis
Malipiero had been.[18]   Thompson never had a role model more
powerful than Malipiero.

Thompson frequently left Rome to visit Malipiero at Asolo,
and was welcomed as a regular family guest. To whatever
extent Asolo was a haven for Thompson, it was, like

everything else about Malipiero, a model for him, too. Even
the layout of Malipiero's studio apparently provided Thompson
in later life both a kind of aesthetic and practical floor
plan for his own studio in his home on Larch Road in
Cambridge. The concrete impact which Malipiero had on
Thompson was three-fold: he impressed upon him the idea that
vocal, and especially choral writing, was an art form of the
highest seriousness of purpose, not to be relegated to a
second place in back of so-called 'absolute music'; Malipiero
introduced him further to the music of Monteverdi, which he
was just beginning to edit; and through his own example he
leavened Thompson's style with his own Neo-classical music
and idiom. Thompson's music for string quartet, The Wind in
the Willows (1924) was much influenced by Malipiero's
Rispetti e strambotti (1920) and Stornelli e ballate (1923),
whose first performance Thompson heard in Rome. Throughout
much of The Piper at the Gates of Dawn (1924), Thompson
combined a dense Bloch-like polytonality with the misty,
glittery impressionism of the work of Respighi (whom he met
at the Academy of St. Cecilia, and found 'delightful') and
Malipiero, especially the third part of Impressioni dal vero
(1922) and Pausa dal silenzio I (1918).[19]

The most direct product of Malipiero's tutoring was the
Five Odes of Horace, which Thompson composed between April
1924 and January 1925. They were first performed by the
choir of the church of San Salvatore in Lauro, on 16 May
1925. Presumably the third, "O Venus, regina Cnidi Paphique"
was performed with piano, since the orchestral score (the
other four are a cappella) was not finished until September,
in Venice. Thompson also began a setting for chorus and
orchestra, later used for the first movement of his First
Symphony, of the Ode Poscimur, (Liber I, XXXII) in December
1924, and in April 1925 a setting of the Ode Vides ut alta
(Liber I, IX, later the second and third movements of the
Symphony). Thompson reported that there were still in 1925
castrati among the singers in the choir at San Salvatore.[20]

In the fall of 1924, Leopold Mannes came to visit Thompson
in Rome. Mannes, as usual, and Thompson, unexpectedly, were
in a 'slump.' They conceived the idea of each writing down a
note on a piece of paper and then writing a set of piano
pieces each around the theme. Mannes wrote A, Thompson G-
sharp, and Mannes F. Upon this crabbed idea, Thompson wrote
his Suite for piano between 31 October and 6 November. The
idea was to write a piece each day. The Suite, which
Thompson decided to publish in the early 1980s, remains his
finest expression in keyboard music.[21]

It was around this time during his Rome years that
Thompson met the woman he was to marry. In 1924 or early
1925, he was in Paris when friends introduced him, at a cafe,

to Margaret Whitney. It is conceivable that they had met in earlier life, since their fathers had both been classmates at Williams College, and Thompson had spent some time around Amherst, Massachusetts when growing up. (In Amherst he came to know a rising young poet, Robert Frost.) But any earlier acquaintance was irrelevant to them. She was to prove an ideal companion, intellectually and socially, and from an early date she was convinced absolutely of the worth of her future husband's talents. A sensitive gouache artist in her own right, she combined great personal beauty with an iron-strong will and critical faculty. It must have been a considerable test of Thompson's own self-image to start a friendship with her.

Although he had arrived in Rome in late 1922, Thompson was the 1925 fellow by Academy reckoning (from the end of the fellowship: Hanson and Sowerby were both '24). The 1926 fellow first appointed was Wintter Watts (1884-1962) who had unsuccessfully competed with Thompson for the Damrosch Fellowship in 1922. He was then the second Parker Fellow. Watts, who had won a Pulitzer traveling scholarship in 1923, and who had taught at the College of the Pacific where Hanson had been Dean before coming to Rome, was not a success at the Academy. Priggish, vain, and obnoxious, he was the bane of the department, wrote little, and that of very poor quality. At the end of the first year of his Fellowship (around July 1925) he was 'retired' by the Academy and sent packing. Thompson was not present for the dénouement, but wrote from Spain, where he was spending two months at Remacha's instigation: "How did Watts finish out the year? I trust you were not put to any greater or even prolonged agonies."[22]

Herbert Elwell (1898-1974), who had been studying with Nadia Boulanger (1887-1979) at Fontainebleau (where he was a classmate of Aaron Copland) was provisionally accepted to fill Watts' vacancy. Thompson liked Elwell, and felt, as senior fellow, that he ought to introduce him around and insure that he would be appointed to the Parker Fellowship. In Venice in August 1925, where Thompson and his mother, Mannes, Billy Richards, and the sculptor Joseph Coletti had rented part of the Palazzo Papadopolo, he got Elwell to work with Malipiero. That final summer, Thompson's family joined him in Rome and Venice and they made their way through much of Europe. By early fall he returned to Rome for his final weeks at the Academy and embarking at Genoa, he headed back to the United States. On board ship, on 16 October 1925, he finished the orchestration of the first of the choral/orchestral Odes, "Poscimur."

Homecoming and Marriage: 1925-1937

In early November, Thompson reached New York. Anxious to
reestablish himself as a working composer, he rented rooms at
180 Sullivan Street, and figuratively hung out his shingle.
He was able to find work in a number of areas. He was
commissioned to set several poems of Merle St. Croix Wright,
a local poet, to music at twenty dollars each. He set five.
The Neighborhood Playhouse engaged him to write a number of
songs for the "Grand St. Follies," and he further
orchestrated the entire show. Richard Boleslavky (1889-1937)
asked him to write about twenty 'numbers' for an American
Laboratory Theatre Production of "The Straw Hat," an English
translation of Un Chapeau de paille d'Italie by Eugene
Labiche (1815-1888).[23] He carried through with the project,
despite the fact that the 'backers' of the show failed to pay
him any but a small part of the initially agreed upon fee.
In New York he also met Aaron Copland, who included him in
his list of "America's Young Men of Promise," in early
1926.[24] He wrote book reviews for New York publications.
Hanson performed Pierrot and Cothurnus in the first season of
the American Composers Concerts at Eastman (1925-1926), and
Thompson felt the entire year was "a great experiment."

His parents' failing health led him back to Boston
frequently, but he had good friends there in the form of the
Huntington Browns and the Coletti family: Joe Coletti was
the sculptor who had been studying in Rome while Randall and
the Browns were there. Coletti later designed the Harvard
Glee Club Medal.

By the fall of 1926, Randall and Margaret Whitney had
decided to get married. "The fact is," he wrote to Felix
Lamond in Rome,

that the most important piece of work that I have done
since my return is to have become engaged. You will
remember, I'm glad to say, how rare and beautiful a
girl Margaret Whitney is. . . . It would be jejune of
me to go into details regarding my happiness in telling
you this, or to try to explain how my very existence is
changed and my plans of life glorified. . . . Margaret
will be Mrs. Lamond's first Academy daughter-in-law.[25]

The wedding took place on 26 February 1927 in Montclair,
New Jersey, near the Whitney family's home. Randall wrote
two Amens for the service. They spent their honeymoon skiing
at Gray Rocks Inn in St. Jovite, Quebec.

After the wedding, they set up housekeeping on Eighth
Street in New York, and Thompson began the first of several

pieces dedicated to his new bride. The Jazz Poem, originally
for piano solo, was an idealized reflection of the age.
Thompson blended a jazz idiom derived from Gershwin (and
probably from Copland's Piano Concerto of 1926, first
performed in Boston in early 1927) with the post-
impressionism with which he had experimented in The Piper at
the Gates of Dawn. His use of vernacular music would become
more systematic and less superficial in later years.

    Thompson was offered, in the late spring or early summer
of 1927, a position at Wellesley College, and with its
proximity to Boston, his family, and known opportunities for
performances, he felt he could not refuse. He did feel
awkward about bringing Margaret to a women's college, but in
the end she agreed to the move. Arriving in Wellesley he
replaced both the aging Hamilton C. MacDougall (1858-?), an
organist who had been dean of the Boston Chapter of the AGO
from 1908-1909, and Howard Hinners (1898-1976), who had been
music instructor. Thompson, appointed Lecturer in his first
year, set about revising, in a subtle way, the curriculum.
"Wellesley is proving a wise move," he wrote to Mannes:

    The harmony class is not all brilliant, but the
    counterpoint class is really intelligent. . . . They
    appear . . . fascinated by it all, which is gratifying.
    The choir is also the glee club, and there is much
    intensive rehearsing. I have bought a lot of Al music
    . . . Lassus, Victoria, Palestrina, Weelkes, Morley, and
    the Rachmaninoff Cherubim Song. Couldn't you send me 40
    copies of something . . . you have written (not for
    Spalding).[26]

His youthfulness and energy attracted many students to the
choir, which sang for morning chapel and for evensong once a
week. For the large number of women's voices he had
available he wrote his antiphonal Pueri Hebraeorum in
November of 1927, a significant work in his development. In
its skillful recreation of Renaissance textures and tonal
qualities, by using parallelism of a kind he was surely not
encouraging in his counterpoint class, and by using mixed
meters, he began in this work to delineate the style and
qualities that would dominate the rest of his compositional
life: austere, rational, classically formal and yet freely
tonal. There were still a few subsidiary influences to work
through.

Unlike his easygoing predecessor, MacDougall, he was a
taskmaster, with a temper that became famous:

    There was a tremendous, exciting difference between
    their conducting styles. Hamilton MacDougall no doubt
    was a good choir conductor . . . [but] . . . my memory

is that we resembled a glee club rather than a serious singing group. . . . Rehearsals with R. T. frequently left me exhausted--sometimes even shaking with the effort we all put into trying to meet his standards-- but tingling with the excitement of undertaking something just beyond our capability, and managing to do the seemingly impossible.[27]

Hanson continued his efforts on Thompson's behalf by repeating his Pierrot and Cothurnus in the second season (1926-1927) of the American Composers Concerts at the Eastman School of Music. His symphonic poem The Piper at the Gates of Dawn was performed in the 1926-1927 and 1927-1928 seasons, and the Jazz Poem, in a revised version called simply "Poem for Piano and Orchestra," was performed on 27 November 1928, with Thompson himself as soloist. Aaron Copland's Organ Concerto (1924) was performed on the same program, and it is a bit difficult today to realize the overwhelming importance of these Rochester concerts for composers of Thompson's generation. He tried hard to make the most of his association with the influential Hanson and with his colleagues and former teachers in Boston and Cambridge. When Ravel came to Boston in early 1928, Thompson was seen by several of his students standing on the platform of the Boston and Albany rail station in full morning dress, heading off to meet him at a Harvard reception (probably before his American debut with the Boston Symphony on 12 January 1928). At this reception Thompson was introduced to Serge Koussevitsky, to whom he sent The Piper at the Gates of Dawn. Koussevitsky was enthusiastic about the work, and it was performed by the Boston Symphony on 28 March 1929.

What time he had for composition during his first year at Wellesley evaporated completely during his second when he was appointed Assistant Professor. His first child, a daughter, Varney, was born in 1928. She kept him and Margaret busy. In the spring of 1929, he was asked to take over the Canon and Fugue class at Harvard, replacing Heilman, who had suffered a nervous breakdown. He found this hectic schedule unsatisfactory, however. In early 1929, with a view to finding more time to compose, he applied for a Guggenheim Fellowship, which was awarded in March.

Thompson resigned from Wellesley at the end of the spring term of 1929. Despite the Fellowship, the Thompsons planned to stay in America until the following February, when they planned to leave for France. In the summer of 1929, with a year-old baby, and another expected in the fall, the Thompsons, at E. B. Hill's instigation, retreated to Francestown, New Hampshire, and here Thompson was able to attack a number of projects which had lain fallow. The first of these was a setting for women's voices of four poems from

Stephen Vincent Benét's Tiger Joy, which Thompson called Rosemary (his third child was later to be so called). Benét was delighted with the settings, and they became good friends.

The next project was a revision of the orchestral ode Poscimur, which he had finished in 1925. Believing that it would never reach the concert stage, he rescored the work, omitting the baritone solo and chorus and adding extra woodwinds and an organ part. Why he chose to do this is unclear, but in September or early October Hanson seems to have asked him for a new orchestral work to be played in the second half of the 1929-1930 season. Thompson returned to the sketches he had made in 1925 for Vides ut alta and, orchestrating them for the first time, called the work his First Symphony. It was performed by Hanson in Rochester on 20 February 1930, to a rapturous reception. Thompson, critically aware even then, did not disclose the fact that it was a transcription of earlier works, simply stating in the program note that "Sketches for this symphony were made in Rome and Venice in 1925. It is in free form, not following any conventional symphonic pattern. . . ." The critics, typified by Stewart Sabin of the Rochester Chronicle, were reserved: "It is an interesting work--has moments of beauty even to the prejudiced ears of the classicist." But the audience was overtly enthusiastic. Hanson arranged for the audience at each concert to vote, on special papers, for one work to be published at Eastman's expense. Thompson's Symphony won easily over works by Gertrude M. Brown (b. 1907) and Mark Wessel (1894-1973).[28]

By May, 1930, the Thompsons reached Paris, where Randall hoped to spend his second Guggenheim Fellowship year. He had been reappointed in early 1930. Perhaps the acclaim which Copland, Elwell, Roy Harris, Virgil Thomson, and so many other composers of his years had returned home voicing led him there. Perhaps it was Margaret's own love of France and le style. At any rate, it did not prove satisfactory. "The truth is," he wrote to Lamond,

> we've given up on Paris . . . so we are going to Gstaad . . . where I found [Frederick] Jacobi just leaving and only too glad to turn over his studio and piano to me. It really is a heavenly place. . . .[29]

Thompson loved Gstaad and the Swiss, and eventually bought property there, where many of his later works were composed. Between July 1930 and February 1931 he composed his Second Symphony in Gstaad, undoubtedly the best known of his non-choral works. His sketch book one day was accidentally left on a bench in the middle of an alpine field, where he had gone to work in the sun. At midday a terrific thunderstorm broke, lasting a few minutes. When Thompson ran back to the bench (no easy feat at 3500 feet above sea level), he found the sodden booklet intact. The sketches were in pencil; had they been in ink, they might have been completely lost.

In the Second Symphony, he accomplished two things: he wrote an integrated work of large dimensions along the 'Classical' model, which some critics of the First Symphony had suggested he might not be capable of, and he put into his music an element of nationalism in its most obvious sense, which had been explored in the Jazz Poem of three years earlier. The parts of the symphony which attracted most attention (and still do), the languorous, pop-song slow movement, the Gershwinesque Trio of the Scherzo, and the ragtime Finale, are catchy, but belie the fact that the first movement is where Thompson's skill is best shown. The construction here is extremely tight, the rhythmic motive as coiled with tension as a cotton string after a rainstorm, and Thompson pointedly called the Symphony an E minor symphony: this is the only movement in that key. Where Thompson uses a 'popular' device, he does so with a sound reason: the 'blue note' (B-flat) sounded by the horn against the C major chord of the end of the second movement, is not there for fun. It leads into the G-minor scherzo which follows, a rhythmic labyrinth in seven-four time which has been the downfall of many orchestras.

Thompson returned to New York in the spring of 1931, in time for a second performance at Rochester on 21 May of his First Symphony. It was at or shortly after this performance that an unfortunate incident occurred, the ramifications of which could hardly have been imagined at the time. After the performance in Kilbourn Hall, Thompson went to see Hanson in the Green Room, to offer contratulations and to collect the score, which Hanson had had for over a year (in part to give C. C. Birchard time to engrave this score). When Thompson asked for it back, Hanson told him that, as it had been published at the Eastman School's expense, it was now property of Eastman and had been sent along with the parts to the Library. For good measure, Hanson mentioned that the seal of the University of Rochester had been embossed on the title page. Thompson never forgave Hanson for this high-handedness, which he called 'theft.' The rupture of their professional relationship was never really healed, to the personal loss of both men. Despite this, curiously, he allowed Hanson to give the first performance of the Second Symphony, on 24 March 1932, and had no objection to accepting an honorary doctorate in music from the University of Rochester in 1933.[30]

By the fall of 1931, the family had settled once again in New York, where Thompson had been appointed guest conductor

of the Dessoff Choirs, taking the reins over from the ailing
founder, Margarethe Dessoff (1874-1944), of the Madrigal
Choir and Supervisors' Chorus at the Juilliard Graduate
School.   These appointments secured his reputation as a
choral conductor.   In a sense, it also marked the end of his
youthful period and the beginnings of true maturity.
Indirectly, it also led him into an academic career, far
different from the career of an independent composer, which
he had hitherto planned to pursue.

Upon his return from Europe he wrote an interesing, if
short-winded and sketchy, assessment of "The Contemporary
Scene in American Music" for the Musical Quarterly (January
1932) which gives an insight into his thoughts about being a
composer and an American at the time.   While essentially a
casual index of his opinions of several dozen of the leading
figures of the day, it shows that, in the wake of the Jazz
Poem and the Second Symphony, Thompson felt the common
imperative of the 1930s was for American composers to write
music that sounded distinctly 'American':

Romanticism, with its attendant "cult of the
individual," has prevented us from having a school of
composers who display group feeling or marked
similarities of style.   Among our composers, the itch
to be different amounts to a plague. . . .

The spirit of George Herbert Palmer (still alive at the
time) looms large over Thompson's thoughts here.   His views
on jazz are worth attention in light of his own recent
compositions:

Jazz is a historical fact.   It may pass or gradually
evolve into something else, but already it is part of
our heritage.   To force it out of one's musical
consciousness is repression. . . .   As for the
limitations of its form, they are the result of the
uses it has been put to . . . in the Pianoforte
Concerto of Copland there is a close-knit development
of jazz themes and Copland proved once and for all that
jazz and larger forms are not incompatible.

Thompson might well have been preparing for the critical
onslaught he expected would greet the Second Symphony, which
was given its first performance in Rochester by Hanson on 24
March 1932.   It was well received critically, and the work
went on to be one of the most frequently performed of
American symphonies.   During February and March of 1932, on a
commission from the League of Composers, he composed
Americana, a sequence of five choruses based on selected
satirical texts which he found in H. L. Mencken's same-named
column in The American Mercury.   Their 'folksiness' and

slapstick wit had its admirers and detractors. Emerging from
the stage door after conducting the first performance,
Thompson ran into Copland, who merely sniffed, and muttered
"Long live America!"   It was a classic example of the
inherent conflicts in the 'search for nationalism': Copland,
for example, had organized his Young Composers' Group in
1932, which argued, in the apartment of the American composer
Paul Bowles (b. 1910), the ways and means of a consciously
American school of composers. But there was nationalism and
Nationalism: Virgil Thomson and Paul Bowles, with their
foreign training, were viewed here as overly sophisticated.
Thompson, with his Harvard education and years of life
abroad, not to mention gainful employment and marriage into a
wealthy family, would also have been already too
'establishment.' It was a tribute to Copland's sense of fair
play, then, that Thompson was invited to join him at the
First Festival of Contemporary American Music at Yaddo in the
spring of 1932, and to serve on the Central Music Committee
for the Second Festival in 1933.[31]

Between 1932 and 1935, Thompson had little time for
composition. He was appointed to head a committee
established by the Association of American Colleges, to
investigate, with a view towards radical restructuring of
curriculae, the present state of music education in the
country. During those years he traveled extensively,
interviewing students and faculty, observing classes, and
thinking about his own views on education. These had
initially been formed at Harvard by Davison and by Thomas
Whitney Surrette (1861-1941), the popularizer of 'music
appreciation' courses.[32]

When the Committee met in late 1934 to consider the final
draft of Thompson's 'investigation,' they were appalled at
the terrible state of affairs on which Thompson reported with
his usual dry, pungent wit: widespread ignorance and
educational incompetence (one music history teacher could not
recognize the theme from the opening of the Unfinished
Symphony of Schubert); lack of the most basic facilities at
many schools; low standards; grave cases of bigotry and
injustice, both racial and economic, affecting opportunities
for performance; and all manner of harassment, both by
students and teachers. (Conductor to young woman
auditioning: "Are you nervous?" Young woman: "No. Are
you?", is prefaced with the comment "How one girl got into
the chorus.") A clique of committee members, headed by
Howard Hanson, demanded a chance for their dissenting views
regarding some of Thompson's recommendations to appear in
print. The issue of whether or not to grant academic credit
for 'practical subjects,' such as instrumental lessons or
membership in performing organizations, was the greatest
sticking point. Thompson felt the liberal arts education was

debased by this 'manual training,' in which a high level of abuse and 'grade inflation' was always a danger, and which he felt contributed nothing in and of itself to the intellectual and moral development of students. Conservatories trained; the liberal arts institutions educated. The result was that the committee approved a motion for Hanson to write rebuttals to be printed at the end of each chapter. The lingering bitterness which Thompson felt over the score affair of a few years earlier hardened into an irrational hatred of Hanson, whom he privately called "the devil incarnate," not just referring to his robust physique and pointed goatee.

College Music, published in 1935 by Macmillan, established Thompson's educational views: for the overriding supremacy of the liberal arts education, with no credit for merely practical subjects and pursuits, he became a forceful and eloquent spokesman. Although he felt his work had been 'undermined' by Hanson, the Board of Overseers of Harvard University were sufficiently impressed to appoint Thompson in 1935 to the Visiting Committee on Music, of which Mark Anthony DeWolfe Howe (1864-1960) was chairman. Thompson, as secretary, headed a sub-committee on Curriculum. In the fall of 1935, Thompson produced a report influenced by his experiences of the last three years, "A Proposed Revision of the Music Curriculum." It was a complete revision of the catalog entries for the Department of Music, and was accepted.

A minor revolution was taking place. There were meetings at the Thompson home in Belmont [Mass.] and at the [A. T.] Davisons with the younger department members, [A. Tillman] Merritt, [Walter] Piston, and [G. Wallace] Woodworth. The result was the survey course Music 1, The History of Music, that would be taught by Davison.[33]

Such a course is now standard in American universities, but it was then a radical move and, since it originated from Harvard, widely and quickly copied.

After completing the manuscript of College Music, he was delighted to receive another commission from the League of Composers, of which he had become an officer, for a choral work to be performed by the Harvard Glee Club and Radcliffe Choral Society. In March of 1934, the Worcester (Mass.) Art Museum acquired one of the best known versions of Edward Hicks' painting, The Peaceable Kingdom. Thompson saw a reproduction of the painting in the Boston Evening Transcript on 8 September 1934, and drove to Worcester several days later to view it.

Between January and December 1935, Thompson worked on his

'sequence of sacred choruses,' or 'Choruses from Isaiah' as
he initially called it.   Inspired by Orazio Vecchi's madrigal
comedy format (L'Amfiparnaso was the actual model) he
produced an extraordinary work, both in its own right and for
its time.   John Powell (1882-1963) had met Thompson in New
York in the early 1930s, and had introduced him to the shape-
note hymns of the south, which he had used extensively in his
own work, and to the scholarship of George Pullen Jackson
(1874-1953), whose book White Spirituals in the Southern
Uplands appeared in 1933.   Thompson's reaction to Powell and
his work, which he called "an important influence on my own
thinking and feeling about music,"[34] was to write a movement
recreating (without imitating) a shape-note hymn, with the
tune in the tenor voice: "The paper reeds by the brooks."
As in Pueri Hebraeorum he had re-created (without precisely
imitating) the style of Hassler and the antiphonal style of
the Renaissance, in The Peaceable Kingdom he continued that
idea, defining his mature style in the process.   As James
Haar has said, his music is more tonally oriented than the
music of Lasso and Palestrina, but the origins are never
obscure.

     After a hectic year as administrator and composer,
Thompson left for a vacation in Austria, without his wife and
four children.   He stopped in London to see his brother
Daniel, who was director of the Courtauld Institute, and
proceeded to Sankt Anton for three weeks of skiing on the St.
Christoph.[35]   Thompson returned to New York and then Concord,
Massachusetts, in early February, and The Peaceable Kingdom
was first given in Cambridge on 3 March 1936 and was quickly
repeated in New York.   Despite audience enthusiasm, the
critics were mystified.   Accustomed by 1936 to being shocked
by new works, here was something rare, well-crafted and
accessible.   Pathetically ignorant of its musical sources and
antecedents, they now carped about 'lack of originality,'
that great bugbear of small minds.   "Come now," Thompson, in
a letter to his friend the composer Douglas Moore (1893-
1969), imagined himself writing to one of the critics,

     are you a tune detective?   and did you trap me in 30
     minutes of unmitigated plagiarism?   Won't you provide
     me with a key to my sources, if you did?   Or did you
     mean "originality" in some other sense?   And if so, did
     you attach importance to it?   And if you attached
     importance to it, how are you able to accept any of the
     classics?   Are any of them "original" in the sense that
     they bear no resemblance to previous works?[36]

     While many considered this his greatest work, there was an
ominous message to be read in the critical opprobrium.   As
Thompson's eclectic style was becoming defined, it was, to
the detriment of his reputation, being seen in some quarters

as increasingly reactionary and an about-face from the
critical wariness which had greeted his First Symphony only
seven years earlier.[37]   Copland, reviewing the achievements
of the composers he had singled out ten years earlier,
remarked on Thompson's

> well-deserved reputation as an expert craftsman. It is
> curious to observe how a man of Thompson's scholarly
> interest and academic background has come to make a
> definite bid for popular appeal, as in his Symphony No.
> 2. Thompson has the audience very much in mind when he
> composes. This attitude is not without its dan-
> gers. . . . [38]

In the fall of 1936, Thompson was once again appointed
Assistant Professor of Music at Wellesley College. Having
left seven years earlier, it seems appropriate that he should
have again started there on the next twenty years of his
life, in which he was to be principally seen as an academic.
In Concord, Massachusetts, where they lived on Nawshatuck
Hill, he wrote his setting of a poem of Hilaire Belloc, for
the Yale University Glee Club between October 1936 and April
of the following year. Such a long time to compose an eleven
minute work may be explained by the virtuoso piano part,
which gave him considerable difficulty. His foray into
'popular' styles, here Latin American dance rhythms, was
possibly influenced by Constant Lambert's Rio Grande of 1927.
Thompson had bought Lambert's book, Music Ho! upon
publication in 1934, and the score of his ballet, Summer's
Last Will and Testament (1935), possibly after seeing the
premiere in London in January of 1936.

The Academic: 1937-1948

In the fall of 1937 Berkeley, California, became the
Thompson family's new home. Thompson had been offered a
position on the faculty, as professor of music and director
of the University Chorus (which he was to organize), at the
University of California. Invited by Albert Elkus (1884-
1962), who in time would also bring Bloch, Sessions, Arthur
Bliss (1891-1975), and Manfred Bukofzer (1910-1955) to join
the faculty, Thompson found the agreeable climate a pleasant
change from New England, as did Margaret and their four young
children. They were not especially productive years for
Thompson the composer, but honors continued to come his way,
and his reputation grew, especially with his election to the
National Institute of Arts and Letters in 1938. One of his
students at Berkeley, William Denny (1910-1980) sensed this,
and, interesting himself in Thompson's music, orchestrated
Tarantella for him. Thompson wrote The Lark in the Morn, a

setting of a traditional English folksong included in one of
Cecil Sharp's collections, in October of 1938, but other than
that, he appears to have suffered an uncharacteristic dry
spell. This lack of activity, and the fact that he was never
really partial to the moral somnolence of the West Coast,
was a frustration. He was pleased, then, to be offered a
position as Director of the Curtis Institute of Music in
Philadelphia at the end of the 1938-1939 academic year.
Given his known antipathy to the 'conservatory' educational
method, one can even today question why he accepted this
position, which ultimately brought him much grief. Perhaps
it was a family decision or perhaps the prestige of it made
it a purely 'resume-dictated' decision. At any event, he
accepted the offer made by the president, Mary Louise Curtis
Bok (1876-1970) and replaced the administratively ineffectual
Josef Hofmann (1876-1957) in September of 1939.

These two years in Philadelphia ran the gamut from
challenging to comical to macabre, but several of his finest
works were also composed during this time. His efforts to
reform the day-to-day curriculum were noble but doomed to
failure. Students who had been left alone mornings to
practice suddenly found themselves summoned to take part in a
required all-Institute chorus which Thompson rehearsed and
Fritz Reiner (1888-1963) conducted (and for which, naturally,
no credit was given). Students were required to attend
assemblies, to hear distinguished speakers such as Douglas
Moore, Carleton Sprague Smith, Hans T. David (1902-1967),
Serge Koussevitsky (who introduced the idea of the Berkshire
Music Center there) and Sir Thomas Beecham (1879-1961), who
in the words of one person present, "delivered himself of an
unforgettable speech."[39] They were being educated.

As director, Thompson also tried to avert one of the
tragedies of twentieth-century music. In the spring of 1940,
he offered Béla Bartók, then on his second American tour, a
job at the Curtis Institute, which would have required at
most two days of teaching each week. Bartók politely
rejected Thompson's generous offer and one cannot help
feeling that Bartók's attitude, and subsequent poverty-
stricken demise must have reinforced Thompson's worst fears
about conservatory backgrounds.[40]

Thompson did have a group of extraordinary students and
faculty members at Curtis. Among them, Samuel Barber (1910-
1981) was teaching conducting, composition, and
orchestration, and was in charge of a Madrigal Group which
Thompson had suggested he form.[41] The young composer Gian
Carlo Menotti was also there, and Leonard Bernstein (1918-
1990) had come down after graduating from Harvard to study
orchestration with Thompson and, at Thompson's
recommendation, conducting with Reiner. In connection with

Bernstein's presence at Curtis, Thompson encountered the most bizzare experience of his academic life. Bernstein, like Thompson, was suspect from the start, educated humanists being a rarity at Curtis. There was a strong 'anti-Bernstein clique' who felt pushed aside as this Ivy League tyro swept all before him. For one student it was too much. One day this disturbed young man walked into Thompson's office, sat down, pulled a loaded revolver from his coat, and calmly announced that he was going to shoot Leonard Bernstein. Thompson managed somehow to talk him into giving the gun up, and called the police, who led the unfortunate boy away.[42]

In the spring of 1940, the League of Composers, on whose executive board Thompson served from 1939 to 1941, commissioned him again, this time to write a work for oboe, clarinet and viola, for a CBS radio premiere. Busy writing his Annual Report for Curtis, he composed his Suite at night after spending the day teaching or in administrative work. The five movements were chosen to imitate five folkmusic forms: folk dance, mountain ballad, additive-verse children's song, shape-note hymn (with intervening 'preacher'), and running set. In June, Alfred Wallenstein (1898-1983) asked Thompson to orchestrate the piano accompaniment of Americana for a radio broadcast, and during the same month Koussevitsky asked him for a choral piece, a 'fanfare' to be performed as part of the opening exercises of the new Berkshire Music Center. During the first five days of July he worked on the choral 'fanfare' which Koussevitsky had ordered. This in itself had almost not come to pass. Harvard's G. Wallace Woodworth, who was to conduct the chorus at the Institute, had suggested that some of the "noble chorales of Bach" would be the most ceremonially appropriate music to begin with. But Koussevitsky had insisted that, as this was an American music center, and a twentieth-century creation, it would only be appropriate to use a work commissioned from a living American composer. But for Thompson, a fanfare was not possible: France had fallen. He struggled to find some suitable expression for his and the world's anguish at that moment, and later wrote:

> I recall that Louis Baille referred to it in speaking to me as being a very sad piece, and he was absolutely right. The word "Alleluia" has so many possible interpretations. The music in my particular Alleluia cannot be made to sound joyous. In fact it is a slow, sad piece, and . . . here it is comparable to the Book of Job, where it is written, "The Lord gave and the Lord has taken away. Blessed be the name of the Lord."[43]

On Friday of the first week of the Center's exercises (12 July 1940), the Institute Orchestra gave its first concert.

Bernstein, in his public debut as a conductor, conducted Thompson's Second Symphony at the start of the program.   It was an auspicious beginning.

In his second year at the Curtis Institute, a concerted effort was made to undermine the change of educational focus which he had brought to bear on the curriculum.   The All-Institute chorus collapsed, as did Barber's madrigal group, whose principal project ultimately had been the making of a studio recording of Barber's Reincarnations.[44]   In the midst of this, Thompson was sufficiently inspired by teaching a course on the quartets of Beethoven to write one himself. Under a commission from Elizabeth Sprague Coolidge (1864-1953), he composed the First String Quartet in D minor, the most extensive chamber work he would write, in the spring and summer of 1941.   It was 'Neo-Rassumovskii' as he described it, although the strong influence of Ravel can be heard in the syncopated, rhythmic Scherzo; and the first movement shares with the Second Symphony an individual approach to combining the rhythmic drive of neo-classicism with a memorable, folk-influenced, and easily fragmented 'fiddle tune' motive.   How he managed in those days to compose so serene a final movement as in the Quartet is beyond account. The fact was that Curtis and Thompson were essentially incompatible.   Things came to a head when Mrs. Bok decided that she wished to replace Thompson as director with her future second husband, Efrem Zimbalist, Sr. (1889-1985), who served on the faculty as a violin teacher.   In February 1941 Thompson was called on the carpet and given the option of either resigning or being forced out.   Thompson believed that he could only be fired for dereliction of duty or moral turpitude, neither of which he was guilty.   But water seeks its own level, and, fearing the growing crisis and its effect on his career, he decided that he would have to leave.   His resignation, after only two years, caused a sensation in the musical press.   'Educational differences' were given as the reason, and indeed these lay at the heart of his unhappiness at Curtis, but he bridled for the rest of his life at the old-fashioned propriety that kept the real, tawdry story from emerging.   He also felt abandoned by his colleagues.   He took some comfort, several hours later, when Reiner, in a tersely worded statement, tendered his resignation in sympathetic protest.[45]

To be out of a job, under unusual circumstances, in the midst of a World War, was an unenviable position to be placed in.   But fortune here favored Thompson, and he was offered the post of head of the music department of the School of Fine Arts at the University of Virginia in May 1941.   The august, distinguished, and scholarly milieu in which Thompson found himself in the fall could not have been more different from his experience at the Curtis Institute.   The

Jeffersonian 'Academic Village' could not have been more
perfectly constructed to Thompson's classical specifications,
both internally and externally, and for the next four years
it seemed as though he had found his niche. But the truth
was, that the War had siphoned off a considerable number of
students, it was a time of severe national anxiety, and these
years did not prove to be especially productive.

At the height of the Curtis fiasco, the League of
Composers and CBS commissioned him to write an opera,
suitable for radio broadcast and for performance by college
operatic ensembles with limited resources. The concept had
initially been Thompson's own, and as he later put it, "they
said, 'It's such a good idea, why don't you write the first
one.' And so I did." Solomon and Balkis, based on one of
the Just So Stories by Rudyard Kipling ("The Butterfly That
Stamped") was written between August and November 1941, and
first broadcast over CBS in March 1942. Subsequent staged
performances at Harvard and Juilliard failed to establish it
as a repertory piece. Thompson's only real opera, it has a
static quality that perhaps indicates too much its radio
origins. But it is the most intensely and deliberately neo-
classic of Thompson's compositions, sharing much in common
with works like Menotti's Amelia al ballo (1937) and The Old
Maid and the Thief (1939), which Thompson would have heard at
Curtis, and, as mentioned earlier, Malipiero's three mini-
operas on stories by Goldoni.

On 30 October 1941, Thompson received the Coolidge Medal,
'for services to chamber music' for his First String Quartet,
in a ceremony at the Library of Congress in Washington, D.C.
The Coolidge Quartet gave the first performance, and
Alexandre Tansman and Benjamin Britten were also awarded
Coolidge Medals in the same program. In a lengthy speech,
Elizabeth Sprague Coolidge gave the first medal to Tansman,
extolling the heroism of his native country, Poland, and its
gallant resistance to Nazi aggression. Britten, who was
called up next, was reminded of the crucial efforts Britain
was making in the war effort, and the United Kingdom was
praised as the last defense against the Axis powers in
Europe. Finally, Mrs. Coolidge walked over to Thompson,
handed him the medal in its case, and said, dryly "Here,
Randall. This is for you."

During his four years in Virginia, Thompson finished only
a single surviving original work. The Testament of Freedom,
after Alleluia probably Thompson's most often performed
composition, was not only a war effort work but also a
gracious homage to the humanitarian ideals of Thomas
Jefferson. The texts suited the times admirably, but they
are not as belligerent as a casual glance might suggest: "We
fight not for glory or for conquest. . . ." Thompson

composed the work partially for the war effort, but principally for the Jefferson Bicentennial. However, given the militaristic sweep and tone of the music, it is easy to lose sight of this key, essentially peace-loving ideal. It was in Virginia that Thompson met the young musicologist, Stephen D. Tuttle (1907-1954), whose close friend he became, and who conducted the premiere of the Testament on 13 April 1943, with Thompson at the piano. Originally, he had written a four-hands accompaniment and a lengthy introduction, later reduced to a single player and five chords which rhythmically 'spell' Tho-mas Jef-fer-son. Thompson has often been criticized for this work. Its enormous popularity hurt him after the war, when it was held up to ridicule and missrepresented as a characteristically maudlin work by a second-rate mind. His significant previous achievements were belittled and lost in the shuffle that occurred in the world of contemporary music with the advent of the serial schools. As late as 1942, Quincy Porter could still say of him "He rides eloquently through the present on the fine stagecoach of our ancestors. One may see more at this speed of travel . . . . The important thing is that he is writing music which, regardless of style, has a well justified place in our musical life. . . ."46 By the end of the war, especially after The Testament of Freedom, it is doubtful that this attitude could be so easily advanced.

Even so, he was sought after for his known skill and reliability both as a composer and administrator. In 1944, Thompson received the Ditson Award from the Alice M. Ditson Fund at Columbia University, which carried with it a commission for an orchestral work. He sketched four movements, but the pressure of teaching and formal problems with the music kept him from proceeding further at this time. In 1945 he was named Director of the League of Composers, a post he retained until 1948. Virginia, and especially the Blue Ridge Mountains, held a special place in Thompson's affection. But despite this he resigned abruptly from Virginia at the start of the 1945-1946 academic year, and in 1946 accepted an offer to join the music faculty at Princeton University. It was part of an inexorable trek northwards.

At Princeton, he was invited to deliver an inaugural address, which he called, "Music, Popular and Unpopular." Here he summed up what had become his artistic creed: "A Composer's first responsibility is, and always will be, to write music that will reach and move the hearts of his listeners in his own day," that American composers had a responsibility to reject the "literal and empty imitation of European models" and return to "our own genuine musical heritage in its every manifestation, every inflexion, every living example."47 These concepts, central to Thompson's by then settled aesthetic (and derived largely from Palmer),

that composers have a responsibility to their audiences, that
there is a difference between American and European models,
and the implication that many composers had abandoned this
essentially moral view of a composer's world, could not have
been popular even in 1946. 'European models' is a veiled
reference to serialism: even then, Thompson saw a kind of
artistic hegemony encroaching on the liberal arts educational
establishment. But that there would soon be no place for his
music in this establishment did not occur to him, and that
the marketplace of ideas was being closed down for
contemporary composers would have struck him then as
impossible. In writing the address, he doubtless thought of
his music in terms of 'popular'; by the time he gave the
address, his music in the eyes of many of his colleagues was
decidedly 'unpopular.' The Classical concept of the artist
as 'craftsman,' an idea he owed to Bloch, to Malipiero, to
ancient Rome, and to the Renaissance, was swiftly swept away
after the war by the regressive nineteenth-century Romantic
aesthetic of the artist as 'artist,' serving only his own
expressive or intellectual needs, a central, controlling
factor in the self-justification of the music of post-war
schools of composition. Craftsman, even as used by Copland
in 1936 to describe Thompson, had become a back-handed
compliment at best, a polite indication of unfashionableness
verging on superfluity.[48]

    At Princeton, Thompson taught for two years, and began in
earnest to compose one of his most deeply felt, emotionally
fraught, and curiously neglected works. From the sketches he
had made for the Ditson Foundation commission in 1944, he
began to write his Third Symphony in A minor in August of
1947. This was not an easy work for him to write, and he at
one point asked the Ditson Foundation to relieve him of the
commission, offering to return the fee they had paid him.
They generously gave him more time, and the reward was great.
Although composed after the War, the sketches on which it is
based were written at the height of the conflict. Even the
most cursory comparison of the Third Symphony (and, let it
not be forgotten, Alleluia) with The Testament of Freedom
will show what Thompson's artistic expression of the War
experience was. There is no jingoism here, the polytonal
clashes of the first two movements are hardly 'popular'
devices, and at least in the first half it is a work full of
doubt and inner struggles. Only in the spacious third
movement, an ecstatic distillation of a summer spent in the
Blue Ridge Mountains, does the music move towards optimism.
The breezy finale nearly trivializes the work, but like
Haydn, whose later symphonies provided the model for much of
this work, Thompson created a texture of simplicity to belie
the complex canonic devices employed.

    Between the beginning of work on the Third Symphony and

the end, Thompson made another major career move. In the
fall of 1948, he returned to Harvard as Professor of Music,
where his official teaching career would later end. It was a
homecoming that had mixed, but ultimately satisfying
blessings attendant upon it.

Harvard Redux: 1948-1965

    The Third Symphony was to be Thompson's finest essay in
purely instrumental form, with regard to emotional intensity
and intellectual rigor. After this, and during his long and
successful tenure at Harvard, he composed but one other
orchestral work, and the works which tumbled from his pen
during the next decade and a half were with few exceptions
vocal, and mostly choral. How much of this was due to his
own predisposition, and how much due to the fact that he had
clearly become 'pegged' in the public imagination as a choral
composer, is hard to say. One inescapable fact is, that as
the years drew on, his works were commissioned by less and
less prominent bodies in the musical world, and his
willingness to write for them was taken as a sign in some
quarters that he was not 'serious,' or worse, that he was not
to be taken seriously. That professional jealously was
involved here may be indicated by the fact that his
popularity among choral musicians grew in inverse proportion
to the national and international influence and reputation
which was promised him before 1945, and that even today his
non-choral works, almost all composed before 1945, are
virtually unknown. By 1948, American music had entered a
dark period of "partisan polemic," "categorical positions,"
"a priori arguments," and "absolute judgments," polarizing
composers between "the propriety of writing tonal music in
the mid-twentieth century, [and] the legitimacy of the method
and practice of serialism. . . ."[49] Thompson, along with
many composers of his generation, was for the time being
caught on the losing side of these specious arguments. His
increasing popularity in areas of non-professional and
educational music-making went some way to assuage a very real
anger he felt at being ignored by what he termed the
'highbrows' of American music.

    At Harvard, he had the satisfaction of seeing his work of
the thirties paying handsome dividends. He continued
teaching his favorite subjects, orchestration, fugue,
composition, and analysis (the Beethoven quartets) which he
always felt stimulated his own work.[50] In the summer of
1949, Koussevitsky asked him to compose a choral work, having
been given the discretion by the Boston Symphony Orchestra to
name the composer who would write a piece to honor the
twenty-fifth anniversary of his directorship. It was an

indication of Koussevitsky's esteem for Thompson that he
chose him, and that the work was specified for the chorus of
the Berkshire Music Center and the Boston Symphony. Thompson
had little time to write and felt that he was composing "at
the point of a gun." In a parcel of cuttings and text
fragments which he had assembled over the years, he found a
fragment from 2 Samuel, which he had discovered in a hotel
Gideon Bible, while on one of his many cross-country trips at
the time he was writing College Music. They were now an
homage to Koussevitsky the musician as much as anything else:
"Now these be the last words of David,. . . the man who was
raised up on high,. . . He that ruleth over men must be just
. . . ." The first performance of The Last Words of David
was given at Tanglewood on 12 August 1949.

While the return to Cambridge proved pleasant for the
Thompson family, and while they were able to move into a
large and convenient house on Brattle Street, only steps from
the old Dana house where Thompson had lived thirty years
earlier, his teaching absorbed him exclusively for several
years. In the middle of the 1951-1952 academic year, he was
appointed the first Walter Bigelow Rosen Professor of Music,
and in the fall of 1952 became chairman of the department.
Still dissatisfied with the curriculum, he set out to change
it, but this time with the support of his colleagues for the
first time in his life. The result was a slight swing
towards a greater emphasis being placed on history, at the
expense of theoretical studies. His major achievement during
the five years of his chairmanship was the building of the
Eda Kuhn Loeb Music Library, a model of what a music library
should be. It is still in use, though enlarged somewhat,
today. At the end of the 1953-1954 academic year, Thompson's
old teacher, Davison, retired, and as a parting tribute
Thompson set a fragment of another Horatian ode, Felices ter.
It is an instructive example of the meaning of 'originality':
written to strict contrapuntal rules, of the Jeppesen-
Palestrina order, it sounds nothing like Palestrina, but is
pure Thompson, somehow timeless and identifiably twentieth-
century American. Added by Thompson's publisher to the
earlier and unrelated Five Odes of Horace, it deserves to
stand alone.51

From this point, Thompson's career became one of hitherto
unknown regularity, generally teaching during term and
composing on commission during vacations, principally at his
chalet in Gstaad. In the summer of 1953, he sketched his
'symphonic fantasy,' A Trip to Nahant, his last orchestral
work, that had originated as an informal commission from
Eugene Ormandy. The title was taken from an eighteenth-
century fiddle tune (not used in the work) which Thompson had
come across and whose title amused him. Thompson appended a
lengthy program to this lengthy work, which in the end was

hardly the 'overture' which Ormandy had originally suggested. Thompson complained to Henry Pleasants:

> After the first rehearsal he [Ormandy] wrote me that it was 26 minutes long and would I please reduce it to 17 . . . . I am to attend the final rehearsal. Heaven only knows what I shall hear. . . . [52]

At the first performance in Philadelphia in March 1955, Ormandy cut the work severely, but at subsequent performances the following year in Boston under Munch, it was played in its entirety. The quiet, understated ending had disturbed Ormandy, who told Thompson with irritation, "you lost five minutes of applause because of that."

In response to a private commission from Nicolas Brown, of Providence, Rhode Island, he wrote his Mass of the Holy Spirit in Gstaad during the summers of 1955 and 1956. An English Mass or Communion Service, it is perhaps too discursive for service use, but is an outstanding example of the peculiarly Thompson-esque assimilation of musics from the past high ages of choral composition, specifically the Italian and English Renaissance and German Baroque eras, recast in an introverted but instantly audible contemporary idiom.[53] It is a continuation of the string of such works which began with Pueri Hebraeorum in 1928.

In 1956, Nadia Boulanger was given the Harvard Glee Club Medal. Thompson remained one of the few significant American composers of his generation who did not study with her. Nor had he ever wanted to. He found her autocratic, missionary-like zeal for her students foolish, and possibly dangerous. At the dinner honoring her, Thompson was nearly caught off-guard when someone asked him loudly if he had ever studied with 'Mademoiselle.' He replied, "No. But she taught me a lot."[54] When she died, he wrote "She was always very kind to me, but I wonder what her total record will reveal in stature and feeling. How glad I am that I went to Rome when so many others turned to the rue Ballu."[55]

During the 1951-1952 academic year, Thompson had taught a semester-long course called The Age of Handel. When he was commissioned in 1956 by the Virginia 350th Anniversary Commission to compose a work in honor of the first permanent English settlement in the New World, he leaped at the chance to set Michael Drayton's Ode to the Virginian Voyage in a neo-Handelian vein. In the summer of 1956 he worked on the music in Gstaad, finishing the score during the semester break in late January of 1957. What Handel (1685-1759) had to do with the world of 1607 was a point which did not seem to trouble Thompson. It was an occasional work, and the eighteenth-century, 'Merrie England' tone of the music was an

apparently acceptable anachronism.   The high points of this
score are the ingenious double inversion setting of the hymn,
St. Anne, and the extraordinary 'madrigal,' "And in regions
far," which deserves to be known and performed apart from the
whole.[56]

Despite the many commissions which came his way, he did
not altogether abandon personal considerations when it came
to deciding what sort of work he would write.   In the summer
of 1954, he had come across two fragments of biblical text in
the London Times, which as he later said "led to thinking
about the possibility of a dramatic work . . . about life and
death."   The impetus for this cogitation had been meeting the
son of old friends, a young choral conductor named Frederick
S. Pratt II, who was terminally ill, and who had come to talk
with Thompson in June 1954 about the possibility of finding a
job.   In the fall of 1954, Thompson had settled on the idea
of a Requiem for double chorus, in which the conflict
inherent in the life/death struggle would be audibly played
out between the choirs.   The final plan for the work was not
settled until just before Pratt's death, and Thompson's
explanation of the projected work reached Pratt's home the
day after he died.[57]   In such tragic circumstances the work
remained unwritten, while the Mass and the Ode were composed.

The projected Requiem waited another two years.   At the
end of the 1956-1957 academic year, Thompson stepped down as
chairman, was awarded, along with Albert Schweitzer (1875-
1965), the Harvard Glee Club Medal, and went on a year's
sabbatical.   Thompson spent the summer in Gstaad, where he
met Gérard Souzay, the distinguished baritone, for whom he
spontaneously wrote one of his few art-songs, The Passenger.
The song is set to words by Mark Anthony DeWolfe Howe,
Thompson's old colleague from the visiting committee at
Harvard in 1935.   Thompson attached great importance to this
song, and he identified closely with its "real sense of
achievement."[58]   This is evident in the inclusion of an ur-
Thompson motive in the piano accompaniment, marked 'Come un
Alleluia lontano.'[59]

During the summer of 1957, David Boyden at the University
of California asked Thompson to write a work for the May T.
Morrison Festival of Music for the dedication of the new
music buildings.   Thompson was the logical choice, as he had
founded the University Chorus there twenty years earlier.   He
had found the opening he had been waiting for.   In October
Thompson began to assemble the texts, which took six weeks,
before composition was begun in November and finished the
following March.   He described the massive five-section work
that resulted as "an extension of the idea that prompted the
writing of The Peaceable Kingdom," that is, the madrigal
sequences of Vecchi and Banchieri.   It was the transferral of

this technique to a sacred work which intrigued him, and he
went on to say

> The Requiem goes further than The Peaceable Kingdom in
> religious drama-like treatment of the double chorus.
> In the latter, the two choruses sing as one [i. e.,
> with the same moral intent]; in the Requiem they
> represent opposing forces, individually personified
> throughout the work.[60]

Although not his longest work, which was still to come, this
so-called 'Dramatic Dialogue' is little performed.   It is a
Mahlerian undertaking to perform eighty, uninterrupted
minutes of a cappella music, and the work has become best
known through separate performances of Part IV, "The Garment
of Praise."[61]

From the profound emotional depth plumbed in the Requiem,
Thompson's next commission was a pleasant reversal in some
ways.   In 1958, the Town of Amherst, Massachusetts, where his
father-in-law had settled and where his own father had
attended Williams College, asked him to write a work to
celebrate the 200th anniversary of the town's incorporation.
Robert Frost's poetry, because of his association with
Amherst, was appropriately suggested, especially as Frost and
Thompson had known each other for years.   But the poem which
the Town put forward, The Gift Outright, troubled Thompson.
He had qualms about its lamentably imperialistic tone, and
explained gently that the 'manifest destiny' rhetoric of its
lines ("The land was ours before we were the land's . . . "),
would hardly be suitable to the commemoration of a charter
granted by George III.[62]   In its place he substituted seven
poems of his own choosing, writing in a light, easy-to-take
style, not without pathos or a genuine sincerity of feeling
called forth by the better poems, such as the well-known
final chorus Choose something like a star.   At the conclusion
of the premiere on the 18th of October in 1959, Frost rose
spontaneously from his seat and bellowed, "Sing that again!"
Thompson often did this at later performances, to the
amusement of the audience and the confusion of conductors,
who thought he meant the whole work!

In 1959, Thompson was sixty, recognized as the 'dean' of
American choral composers, a remarkable success story in many
ways.   Despite the fact that the dreaded 'highbrows'
continued to ignore him and his music, he was in demand in a
way that perhaps no other American composer before him had
been.   It perplexed him to see the path which so many of his
colleagues and students were taking in composition, towards
serial or experimental idioms which had little in common with
his view of the artist as craftsman, who specifically
produces a desired commodity, or of the proper role of

artists in American society.   He defended himself in a
controversial speech at Yale University, when he addressed
the Intercollegiate Music Council in May of 1959:

> My sympathy gives out when they [composers] shake their
> fists at a cruel world and say, "My art is not wanted;
> it is not appreciated; there is no place for the artist
> in contemporary civilization."   . . . The first thing
> they should realize is this: many of the greatest
> composers' greatest works are choral, and they can all
> be sung by amateurs.   If a piece is too difficult for
> amateurs to sing, then the chances are that it is not
> good enough.[63]

One does not have to share Thompson's estimation of other
compositional idioms to see that his view of the role of a
composer in society was one of longstanding and absolute
conviction, unwavering, and as such still worthy of respect
today.   To see that this was not merely posturing, that there
was not the slightest perceptible 'crack in his armour,' is
to give the lie to those who would (and did) suggest that he
was either a fool or a knave to cling to this highly
debatable aesthetic ground.   Whether or not he was blinkered,
he saw himself vindicated by the successful relationship he
had with his growing audience, and the constant stream of
commissions he received.   He was settled in his ways.   As if
to affirm this, in 1959 he settled himself for life in The
Larches, a large and dilapidated house off Brattle Street.
The finest example of Federalist period architecture in
Cambridge (built in 1808), he and Margaret spent years
lovingly restoring it and sculpting its acre of formal
gardens, these inspired by the Jeffersonian walks at
Monticello and Charlottesville.   It was his Asolo.

This sense of settlement had extended to all but one area
of his life.   It is a remarkable fact about so devout a man
as Thompson that, although baptised into the Episcopal
Church, he had never been received into communion by that or
any other organized religion.   The faith life of the composer
of The Peaceable Kingdom and the Requiem was obviously one of
great depth, and, feeling that the time had come to make a
public confession, he had been confirmed in April of 1958 and
became a member of the historic foundation of Christ Church,
Cambridge.   He felt a great sense of gratitude for being
accepted so late in life, and set about finding a suitable
work to compose by way of a 'thanks-offering.'   The Nativity
According to St. Luke was written between July of 1960 and
June of 1961.   The occasion it celebrated was the 200th
anniversary of the dedication of Christ Church, but the work
took on enormous psychological and religious importance for
Thompson.   'A Musical Drama in Seven Scenes,' it is really
his second opera, a chancel drama full of skillful and

radiant music, depicting indeed what he once described as "a world without dissonance in it." The first performances in December of 1961 were extravagantly produced, but the work failed to gain the foothold in the popular imagination he had wished for it. Over the years it became an increasingly bitter disappointment for him, as he had hoped that at best the work would join the ranks of Britten's A Ceremony of Carols and Menotti's Amahl as a Christmas 'standard,' or at least that it would become an annual fixture at Christ Church. It was never revived there, although performances have been sporadically mounted by enterprising congregations, including one in Japan which intrigued Thompson enormously.[64]

At the end of the 1961-1962 academic year, Thompson went on a leave of absence from Harvard. It gave him an opportunity to rest, and also to attend to several small commissions. Chief among these is the cantata, A Feast of Praise. This curious and almost unknown piece for chorus, brass ensemble and harp is notable primarily for Thompson's only extended use of non-triadic (here, quartal) harmony. Commissioned by Stanford University, Thompson conducted the premiere in August of 1963. Between the unexpected chordal idiom and the irregular metrical schemes, it must have been quite a shock to audiences expecting another Alleluia.

When he returned to Harvard in the fall of 1963, he once again taught Fugue and Choral Composition, his favorite subjects. He was "a born teacher and he believed in the inspiration of the moment when he taught. . . ."[65] It was his practice to work aloud at the board, and have a teaching assistant take down the compositions as they grew. A very sizeable group of organ and keyboard pieces were amassed over these years in his Tonal Counterpoint and Fugue classes. He published a selection, Twenty Chorale Preludes, Four Inventions and a Fugue later, in 1969.

The 1964-1965 academic year was Thompson's last before retirement. Very much at the height of his powers, he was commissioned early in 1964 to compose a work for the 150th anniversary of the founding of the Handel and Haydn Society, the composition of which occupied him during the summer and fall semester, and early months of 1965. The Passion According to St. Luke was a corollary to The Nativity, although Thompson searched long and hard before settling on the Passion story for the work. It is his longest and most ambitious single work, and three points may merit special consideration. Unlike most Passion settings, Thompson's Passion opens with the triumphant entry into Jerusalem. Secondly, the use of the chorus as narrator or evangelist is unusual, but perfectly in keeping with Thompson's keen interest in choral writing. It was probably suggested by the similar use of the chorus in Malipiero's La Passione, which

Thompson knew as he had an inscribed copy in his library. Thirdly, it, along with The Nativity, is one of Thompson's few settings of New Testament text. With the exception of a very few passages in the Requiem, and the brief Glory to God in the Highest of 1958, he had been exclusively a setter of Old Testament texts.[66] The premiere, in March of 1965, was well received, in spite of the abyssmal level of performance to which the Handel and Haydn Society had sunk in those years. This premiere was followed by another important milestone less than a month later, when the combined choruses and orchestras of Harvard and Radcliffe presented a concert in honor of Thompson upon his retirement. For this occasion on the 23rd of April in 1965, he had scored Frostiana for chamber orchestra, and the concert included the Odes of Horace and The Last Words of David, all conducted by the composer. It was a fitting valedictory to one whose efforts fully entitled him to rest upon his laurels.

The Laureate: 1965-1984

Retirement for Thompson did not, however, mean resting from his labors. Freed from his teaching, but principally from his administrative commitments, he continued to lecture widely during the last two decades of his life. He also accepted commissions. Two came his way in 1966-1967, fulfilled with differing results. The Harvard Musical Association commissioned him in 1966 to compose a work for its 130th anniversary, and in early 1967 he wrote his Second String Quartet. It proved to be a very different work from his First, composed a quarter century earlier. There is a lightness of touch, and a sense of restraint in this lovely piece which is missing in the earlier quartet. The third movement is one of Thompson's most inspired ideas, with the first violin soaring at the end to a breathtakingly high C-sharp. It is a work which makes one consider whether all the previous years of relentless choral composition were all that well placed. The next commission he filled brings to mind similar misgivings. For the centennial of the New England Conservatory, he was commissioned to compose a work for mixed choir with a chorus of children's voices, and he wrote A Psalm of Thanksgiving in Gstaad between August and November 1967.[67] The first performance, in the midst of a freak November blizzard, was poorly attended and presaged the neglect into which the work has fallen, in part because of the slightly awkward forces employed, and in part because of a certain mechanical, workaday quality of the melodic invention, which is especially noticeable in his treatment of Crüger's Nun danket alle Gott. It is interesting to see, nevertheless, how Thompson combined passages from both the King James Version and the Book of Common Prayer translations of Psalm 107, and how he set that most famous of texts, "They that go down to the sea in ships." Inevitably, it suffers from the same kind of over-parodying that distracts in the Ode to the Virginian Voyage.

In early 1968, plans were made at Harvard to publish a volume of newly composed works in honor of G. Wallace Woodworth, who had been Thompson's close friend and colleague for over forty years. For the occasion, he wrote a setting of The Eternal Dove, to a text by Joseph Beaumont (1615-1699), incorporating into it passages from the Mass of the Holy Spirit, whose first performance 'Woody' had conducted. It was thus a kind of reversal of the 'parody Mass' idea, here creating the motet from material in the Mass, an idea of which Thompson was quite proud. The concluding "Hallelujah" was also a reference to Woody's direction of the first performance of Alleluia in 1940.

By 1968, the Alleluia of 1940 had become the best selling piece of American choral music ever published, a position it still holds today. Thompson's publisher, E. C. Schirmer Music Co., in Boston, had passed in 1966 to the directorship of Robert MacWilliams, who greatly expanded and updated much of the firm's catalog and its approach to publishing. The relationship they had with Thompson is unparalleled in the history of American music.[68] It was also in the spring of 1968 that Thompson, musing in his study at Larch Road one day, made a fascinating discovery: that all of Alleluia had been, quite unintentionally, written in four-part invertible counterpoint. "My excitement would be hard to describe," he later said, and he at once set about recasting the versions for men's and women's voices alone, which had long escaped his or his colleagues' efforts to produce.[69]

The popularity of Alleluia was something which Thompson took with great equanimity. In 1968 he accepted a commission from Saint Thomas Church Choir School in New York for a work for treble voices and chamber orchestra, to mark the fiftieth anniversary of the school's foundation. During later discussions regarding the commission he mentioned that he had selected texts for the work from Robert Herrick, and had applied to the poet Richard Wilbur for permission to set one of his translations. The commission committee at Saint Thomas' were enthusiastic about these choices, yet at one point found the courage to ask if, just possibly, the last movement might not be a setting of the word, "Alleluia." Thompson thought on the phone for a moment, and then said, "Well, you know: my Alleluias don't come cheap!" In the course of composition in late 1968 and early 1969 in Gstaad, he arranged the text of the final movement so that it could be sung as a second "Alleluia," but it has never achieved the same popularity.

As he reached his seventieth birthday, there were the vague stirrings of renewed national interest in Thompson and his music, propelled especially by the buildup towards the nation's Bicentennial in 1976.   In 1969, the University of Pennsylvania bestowed an honorary doctorate on him, the second of four he would eventually receive.   He was again honored with honorary doctorates, from Allegheny College in 1973, and from New England Conservatory in 1975, when a rare performance of his First Symphony was given to celebrate the event.   In 1974, the American Choral Foundation honored him with a special issue of American Choral Review devoted to writings on his music.

These years were attended with personal difficulties.   Of the two unaccompanied settings of poetry of George Herbert, composed in 1970-1971, the poignant and moving Bitter-Sweet was composed as a memorial to Thompson's grandaughter, Katie, who had died very young.   The tersely jubilant setting of Antiphon followed as a pendant about a year later.   They show that Thompson was still, at seventy, in complete control of his creative powers, although the text of Bitter-Sweet was clearly more personal and brought forth a higher level of inspiration.   The same sense of loss and regret ran through several other works of these years, especially Fare Well, his Walter de la Mare setting of 1973.   His health had begun to suffer, and by the time he accepted a commission in 1974 for a Bicentennial theme work for the Town of Concord, he needed an amanuensis to help him complete the full score of A Concord Cantata.   In 1975 while on vacation in California, he suffered a stroke.   His eyesight and coordination were further impaired, and a memory deficit added to his health problems.   A tedious year of recovery and rehabilitation led to some significant improvements.

In the fall of 1976, Thompson met David Francis Urrows, then a student of Harold Shapero and Arthur Berger at Brandeis University.   An invitation to discuss music in general led to private lessons in composition in exchange for copying and secretarial work.   In 1975, Thompson had accepted a commission from the Rocky Ridge Music Center in Colorado for a three movement work for chorus and orchestra. Thompson's stroke and subsequent recovery had put off composition of the piece, but with Urrows' help as amanuensis he began to assemble the texts and compose again.[70]   In the summer of 1977 he wrote Two Worlds, and decided to revise and include in the work, now projected to be four movements, his 1918 composition The Light of Stars.   Also inserted into the growing work was the 1957 song, The Passenger.   Finally, Siciliano, a song from theater music which he had written for his Boston club, was chosen, making a fifth movement.   Work on the song cycle for Rocky Ridge was interrupted by another commission, from the Kentucky State Music Educators

Association, for whom he wrote The Morning Stars for chorus and orchestra while in Gstaad in January of 1978. In the early summer of 1978 he finished The Happy Shore, a setting of Edmund Spenser's sonnet from the Amoretti, the final movement of Five Love Songs.[71] The premiere was given in August, 1978, and although he could not be present, he sent a taped speech in which he thanked the organizers of the festival for their patience:

> It was never my intention to take three years to accomplish what I would have normally accomplished in a single year. . . . From the very beginning of my creative work it has been my ambition not to wait for an angel with a golden pen to guide my hand. On the contrary, my aesthetic resembles the principles laid down, years and years ago [in Rome], namely, to provide what was wanted, needed, and requested, and even, if possible, to transcend the terms which were defined . . . .[72]

In 1979, the American Choral Foundation planned another special issue devoted to his music. In an interview with Urrows, he elaborated on the above-mentioned principles:

> The aesthetic principles I referred to were really adopted as the result of various influences during my three years at the American Academy in Rome. They owe their origin to the bottega system. For example, a printer or an architect in mediaeval society would set up a shop or a booth (bottega) and take orders or commissions . . . always to create something according to the specifications laid down by the patron. . . . They didn't work only when an inspiration came to them. They worked, and in the process of working they were inspired to transcend the stipulations set forth . . . .[73]

These later works are a tribute to Thompson's sense of a composer's responsibility more than important additions to his catalog. The large scale architectonic sweep, never his strong point, was beyond his reach at this time, but the mere quality of his workmanship prevails against odds in a piece like Two Worlds, with its unsettling triplet accompaniment and unusual mixture of modes. The inclusion of three earlier works, two of which were at the time unpublished, in Five Love Songs, is significant. In 1978, Thompson and Urrows excavated Thompson's collection of musical manuscripts from his archives, and sent them to Houghton Library at Harvard, where they remain on deposit. In the process of doing so, a large number of unpublished pieces, which Thompson had not seen for decades, came to light. Impressed with their quality, he decided to publish some of them. Foremost among

these was the Suite of 1924. A short piano work of 1925, The
Boats were Talking, had originally been written as a wedding
present for Leopold Mannes and his first wife, Edie. Upon
publication in 1980, Thompson changed the dedication to
Mannes alone. The Last Invocation, one of the works
submitted for the Rome Prize in 1922, was also sent to E. C.
Schirmer, as was the Scherzino which he had written for Bloch
in 1920.

In 1980, Thompson was named laureate of the Julius Adams
Stratton Prize for Intercultural Achievement, given by the
Friends of Switzerland, of Boston. This coveted award
carried with it the obligation to name a young colleague in
the laureate's field who would receive the Stratton
Fellowship for study or creative work in Switzerland.
Thompson promptly nominated Urrows, who accepted. In 1981,
Thompson was unexpectedly offered the Reynolds Lectureship in
the Humanities by Emory and Henry College, a small Methodist
college in Emory, Virginia. He was asked specifically to
talk on the influence of indigenous music in his own work,
and could not resist the chance to write several short pieces
illustrating how the singing traditions to which John Powell
had introduced him had affected his own style. The pieces
charmed the audience, and he left with a promise to continue
writing a larger work around them. It took two more years to
compose the remaining parts of his final work, Twelve
Canticles. The final canticle (Thompson's use of the term
implied 'sacred song') was a linking of the two Amens of
1927, which he had written for his own wedding.[74] He also
reused melodic material from A Trip to Nahant in the sixth
and ninth canticles, probably unintentionally.[75]

In early 1983, Thompson was named laureate of the Andre
and Clara Mertens Festival of Contemporary Music at the
University of Bridgeport, Connecticut. His increasingly
delicate health made it a difficult trip, but he enjoyed
especially hearing a performance of the Second Symphony
during the week. The premiere of Twelve Canticles was given
on 30 October 1983. Thompson, frail but excited, made the
trip to Virginia to hear the work. Early in the following
year, his eyesight had deteriorated to the point that his
doctors recommended an operation on his cataracts.
Complications ensued, and he was bedridden for weeks,
although he managed to receive a temporary discharge to
attend a concert in his honor at the Longy School of Music in
Cambridge. At this event, a proclamation from Gov. Michael
S. Dukakis was read, proclaiming 21 April 1984 Randall
Thompson Day in the Commonwealth of Massachusetts.
Eventually he was able to return home in May. With Urrows,
he continued to discuss the revisions, with a view towards
publication, of The Morning Stars which they had begun the
previous fall, omitting the orchestra entirely and replacing

it with a few chordal passages for piano in the opening
section only. They also discussed revising and publishing
the Prelude for viola and piano which he had written in 1920
for Raisbeck's Torches. The relevant manuscripts were found
and left with Urrows to prepare fair copies for submission to
E. C. Schirmer. But in June his condition suddenly worsened,
and he was transferred back to Massachusetts General
Hospital. He lapsed into a coma, and after three weeks,
passed away on 9 July 1984. Margaret survived him by less
than a year. In 1985 his personal papers were given to the
Houghton Library, joining his manuscripts, and by the end of
the year, The Larches had been sold, and his gardens and
walks came under the care of other hands.

NOTES

David Francis Urrows is the author of Thompson's biography
and is thus the author referred to throughout these notes.

Childhood and Youth

1. Where otherwise uncredited, all material in quotations is
from conversations with the author, 1977-1984. "Miss
Harris," about whom nothing further is known, may possibly
have been a maternal aunt or other relation of Bertrand
Harris Bronson (Harris was his mother's maiden name).

2. Randall Thompson, recollections for the Vienna Historical
Society, dictated in 1983. After 1912, the Thompson family
does not seem to have stayed at Vienna in the summers.

3. He played it on a recital program preceeding the
Commencement Exercises at Lawrenceville on 11 June 1916. Van
Dyck died of septicemia caused by an alveolar abscess on 25
January 1916.

The Cosmopole

4. "My life," he said on a number of occasions, "has been an
attempt to strike back!"

5. Hocking, William Ernest. "Palmer, George Herbert." The Dictionary of American Biography, 20 volumes, edited by Dumas Malone. New York: Charles Scribner's Sons, 1934. XIV, 180-83. See for a précis of Palmer's thought and life. "Few have been so gifted in the capacity for reaching objective estimations of personal ability."

6. Mannes, Richards, and Thompson were fast friends, and a bit of a known trio at Harvard in these years. The poet David McCord (Harvard, '21) told the author of evenings spent in one of the Harvard dormitories, where in one room he and Mannes would be, say, making a telescope, and in the other, Richards and Thompson would be playing chamber music. Richards appears also to have played the cello. Both Mannes and Richards later killed themselves. When shown, around 1980, a photograph of the three friends at Harvard, Thompson quipped to the author: "Both suicides. It's a wonder I didn't do myself in, too."

7. Dana, son of the author of Two Years Before the Mast, was widower of Edith Longfellow, daughter of the poet.

8. The publication includes prelude music and a song by "Randall Thompson," so by this point Ira had been dropped for good.

9. Sessions (Harvard, '15) was on the faculty of Smith College at this time. Thompson had come to know Sessions at Harvard. In the fall of 1921, Sessions went on to become Bloch's assistant at the Cleveland Institute of Music.

10. The initial distribution of the fellowships was an awkward matter, and has never been accurately documented. The version of events given in the standard history of the American Academy in Rome (Valentine, Lucia N. and Alan Chester Valentine. The American Academy in Rome, 1894-1969. Charlottesville: University Press of Virginia, 1973) as well as in other sources, particularly those concerning Sowerby, gloss over the matter and suggest that all three fellowships were competitive. In fact they were not. Thompson reported to the author that there was distinct coolness on this score between Sowerby and the other two men, who felt that Sowerby had not really earned but rather 'engineered' his fellowship. Time has perhaps shown Sowerby to have been the least talented. See below in re Wintter Watts.

11. Sessions was known to be Bloch's favorite pupil at the time.   It is possible that Sessions had also applied for the Rome Prize, and that this was Bloch's not-so-subtle way of stonewalling with Thompson.   Sessions did receive the Rome Prize in 1928.   Sessions' relationship with Bloch is discusssed in: Nott, Michael.   "Roger Sessions's Fugal Studies with Ernest Bloch: A Glimpse into the Workshop." American Music Vol. 7, no. 3 (Fall 1989), 245-59.

12. Letter of George Herbert Palmer to the American Academy in Rome, 27 February 1922.   By permission of the Houghton Library, Harvard University.

The American Academy in Rome

13. Quoted in: Sachs, Harvey.   Music in Fascist Italy. (London: Weidenfeld and Nicholson, 1987), 104.   Also see: Nicolodi, Fiamma.   Musica e musicisti nel ventennio fascista. (Fiesole: Discanto, 1984).

14. Details given here about Lamond (Pronouced LAY-mond) are from my own research at Teacher's College and Columbia University libraries in New York.   The details given in the Valentines' The American Academy in Rome, 1894-1969, the obituary in The New York Times (17 March 1940), and a derived notice in The Diapason (1 April 1940) are full of inaccuracies about his life and career.

15. Not Trinity Church, on Wall Street.   Trinity Chapel was on West 26th Street, and is now the Serbian Orthodox Cathedral of St. Sava.

16. He dedicated his first major composition in Rome, the extremely Bloch-like Piano Sonata in C Minor, to Felix Lamond, and later dedicated his symphonic poem The Piper at the Gates of Dawn to Mrs. Lamond.

17. Elizabeth (Mrs. Huntington) Brown, letter to the author, 28 July 1987.

18. Malipiero had taken down in dictation the last two of Smareglia's operas, and Thompson met the aging, blind Smareglia through Malipiero.   His music is still something of a cult item in Venice.

19. The list of Thompson's later works which were influenced or even directly modeled on works by Malipiero is lengthy: to mention a few, Thompson's setting of Horace's ode Poscimur (later the first movement of his First Symphony) echoes the above-mentioned orchestral works and the Rispetti; the semi-comic opera Solomon and Balkis (1942), with its brilliant Scarlatti-esque dash and vigor, has much in common with Malipiero's Tre commedie goldoniane (1920-1922).   Finally, Thompson directly borrowed the idea of using the chorus as narrator or evangelist in his Passion According to St. Luke (1964) from Malipiero's La Passione of 1935, a copy of which Thompson received from the composer.

20. This account of the castrati was told by Thompson to many people, including the author.   For a full discussion of the genesis of the two Odes later reworked for the First Symphony, see the author's article "A 'Lost' Choral Masterwork by Randall Thompson" in the American Choral Review Vol. XXXII, no.1/2 (Winter/Spring 1990), 8-16.   Thompson told the author (and I have stated in the mentioned article) that Gustav Holst, on a brief visit to Rome, saw these pieces and gave him helpful comments on them.   However, I have not been able to find any record of a visit to Rome by Holst in 1924. It is more likely that Thompson met Holst in London in the summer of 1924.   Thompson attended the Three Choirs Festival that year, and traveled through England and Scotland.   He also met Herbert Howells who, among other rising composers in the musical world of England, could well have introduced them.

21. The Suite, engraved in the early 1980s and the proofs corrected by the author, is expected to be issued in 1991 by E. C. Schirmer Music Co.   What became of Mannes' compositions on the theme is unknown.

22. Letter of Randall Thompson to Felix Lamond (San Sebastian, no date, but July or August 1925).   By permission of the American Academy in Rome.   Interestingly, Watts does not appear in any public records of Fellows of the Academy.

Homecoming and Marriage

23. Boleslavky founded the American Laboratory Theatre with Maria Ouspenskaya, as a kind of cooperative, vaguely socialist artistic venture.   Labiche wrote his once-popular farce in 1851.

24. Copland felt Thompson's "very excellence of workmanship seems to be offered in lieu of a more personal style," and that the "Invocation to Venus" [O Venus, regina Cnidi Paphique, from the Odes of Horace] and "especially his string quartet [The Wind in the Willows] are the works in which he seems nearest to the achievement of a personal idiom." See "America's Young Men of Promise." Modern Music Vol. III, no. 3 (March-April 1926), 14.

25. Letter of Randall Thompson to Felix Lamond, 11 November 1926. By permission of the American Academy in Rome.

26. Letter of Randall Thompson to Leopold D. Mannes, 18 October 1927. By permission of the Houghton Library, Harvard University. Several of his former choristers recall singing Mannes' setting of Shelley's The Moon, and Daniel Gregory Mason's The Mirror. Mason and Thompson were both inducted into the National Institute of Arts and Letters in 1938, and shared a great love of Beethoven's chamber music. Thompson, who modeled his First String Quartet on the Rassumovskii quartets, was later consulted extensively when Mason wrote his book, The Quartets of Beethoven, published in 1947.

27. Letter of Elizabeth Curtiss Willis (Wellesley, '28) to the author, 26 May 1988.

28. Thompson told many people that it was Olin Downes' negative review of the premiere in The New York Times that goaded him, in the summer of 1930, to compose his popular Second Symphony as a riposte. However, Downes did not review the First Symphony until a second Rochester performance on 21 May 1931. See: Downes, Olin. "Chadwick Work Played at Festival: 'Rip Van Winkel' Overture well received at Eastman School Event." The New York Times (22 May 1931), 28. In his review Downes complained about the "cloven hoof of Ernest Bloch, Mr. Thompson's teacher . . ." appearing in the work, and that "we believe that it will be discarded by Mr. Thompson in a later day." Thompson seems to have composed the Second Symphony without prodding from Downes. He may well have confused the reviewers. Of Brown little is known. Wessel was one of the first American students of Schoenberg in Vienna. Thompson praised Wessel's Symphony-Concertante for Horn, Piano and Orchestra in his 1932 Musical Quarterly article, "The Contemporary Scene in American Music."

29. Letter of Randall Thompson to Felix Lamond, 1 June 1930. By permission of the American Academy in Rome. Jacobi (1891-

1952) was director of the American section of the International Society for Contemporary Music, and Thompson was enthusiastic about his use of American Indian themes in his music of the 1920s.

30. Thompson related this story exactly as it appears here, to the author. The score was at the Eastman School's Sibley Music Library until after Hanson's death on 26 February 1981. It was then transferred to Houghton Library, Harvard University. The seal, which reads "University Library/Rochester," is clearly visible on the title page. As Thompson did not see the score between 1930 and 1981, I believe this story to be essentially true as reported. Unlike Thompson, Hanson gradually forgot about the incident, and maintained a curious one-sided correspondence with Thompson into the 1970s.

31. Thompson had no works performed at Yaddo during the first two years. His perennially popular Velvet Shoes (1927) was performed and recorded in the 1937 Festival. For details about the Young Composers Group see: Copland, Aaron and Vivian Perlis. Copland: 1900 Through 1942. (New York: St. Martin's/Marek, 1984). On page 203 of this work a group photograph of the 1932 Yaddo Festival shows Thompson with cigarette in hand, fifth from the right and to the immediate left of Paul Bowles.

32. Surrette had established a summer music school in Concord, Massachusetts, in 1914 and was involved with Davison in the editing and publishing of useful editions of music, especially choral music, for younger voices, a dearth of which existed before and after the First World War. Much of this was published in the well-known Concord Series by E. C. Schirmer Music Co., founded in Boston in 1921. It was through Surrette and Davison that Thompson became associated with Schirmer. His first publication had been Pueri Hebraeorum in 1923. Surrette was also the advisor on music to the Guggenheim Foundation.

33. Forbes, Elliot. A History of Music at Harvard to 1972. Cambridge, Mass: Department of Music, Harvard University, 1988.

34. Interview with Randall Thompson by Jean Bonin, 18 October 1973. Oral History Collection, University of Virginia; Manuscripts Department of the Alderman Library. Charlottesville, Virginia. Accession No. of Collection: 9800.

35. It was here, on the St. Christoph, that the photograph which appeared on the jacket of Maurice Abravanel's 1978 recording of Thompson's First Symphony on Angel was taken in mid-January 1936.

36. Randall Thompson to Douglas Moore, 22 April 1936. The letter is reproduced in part in: Norman, Gertrude, and Miriam L. Schrifte, eds. Letters of Composers: An Anthology. New York: Grosset and Dunlap, 1946. In the 1932 Musical Quarterly article referred to above, Thompson wrote: "Owing to the Cult of Individuality, we have an irrepressible fondness for spotting 'similarities.' The habit is so widespread that it extends from the most casual listener to the most intelligent critic. . . . Why can we not realize once and for all that detection of similarities belongs to the realm of musicology? [my emphasis] There, for historical reasons, it is highly important. But in contemporary criticism it is deadening . . . it is with their uninhibited use of current artifice that they [composers] have expressed the spirit of their times and, sometimes, achieved universality."

37. The remarkable volte-face of American music critics in the 1930s, from shocked conservatives to jaded avant-gardistes, is a topic worth considerable study. Thompson, in his article "The Second Year at Yaddo" in Modern Music Vol XI, no. 1 (November-December 1933), 40-42, had observed a reciprocal turn around in the styles of the composers present: "the radical kicking and screaming of last year have turned to a stately tread and decorous speech. Gone the nonconformity, gone the hearty satisfaction of smashing everything in sight; gone the passionate conviction, gone the spirit of the Mohawk trail. . . ." His observations were correct, if uttered with sarcasm which, I think, no one then or since has picked up on. But few then saw or could explain the critical side of that coin. One who did, and whose writing, I think, had a great influence on Thompson, was Constant Lambert (1905-1951) and especially his influential book Music Ho!: A Study of Music in Decline first published in 1934. See in particular the chapter: "The Revolutionary Situation," p. 32 of the London, Hogarth Press, 1985 edition.

38. Copland, Aaron. "Our Younger Generation--Ten Years Later." Modern Music Vol. XIII, no. 4 (May-June 1936), 5-6. This is a strange opinion coming from Copland, who two years later would write Billy the Kid.

The Academic

39. Letter of Dr. Alfred Mann to the author, 6 January 1990. Mann was, as a staff musicologist, another of the 'novelties' which Thompson introduced.

40. Stevens, Halsey. The Life and Music of Béla Bartók, rev. edition (London: Oxford University Press, 1964), 38. See for Thompson's description of the incident.

41. Mann, Alfred. "Madrigal Awards." American Choral Review Vol. XXIX, no. 1 (Winter 1987), 24-26. See for further details of Thompson's short-lived choral projects at Curtis.

42. Bernstein, Leonard. Findings. (New York: Simon and Schuster, 1982), 320-23. The story is recounted in Bernstein's work.

43. Letter of Randall Thompson to Lydia P. Veazie, 25 July 1977. By permission of the Houghton Library, Harvard University. Thompson's preferred tempo was M. M. = 60.

44. Mann, Alfred. "Madrigal Awards." American Choral Review.

45. For contemporary reaction see: Philadelphia Inquirer, 21 Feb. 1941; Philadelphia Inquirer, 22 Feb. 1941; New York Times, 21 Feb. 1941; Evening Bulletin, 25 Feb. 1941; Record, 21 Feb. 1941, p. 12. Reiner claimed at the time that the two resignations were unconnected. Upon learning of Thompson's resignation, Roy Harris sent him a telegram which read: "Bravo congratulations on your stand for music. Fraternally, Roy Harris." Randall Thompson papers. By permission of the Houghton Library, Harvard University.

46. Porter, Quincy. "American Composers, XVIII: Randall Thompson." Modern Music Vol. XIX, no. 4 (May-June 1942), 240-41. My emphasis.

47. Inaugural address, Princeton University, 1946. Quoted in: Forbes, Elliot. "The Music of Randall Thompson." Musical Quarterly Vol. XXXV, no. 1 (January 1949), 1.

48. The topic of 'the devaluation of the past' and the supression of the 'traditional' wing of twentieth-century American music after 1945 is treated fairly and responsibly in: Tawa, Nicholas. A Most Wondrous Babble: American Art Composers, Their Music, and the American Art Scene, 1950-1985 (Westport, CT: Greenwood Press, 1987).

Harvard Redux

49. Meyer, Leonard. Music, the Arts, and Ideas (Chicago: University of Chicago Press, 1967), 238. I have somewhat removed from context, though not changed the basic intent of Prof. Meyer's words here.

50. For additional details concerning Thompson's teaching of specific courses at Harvard, which are beyond the range of this study, see: Forbes, Elliot. A History of Music at Harvard to 1972.

51. The cover of the original edition read Five Odes of Horace. It was altered to 'Six' in 1956. Felices ter fits neither emotionally nor tonally with the other five. This should in itself disprove the oft-stated allegation that over the years Thompson's compositional style 'never changed.'

52. Letter of Randall Thompson to Henry Pleasants, 7 February 1955, Pleasants Collection, Boston University Library. By permission of Henry Pleasants. Pleasants, author of The Agony of Modern Music, had been a student at Curtis during Thompson's directorship.

53. This work has been discussed at length in: Haar, James. "Randall Thompson and the Music of the Past." American Choral Review Vol. XVI, no. 4 (October 1974), 7-15. Haar was a student of Thompson's at Harvard when the Mass was being written.

54. Compare the comments of another non-Boulanger student, Roger Sessions, in: Copland, Aaron and V. Perlis. Copland: 1900 Through 1942, 149-50.

55. Letter of Randall Thompson to the author, 25 October 1979. Private collection. Thompson, even if he had known about it (which I doubt he did) did not apply to go to

Fontainebleau for the simple reasons that it was established almost concurrently with the Department of Musical Composition at the American Academy in Rome and that Thompson was involved with his Master's degree in 1921-1922.

56. The inverse contrary imitation setting of St. Anne was originally composed in 1942 at the University of Virginia for a blind student in Thompson's counterpoint class. It was later rearranged for double choir, or choir with organ (or other instruments) alternatim in 1972, as The Mirror of St. Anne.   The 'madrigal,' And in regions far, is unfortunately not published separately from the full vocal score.

57. Thompson's thorough analysis of the work and description of its origins may be seen in "Notes on a Requiem," American Choral Review Vol. XVI, no. 4 (October 1974), 16-32.

58. Urrows, David Francis. "Five Love Songs: Reflections on a Recent Work."   American Choral Review Vol. XXII, no. 2 (April 1980), 28-38.   Interview with Randall Thompson and D. F. Urrows.

59. This "Alleluia" motive was later used in the final chorus of the Requiem, and throughout Five Love Songs (1978), into which The Passenger was intercalated.

60. Thompson, Randall. "Notes on a Requiem." American Choral Review.

61. Performances of separate sections were sanctioned by Thompson. First performed in 1958, a study score was issued in 1963, but the vocal (octavo) edition was not published until 1974.

62. When he came to include "The Gift Outright" in A Concord Cantata (1975), he did so only as a last resort.

63. Thompson, Randall. "Writing for the Amateur Chorus: A Chance and a Challenge." American Choral Review Vol. XXII, no. 2 (April 1980), 5-15. Thompson's article was partially reprinted here in this special issue.

64. Although, by general consensus, Thompson's music does not

'travel well,' a number of his works have been well received in Japan.   In addition to <u>The Nativity</u>, <u>The Testament of Freedom</u> has been performed successfully there and elsewhere in Asia.

65. Hughes, David, Leon Kirchner and Elliot Forbes.   [Harvard University] Faculty of Arts and Sciences Memorial Minute, 21 May 1985.   <u>Harvard Gazette</u> (4 October 1985), 4.

66. Whether his reception into the Episcopal church in 1958 had any influence on his choice of texts is an idea worth pondering.   It was clear that the criteria for texts he wished to set were not met by the relatively didactic language of the New Testament.   A by-product of this is the interest which Jewish musicians, congregations, and choruses have expressed in his music, especially <u>The Peaceable Kingdom</u> and <u>Alleluia</u>.

<u>The Laureate</u>

67. Mann, Alfred. "Psalm and Gospel Settings."   <u>Randall Thompson: A Choral Legacy</u>, ed. by Alfred Mann. (Boston: E. C. Schirmer Music Co., 1983), 58-64.   This contains further details of this work.

68. The only mature works of Thompson's which were <u>not</u> published by E. C. Schirmer were the three symphonies, <u>the</u> First String Quartet, two short piano works, <u>Song After Sundown</u> and <u>Little Prelude</u> (all of these by Carl Fischer), and five songs written in 1927 for <u>New Songs for New Voices</u>, a Harcourt-Brace publication.   The popular <u>Velvet Shoes</u> was subsequently taken over by E. C. Schirmer Music Co., along with <u>My Master Hath a Garden</u>.

69. Thompson, Randall. "The Story of an <u>Alleluia</u>."   <u>Randall Thompson: A Choral Legacy</u>, 29-30.

70. In addition to the author, several other young musicians worked with Thompson during these years in various capacities: Marilyn Boenau, Roger Bourland, Bill Hills, Joyce Kouffman, and Amy Wygant.

71. Urrows, David F.   "<u>Five Love Songs</u>: . . ."   <u>American Choral Review</u>.   See for details of this working relationship

in this interview with Urrows and Thompson.

72. Pre-recorded address to the Rocky Ridge Music Center, August 1978. See also: "Five Love Songs: . . ."

73. Urrows, David F. "Five Love Songs: . . ."   Interview with Urrows and Thompson, May 1979.

74. The Amens had also been used in his 1971 suite for string quartet, Wedding Music (also known as Music for a Wedding in Rome), which he had written for his younger son's wedding. The crudely effected joint in the last of Twelve Canticles is very obvious, tonally unsuccessful, and in the present writer's opinion a rare, grave error in judgement.

75. Note also the reuse of melodic material from The Nativity (associated with the Archangel Gabriel) in The Morning Stars of 1978. Thompson also had forgotten that he had set the text of The Morning Stars previously, in his Requiem.

Catalog of Works

This listing is chronological within each category. See Solow, Linda, et al. <u>Boston Composers Project</u> (B185) for the instrumention of Thompson's orchestral works.

The Houghton Library, where Thompson's manuscripts are held, is at Harvard University. They are under the control of the Curator of Musical Manuscripts. Harvard University, Cambridge, Mass. 02138. Tel. 617/495-244

I

Secular Choral Works

E. C. Schirmer has been the sole publisher of Thompson's choral works throughout his long career and the inventory number listed is that of the publisher. Since Thompson's death, a number of works that had not previously been published are now in print. Quite a number of the choral works are published in several voice combinations and it should be noted that Thompson himself, with few noted exceptions, made these arrangements. E. C. Schirmer Music Publishing Co.; 138 Ipswich St.; Boston, Mass. 02215. Tel. 617/236-1935

W1. <u>The Light of Stars</u> for SATB
     <u>1918</u>
     Text: Henry W. Longfellow; <u>Voices of the Night</u> (1839)
     Won the Francis Boott Prize at Harvard in 1919

     E. C. Schirmer-# 3052; 1980

     Premiere: Cambridge, Mass.; 27 May 1919
                Harvard and Radcliffe Choruses
                Archibald T. Davison, conductor

See also Five Love Songs, W23

Manuscript: Autograph probably lost

        Harvard University Archives:
        Holograph manuscript (in uncertain hand)
        Given by Randall Thompson in 1940

W2. Mariner's Song for SATB
     1920
     Text: Thomas Lovell Beddoes
     Based on a theme by Walter R. Spalding

     Manuscript: Houghton Library:
               score; 21 January 1920
               Assignment for Walter R. Spalding

W3. Night for SATB and piano
     1920
     Text: Robert Southey
     Boott Prize Honorable Mention in 1920

     Unpublished

     Manuscript: Lost, or possibly destroyed

W4. The Last Invocation for SSATTB
     1922
     One of three works submitted for the Prix de Rome
     Text: Walt Whitman

     E. C. Schirmer-# 3167; 1989

     Premiere: Boston, Mass.; 10 April 1983
               King's Chapel Choir
               Daniel Pinkham, conductor

     Manuscript: Houghton Library:
               26 Jan.-19 Feb. 1922

W5. Odes of Horace for SATB and men's voices with
     piano/orchestra and without accompaniment
     1924
     Text: Quintus Horatius Flaccus (Horace); Odes

     Dedicated to Hugh Ross and the Schola Cantorum of New
       York

1.   Quis multa gracilis (To Pyrrha) (<u>Odes</u>, I, 5)
       TTBB a cappella
2.   Vitas hinnuleo me similis, Chloe (To Chloe) (<u>Odes</u>, I
       23) SATB a cappella
3.   O Venus, regina Cnidi Paphique (Invocation to Venus)
       <u>Odes</u>, I, 30)
       SSATTBB with piano/chamber orchestra
4.   O fons Bandusiae, splendidior vitro (To the Fountain
       of Bandusia (<u>Odes</u>, III, 13)
       SSATBB a cappella
5.   Montium custos nemorumque, Virgo (Dedication of a
       Pine Tree to Diana) (<u>Odes</u>, III, 22)
       SATB a cappella

E. C. Schirmer: No. 1--# 539
                  No. 2--# 1624; 1932
                  No. 3--# 1623; 1932
                  No. 4--# 1626; 1932
                  No. 5--# 1625; 1932

Premiere: Rome; 16 May 1925
            Choir of San Salvatore in Lauro
            Randall Thompson, conductor
            Ralph R. Calder, piano

Manuscript: Houghton Library:
              April 1924-September 1925; some pieces from
              Rome and some from Venice

W6.   Canons
      1927
      Dedicated to Cecily and Dan [Thompson, Jr.] on the
      occasion of their marriage.

      1.   The lover in winter plaineth for the spring
      2.   Felices ter (Horace, Carminum Book I, XIII)
      3.   Inscription pour une statue de l'amour
      4.   Rima
      5.   Mein

      Unpublished

      Manuscript: Houghton Library; 16-23 Nov. 1927

W7.   <u>Rosemary</u> for SSAA and SSA
      1929
      Text: Stephen Vincent Benét; <u>Tiger Joy</u> (1925)
      Written for Gerald Roberts and the Women's University
      Glee Club of New York

1. Chemical Analysis
2. A Sad Song
3. A Nonsense Song
4. To Rosemary on the methods by which she might become
        an angel

E. C. Schirmer-# 1023; 1930

Premiere: New York, New York; 18 December 1930
            Women's University Glee Club of New York
            Gerald Roberts, conductor

Manuscript: Houghton Library:
             6-25 July 1929; Francestown

W8. Americana for SATB and piano/orchestra
     1932
     Text: Selections from H. L. Mencken's editorial hand in
            the columns of his The American Mercury
     Commissioned by the League of Composers
     Dedicated to the A Cappella Singers of New York
     Orchestrated by Thompson in 1940

     1. May Every Tongue
     2. The Staff Necromancer   a cappella
     3. God's Bottles (SSAA)   a cappella
     4. The Sublime Process of Law Enforcement (SATB)
     5. Loveli-lines (SSAATTBB)

     E. C. Schirmer: score and parts-rental
                      Vocal score, 1932; reissued in 1960

                      Choral score--# 1634
                      Full score--# 1427
                      No. 3--# 2549

     Premiere: New York, New York; 3 April 1932
                League of Composers concert

     Manuscript: Houghton Library: Vocal score-11 Feb.-14
                  March 1932
                  God's Bottles; 20 February 1932

W9. Tarantella (Do you remember an Inn, Miranda?) for TTBB
     and piano /orchestra (orchestration by William Denny)
     1936-1937
     Text: Hilaire Belloc

     Dedicated to Yale Glee Club, Marshall Bartholomew,
        director

E. C. Schirmer-vocal score # 560; 1937

Premiere: New Haven, Conn.; 12 November 1937
            Yale Glee Club

Manuscript: Houghton Library: Vocal score-29 Oct. 1936-
            12 April 1937; Concord

W10.   The Testament of Freedom, A Setting of Four Passages
        from the Writings of Thomas Jefferson for TTBB, or SATB
        and piano, orchestra, or band
        1943
        Text: Thomas Jefferson; A Summary View of the Rights
                of British America (1774); Declaration of Causes
                and Necessity of Taking up Arms (6 July 1775);
                Letter to John Adams (12 Sept. 1821)
        Dedicated to the University of Virginia Glee Club, in
        memory of the Father of the University

        1.   The God who gave us life
        2.   We have not counted the cost
        3.   We fight not for glory
        4.   I shall not die without a hope

        E. C. Schirmer: study score, and vocal score, 1944
                          score, 1971
                          parts-rental

                          # 1424--Band score; 1961 (?)
                          # 1410--Full orchestral score
                          # 3017--SATB, orchestra, band, or piano
                          # 2118--TTBB, orchestra, band, or piano
                          # 2139--First and fourth movements for
                                    men's voices
                          # 3038--First and fourth movements for
                                    mixed voices

        Premiere: Charlottesville, Virginia; 13 April 1943
                    University of Virginia Glee Club
                    Stephen Tuttle, director
                    Randall Thompson, piano

        Manuscript: University of Virginia's Special
                    Collections/Manuscripts of the Alderman
                        Library--orchestration-98 pages
                        piano/vocal score-47 pages
                    (There are about 200 items pertaining to
                    this work, including corrections to
                    mastersheets, piano/vocal score in Braille,
                    Korean translation, programs, etc.)

Houghton Library: vocal score: TTBB and piano
four-hands of The God who gave us
life and I shall not die without a
hope, ca. 1943

W11.   The Testament of Freedom, arrangement for band by John
Corley in collaboration with Thompson.
1960

Premiere: Boston, Mass.; 22 October 1960.
Massachusetts Institute of Technology
MIT Concert Band
MIT Glee Club; Randall Thompson, conductor

Manuscript: University of Virginia
Alderman Library
McGregor (Rare Books) Room
This copy is inscribed by Thompson; 1961

W12.   The Testament of Freedom, arrangement for TTBB and
piano four hands
1943
The God who Gave Us Life; I shall Not Die without a
Hope
(see W10 under Houghton Library)

W13.   Hail, Tuttle! Round for Three Equal Voices
1943
Text: Randall Thompson

Unpublished

Manuscript: Houghton Library

W14.   Felices ter (Thrice happy they) for SATB
1954
Text: Horace; Odes (I, 13)
Dedicated to Archibald T. Davison

This is the sixth Ode of Horace that Thompson set; he
set fives Odes earlier in the twenties. Note that the
"Felices ter" setting of the 1927 Canons (W6) is a
different setting.

E. C. Schirmer-# 2416; 1956

Premiere: Cambridge, Mass.; 30 March 1954
Randall Thompson, conductor (?)

Manuscript: Houghton Library: Music Book, July 29,
               1953-Jan. 16, 1954. See W5

W15.   Ode to the Virginian Voyage for SATB orchestra/piano
        1956-1957
        Text: Michael Drayton
        In honor of the first permanent English Settlement in
        the New World, May of 1607

        1. Sinfonia
        2. You brave heroic minds
        3. Earth's Only paradise
        4. Fanfare and St. Anne's (Rectus et inversus)
        5. In Kenning of the Shore
        6. And in regions far
        7. They voyages attend
        8. Finale: Go and subdue

        E. C. Schirmer: score and parts (rental)
                           vocal score-# 2433; 1957, 1958

        Premiere: Williamsburg, Virginia; 1 April 1957
                     William and Mary College Choir and the
                     Norfolk Symphony Orchestra and Civic Chorus
                     Edgar Schenkman, conductor

        Manuscript: Houghton Library:
                       score-early version; 28 June-4 Aug. 1956;
                         Gstaad
                       Preliminary drafts; June and July 1956;
                         Gstaad
                       Revised version; 29 January 1957;
                         Cambridge

                       University of Virginia's Alderman Library:
                       photocopy of score

W16.   Frostiana for SATB and piano
        1959
        Text: Robert Frost; Come In and Other Poems (1943)
               and You Come Too: A Collection for Young Readers
               (1959)

        Commissioned by The Town of Amherst, Mass. for the
        200th anniversary of its incorporation
        Dedicated to the townspeople of Amherst, Mass. on their
        200th birthday, 1759-1959

1.   The Road not taken--SATB
2.   The Pasture--TBB
3.   Come in--SAA
4.   The Telephone--SAATTBB
5.   A Girl's Garden--SAA
6.   Stopping by Woods on a Snowy Evening--TBB
7.   Choose Something like a Star--SATB; SSAA

Premiere: Amherst, Mass.; 18 October 1959
             Amherst Bicentennial Choir at an Inter-Faith
             Convocation at the Amherst Regional High
             School Auditorium
             J. Heywood Alexander, piano
             Randall Thompson, conductor

E. C. Schirmer: vocal score, 1960

             No. 1--# 2485; 1950
             No. 2--# 2181; 1959
             No. 3--# 2539; 1959
             No. 4--# 2486; 1959
             No. 5--# 2540; 1959
             No. 6--# 2182; 1959
             No. 7--# 2487; 1959
             No. 7--# 2588; 1971

Manuscript: unknown

W17.   Frostiana for SATB and chamber orchestra
        1965
        Text: Robert Frost

        Orchestration especially prepared by Thompson for
        occasion honoring his retirement from Harvard
        University
        See W16 for individual movements

        E. C. Schirmer-# 1450 (orchestra score); 1975
                        parts, 1975

        Premiere: Cambridge, Mass.; 23 April 1965
                     Sanders Theatre
                     Combined chorus: Harvard Glee Club and
                     Radcliffe Choral Society and the Harvard-
                     Radcliffe Orchestra
                     Randall Thompson, conductor

        Manuscript: Houghton Library:
                      score--1-25 April 1965; Cambridge

W18.   Velvet Shoes for SA and piano
         Year: 1960; original solo song written in 1927
         Text: Elinor Wylie; Nets to Catch the Wind (1921)

         E. C. Schirmer-# 2526; 1960

         Premiere: unknown

         Manuscript: unknown

W19.   Fare Well for SATB
         1973
         Text: Walter de la Mare

         E. C. Schirmer-# 2957; 1973, 1974

         Premiere: Merrick, New York; 4 March 1973
                     St. John's Lutheran Church
                     Combined Calhoun, Kennedy, and Mepham High
                     School Choirs

         Manuscript: unknown

W20.   A Concord Cantata for SATB and piano/orchestra
         1975
         Text: Edward Everett Hale, Allen French, and
                 Robert Frost
         Commissioned by the Bicentennial Commission
         Dedicated to the Townspeople of Concord, Mass., 1775-
            1975

         1.   The Ballad of the Bridge (Hale)
         2.   Inscription (French)
         3.   The Gift Outright (Frost; A Witness Tree-1942)

         Premiere: Concord, Mass.; 2 May 1975
                     Concord Chorus
                     Nashua Symphony
                     Willis Traphagen, conductor
                     Edward Gilday, director

         E. C. Schirmer: score and parts-rental # 3003
                           No. 2 and 3--vocal score #3015; 1975

         Manuscript: Houghton Library:
                       piano/vocal score; 16 Feb.-12 March 1975;
                           Gstaad

W21.   Two Worlds for SATB and piano, strings ad libitum
        1977
        Text: Edmund Waller

        E. C. Schirmer-# 3041 (vocal score); 1977

        Premiere: as part of Five Love Songs in 1978 at Estes
                   Park, Colorado by Rocky Ridge Chorale and
                   Orchestra; See W23

        Manuscript: Lost

W22.   The Happy Shore for SATB and piano/string quartet
        1978
        Text: Edmund Spenser; Amoretti (1595)

        E. C. Schirmer-# 3053 (vocal score); 1978

        Premiere: as part of Five Love Songs in 1978 at Estes
                   Park, Colorado by Rocky Ridge Chorale and
                   Orchestra; See W23

        Manuscript: Houghton Library: vocal score
                    In the hand of David Francis Urrows

W23.   Five Love Songs for baritone, SATB chorus, piano/string
           quartet ad lib.
        1978
        Commissioned by the Rocky Ridge Music Center,
        Estes Park, Colorado, as a bequest in memory of
        Tell Ertl.
        Several of these pieces were composed much earlier for
        different occasions and have been listed separately.

        1.   The Light of Stars (Longfellow); SATB a cappella;
        2.   The Passenger (M. A. D. Howe); baritone and piano
        3.   Two Worlds (Edmund Waller); SATB and piano, strings
                ad libitum
        4.   Siciliano; Love is like a wind upon the water
                (Philip Rhinelander); baritone and piano,
                strings ad lib.
        5.   The Happy Shore (Edmund Spenser); SATB,
                piano/string quartet ad lib.

        E. C. Schirmer: No. 1-# 3052; 1980
                        No. 2-# 119; ?
                        No. 3-# 3041
                        No. 4-# 162; 1980
                        No. 5-# 3053

Premiere: Estes Park, Colorado; 6 August 1978
            Rocky Ridge Chorale and Orchestra

Manuscript: See separate pieces

II

Sacred Choral Works

W24.   Anniversary; Hymn tune written for the Lawrenceville
       School Hymnal, # 276
       1915 (?)

       Manuscript: Lost
                     Printed copy at Houghton Library

W25.   As of Old for SATB
       Text by the composer
       1915

       Manuscript: Lost
                     Printed copy at Houghton Library

W26a. Two Amens for SATB
       1927
       Thompson wrote these for his wedding

       E. C. Schirmer-# 4386 in Collected Amens
                     # 3078

       Premiere: Montclair, New Jersey; 26 February 1927

       Manuscript: Houghton Library: Two Amens are in a
                     notebook called Fragments

       Note: These were also reworked as Number 12 of the
               Twelve Canticles.   See W50

W26b. Two Amens for String Quartet; transcription of SATB
       1971

       Transcribed for Randall Thompson, Jr.'s 1971 wedding
       at Villa Aurelia in Rome.   See W77 (Wedding Music;
       Suite of Eight Pieces)

W27. <u>Pueri Hebraeorum</u> for SSAA/SSAA; also later for
      SATB/SATB
      1928
      Suitable for Palm Sunday

      Premiere: Wellesley, Mass.; 5 February 1928
                 Wellesley College Choir
                 Randall Thompson, director

      E. C. Schirmer: SSAA/SSAA-# 492; 1928
                       SATB/SATB-# 3082; 1986

      Version for double chorus SATB a cappella, or
      with keyboard or instruments (the voice parts
      may be doubled by two quartets of
      instruments, but each quartet should include
      similar instruments.) The version for mixed
      chorus was written in 1980 for the School of
      Choral Studies, New York State Summer School
      of the Arts, in Freedonia, New York. Abraham
      Kaplan was the Musical Director. Thompson
      conducted the first performance of this
      arrangement.

      Manuscript: Houghton Library: vocal score for women's
                   voices; 5-14 Nov. 1927; Wellesley

W28. <u>The Peaceable Kingdom</u> for SATB and SATB/SATB
      1936
      Text: Old Testament-Book of the Prophet Isaiah
      To G. Wallace Woodworth and the Harvard Glee Club and
      the Radcliffe Choral Society
      Commissioned by the League of Composers for the Harvard
        Glee Club and Radcliffe Choral Society

      1. Say ye to the righteous-Isaiah III: 10, 11; LXV: 14
      2. Woe unto them-V: 8, 11, 12, 18, 20-22. XVII: 12
      3. The noise of the multitude-XIII: 4, 5, 7, 8, 15,
            16, 18
      4. Howl ye (SATB/SATB)-XIV: 6; XIV: 31
      5. The paper reeds by the brooks-XIX: 7
      6. But these are they that forsake the Lord; For ye
            shall go out with joy (SATB/SATB)-LXV: 11; LV:
            12
      7. Have ye not known?-XL: 21
      8. Ye shall have a song (SATB/TTBB)-XXX: 29

      Premiere: Cambridge, Mass.; 3 March 1936
                 Harvard Glee Club and Radcliffe Choral
                 Society
                 Performed at the Twelfth American Music

Festival at the National Gallery of Art,
Washington, D.C.; sung by the choir of St.
John's Church, Georgetown; 26 May 1955

E. C. Schirmer-# 1730   vocal score; 1936
                         vocal score, 1963

        No. 1--# 1747
        No. 2--# 1748
        No. 3--# 1749
        No. 4--# 1750
        No. 5--# 1751
        No. 6--# 1752
        Nos. 7 and 8 published together--# 1753

Manuscript: Houghton Library:
             score; Say ye to the righteous and Woe
             unto them; 10 Jan-19 July 1935
             score; Paper reeds by the brooks, The
             Noise of a multitude and Howl ye; 14
             July-Sept. 1935
             score; Have ye not known; 25 Dec. 1935
             Printed score and photocopies

Note: Robert Sanders made an orchestral accompaniment
        for The Peaceable Kingdom in 1941; Thompson
        withdrew it. Manuscript is housed at E. C.
        Schirmer.

W29.   Alleluia for SATB
       1940
       Arrangements by the composer for SSAA and TTBB were
       made in the late 1960s.
       Written for the Opening Exercises of the Berkshire
       Music Center in 1940; Serge Koussevitsky, Director

       E. C. Schirmer: score, 1940
                         score, 1968

                         SATB-# 1786
                         SSAA-# 2593
                         TTBB-# 2312

       Premiere: Lenox, Mass.; 8 July 1940
                   Berkshire Festival Chorus
                   G. Wallace Woodworth, conductor

       Manuscript: Houghton Library: copy of original version
                     sung at Tanglewood in July, 1940; 1 July
                     1940; Ozalid copy; annotations and
                     revision added at a later date

W30. Nowell for SATB
      1947
      Written for a theory class at Princeton; was later
      incorporated into The Nativity According to St. Luke

      E. C. Schirmer: TTBB-# 2300
                      SSAA-# 2567
                      SATB-# 2643

      Premiere: In class at Princeton University; 1947

      Manuscript: Houghton Library: With fragment of score
                   on verso; 10 Dec. 1947

W31. Now I Lay Me Down to Sleep: Motet for SSA
      1947
      Text: from The New England Primer (1784)

      E. C. Schirmer-# 1985; 1954

      Premiere: Princeton, New Jersey; 8 May 1947
                 in class at Princeton University

      Manuscript: unknown

W32. The Last Words of David for SATB or TTTB with
      piano/orchestra/band
      1949
      Text: Old Testament-II Samuel 23: 3-4
      Commissioned by the Boston Symphony Orchestra in honor
      of the 25th Anniversary of the Directorship of Serge
      Koussevitsky
      Dedicated to Serge Koussevitsky

      E. C. Schirmer: vocal score, 1950
                      full orchestral score-rental, 1950
                      parts-rental, 1950

                      TTBB-# 2154
                      SATB-# 2294

      Premiere: Lenox, Mass.; 12 August 1949
                 Berkshire Music Center Student Body and
                 Boston Symphony Orchestra
                 Serge Koussevitsky, conductor

      Manuscript: Houghton Library:
                   preliminary draft; 27 June-4 July 1949
                   scores for orchestral parts; 8 Dec. 1949

Mugar Memorial Library/Dept. of Special
Collections; on deposit by the Boston
Symphony Orchestra;
Boston University
Manuscript; bound in half leather, green
and blue-grey green
in composer's hand on page 2:
"This work was commissioned by the Boston
Symphony Orchestra, by vote of its Trustees,
for Dr. Serge Koussevitzky, in honor of his
25th year as its incomparable Director, and
is affectionately dedicated to him in
appreciation of his musicianship and of his
friendship by The Author."

Note: This manuscript was used by Koussevitsky.
This work was used as the conclusion to the State
Department's film Tanglewood in the Voice of America
Series in the Summer of 1949.

W33.   Mass of the Holy Spirit for SATB
1955
Dedicated to the Choir of St. Stephen's Church in
Providence, Rhode Island
Commissioned by Nicolas Brown

Suitable for communion service, especially at
Whitsuntide.

Kyrie (SATB with SAT soli a cappella)
Gloria (SATB and SSAA/TTBB
Credo (SATB)
Sanctus (SSAATTBB)
Benedictus (SATB)
Hosanna (SATB)
Agnus Dei (SATB)

E. C. Schirmer: vocal score, 1956
                  vocal score, 1957

                  Kyrie-# 2463
                  Gloria-# 2464
                  Credo-# 2465
                  Sanctus-# 2466
                  Benedictus-# 2467
                  Hosanna-# 2468
                  Agnus Dei-# 2469

Premiere: Cambridge, Mass.; 22 March 1957
           Sanders Theatre
           Harvard Glee Club and Radcliffe Choral

Society
G. Wallace Woodworth, conductor

Manuscript: Houghton Library:
Preliminary draft; 1955
Manuscript; 24-28 June 1955
Benedictus draft; 30 June-2 July 1956

W34.   Glory to God in the Highest for SATB
1958
Text: New Testament-Luke 2: 14
Dedicated to Harold C. Schmidt

E. C. Schirmer-# 2470; 1958

Premiere: Unknown

Manuscript: Probably lost

W35.   Requiem: a Dramatic Dialogue in five parts for
SATB/SATB
1958
Text: from the Bible
Commissioned for the May T. Morrison Festival of Music
by the University of California at Berkeley for the
dedication of new music buildings
Dedicated to the University of California Chorus and
its conductor Edward B. Lawton

Part I: Lamentations
Part II: The Triumph of Faith:
             1. Why make ye this ado?
             2. What man is he that liveth and shall not
                see death?
             3. Good tidings to the meek
Part III: The Call to Song:
             1. Be filled with the spirit
             2. O let the nations be glad
             3. Sing unto Him
             4. Utter a Song
Part IV: The Garment of Praise
             1. Sing with the spirit
             2. Let everything that hath breath
             3. Let them give glory
             4. Praise Him all ye stars of light
             5. I am their music
Part V: The Leave-Taking
             1. Ye were sometimes darkness (Walk as
                children of light
             2. The Lord shall be unto thee

3. Return unto thy rest
4. Thou has given him
5. Amen and amen, alleluia

E. C. Schirmer: # 2459 (vocal score); 1963
                parts-rental

Optional double string ensemble, duplicating
the voice parts, is available on a rental
basis

. Good tidings to the meek-# 2638
. The Garment of Praise-# 2639
. Ye were sometimes darkness (Walk as
    children of light)-# 2640
. The Lord shall be unto thee-# 2641
. Thou hast given him-# 2642
. Amen and amen, alleluia-# 2673

Premiere: Berkeley, California; 22 May 1958
           University of California Chorus
           Edward Lawton, conductor

Manuscript: University of California, Berkeley
             The Music Library:
             Pencil holograph; Cambridge 20 Nov. 1957-
             March 21, 1958
             Manuscript full score in ink, 133 pages
             Holograph dated 18-21-III-58
             Copy prepared by professional copyist
             c. 1958 by E. C. Schirmer

W36. The Gate of Heaven for SSAA; later for SATB
      1959
      Text: Psalm 122: 1; Habakkuk 2: 20; Genesis 28: 17
      Written for the dedication of the Jessie Ball DuPont
      Chapel at Hollins College

      E. C. Schirmer: vocal score, 1961
                       SSAA-# 2531
                       SATB-# 2490
                       TTBB-# 2175

      Premiere: Hollins, Virginia; 22 February 1959
                Hollins College Choir (SSAA score)
                Boston, Mass.; 18 June 1961
                Trinity Church, Copley Square
                American Guild of Organists-Regional
                Convention
                Randall Thompson, conductor (SATB score)

          Manuscript: Houghton Library: SSAA score
                       sketches in Music Book; 9 Jan.-19 March
                       1959

W37. The Lord is My Shepherd for SATB or SSAA and
      piano/organ/harp
      1962;1964
      Text: Old Testament-Psalm 23
      Commissioned by students, family, friends in memory of
      Dorothy C. Drake, conductor from 1953 to 1961 of the
      Chapin School Choral Club

          E. C. Schirmer: SATB # 2688; 1962
                           SSAA # 2578; 1964

          Premiere: New York, New York; 1 May 1964
                    Chapin School Choral Club
                    Randall Thompson, conductor

          Manuscript: Houghton Library:
                       SSAA; 25 Jan.-8 March 1964

W38. The Best of Rooms for SATB
      1963
      Text: Robert Herrick

      Written for the Northwestern University Chorus,
      Evanston, Illinois

      E. C. Schirmer-# 2672

          Premiere: Evanston, Ill.: 7 April 1963
                       Northwestern University Chorus
                       Randall Thompson, conductor

          Manuscript: Houghton Library:
                       score; 15-24 Jan. 1963; Gstaad

W39. A Feast of Praise: Cantata for SATB with brass choir
      and harp or piano
      1963
      Text: (see individual sections below)
      Commissioned by Stanford University's Department of
      Music
      Dedicated to Harold Schmidt, Director of Choral Music
      at Stanford University

          1. The Stars in their Watches-Baruch 3: 34
          2. Nocturne-Psalm 81: 3

3.   God is Gone Up with a Shout-Psalm 47: 5-7

E. C. Schirmer-# 2675 (vocal score); 1963
        Parts for harp, horns, trombones I and II
(separate and together) and tuba available separately.

Premiere: Stanford, California; 11 August 1963
           Stanford Summer Chorus
           Dinkelspiel Auditorium
           Randall Thompson, conductor

Manuscript: Houghton Library:
             The Stars in their Watches
             8-16 July 1963; Cambridge
             Nocturne; 10-21 July 1963; Cambridge
             God is gone up. . .; 25-27 July 1963
             Cambridge
             Brass and harp parts; 1963

W40.   Hymn: Thy Book Falls Open Lord
       1964
       Text: David T. W. McCord; Harvard University Hymnbook
       Accompaniment for band for use at the 1964 Harvard
       Commencement, 1964

       Premiere: Cambridge, Mass.; 11 June 1964
                 Harvard Commencement Exercises

       Manuscript: unknown

W41.   The Passion According to St. Luke: An Oratorio in ten
       scenes for soloists (baritone, tenor), SATB, and
       orchestra
       1964
       Text: New Testament-Luke 19, 22, 23
       Written for the 150th Anniversary of the founding of
       the Handel and Haydn Society

       1.   The Entry into Jerusalem
       2.   The Passover
       3.   The Institution of the Lord's Supper
       4.   The Agony in the Garden
       5.   Peter's Denial
       6.   The Mocking of Jesus
       7.   The Trial
       8.   The March to Calvary
       9.   The Crucifixion
       10. The Entombment

E. C. Schirmer-# 2695 (vocal score); 1965
            score and parts-rental

Premiere: Boston, Mass.; 28 March 1965
            Symphony Hall
            Handel and Haydn Society and Cambridge
            Festival Orchestra
            Edward Gilday, conductor

Manuscript: Houghton Library:
              original draft; 1 July 1964-1 Feb. 1965;
              Gstaad
              revisions and photocopies; 1965
              printed sheets, annotations, and
              revisions; Jan.-Feb 1965; Gstaad
              Libretto; 1964
              vocal score

W42.   A Psalm of Thanksgiving for SATB, children's chorus,
       orchestra, piano/organ
       1966-1967
       Text: Old Testament-Psalm 107; both King James and
       Book of Common Prayer versions
       Commissioned by Mrs. Lucy B. Lemann
       Dedicated to Dr. Maurice Fremont-Smith

       Orchestral Chorale Prelude: Nun danket alle Gott (based
       on the chorale by Johann Crüger)
       O give thanks unto the Lord
       They wandered in the wilderness
       Such as sit in darkness
       Foolish men are plagued
       They that go down to the sea in ships
       He turneth the wilderness
       Now thank we all our God

       E. C. Schirmer-# 2746 (vocal score); 1967
                   score and parts-rental

           Now thank we all our God-# 4008

       Premiere: Boston, Mass.; 15 November 1967
                   New England Conservatory of Music:
                   Chorus, Children's Chorus
                   Symphony Orchestra
                   Randall Thompson, conductor

       Manuscript: Houghton Library: full score;
                     7 Oct.-1 Nov. 1967; Gstaad   piano/vocal
                     score; 11 Aug.-1 Oct. 1967; Gstaad; Nun
                     danket: Chorale Prelude; 20 July 1966

W43.   The Eternal Dove for SATB
        1968
        Text: Joseph Beaumont

        Dedicated to G. Wallace Woodworth

        E. C. Schirmer-# 2782; 1971

            The Eternal Dove also published in:
            Department of Music; Harvard University; 1972
            Words and Music: The Composer's View; A
            Medley of Problems and Solutions Compiled in
            Honor of G. Wallace Woodworth by Sundry
            Hands. Edited by Laurence Berman.   Editorial
            Committee: Elliot Forbes, David G. Hughes,
            Nino Pirrotta, John M. Ward.

        Premiere: Cambridge, Mass.; 17 May 1970
                    Harvard University Choir
                    John R. Ferris, director

        Manuscript: Houghton Library:
                      score; 9 March 1968

W44.   The Place of the Blest for SSAA, piano/chamber
        orchestra
        1969
        Text: Robert Herrick
                Richard Wilbur; Things of this World (1956),
                original text from an Anglo-Norman Bestiary of
                1120 by Philippe de Thaun
        Written in honor of the 50th Anniversary of the
        Founding of the Boys Choir of the Saint Thomas Church
        Choir School
        Dedicated to the Saint Thomas Choir School
        William Self, organist and Master of the Choir

        1.   The Carol of the Rose (Herrick)
        2.   The Pelican (Wilbur)
        3.   The Place of the Blest (Herrick)
        4.   Alleluia, Amen

        E. C. Schirmer: vocal score, 1971
                          score, 1971
                          score and parts-rental

                          No. 1--# 2800
                          Nos. 2 and 3--# 2801
                          No. 4--# 2839

      Premiere: New York, New York; 2 March 1969
                  Saint Thomas Church Boys Choir
                  George Bragg, conductor

      Manuscript: Houghton Library:
                  early drafts; 27 Dec. 1968
                  score; Jan. 1969; Gstaad
                  score; 27 Dec. 1968-17 Feb. 1969; Gstaad
                  photocopy, revisions; 29 Jan. 1969; Gstaad

W45. Two Herbert Settings for SATB
      1970-1971
      Text: George Herbert

      Bitter-sweet is dedicated to the memory of Thompson's
      granddaughter, Katie

      1.   Bitter-sweet
      2.   Antiphon

      Premiere: Bitter-sweet
                  New York, New York; 25 October 1970
                  Church of the Incarnation Choir
                  Thomas Dunn, conductor

      E. C. Schirmer-# 2904 (Bitter-sweet); 1971
                   # 2915 (Antiphon); 1972

      Manuscript: Houghton Library:
                  Bitter-sweet (among uncatalogued items)

W46. Mirror of St. Anne: An antiphonal setting in Inverse
      Contrary Imitation for SATB/SATB. This was originally
      the orchestral interlude in Part IV of Ode to the
      Virginian Voyage See W15
      1972
      Text: Isaac Watts

      E. C. Schirmer-# 2921; 1972

      Premiere: unknown

      Manuscript: Houghton Library:
                  Mimeographed copy of manuscript

W47. A Hymn for Scholars and Pupils for SSAA and small
      orchestra or flute and piano
      1973
      Text: George Wither

"An Hymn for Schollars and Pupils"
Dedicated to Elizabeth and Carlton Sprague Smith
Written for "The Challenge of Excellence"

E. C. Schirmer: vocal score, 1975
                  SSAA-# 2829

Premiere: Washington, Conn.; 8 June 1973
            Wykeham Rise School Choir
            Randall Thompson, conductor (?)

Manuscript: Houghton Library:
              score (SSAA); 12 Feb.- March 1973
              printed sheets with revisions; 1975

W48.   A Hymn for Scholars and Pupils for SATB, organ and
       chamber orchestra with double bass and trombone parts
       added (See W47 above)

       E. C. Schirmer-# 2958; 1975

       Premiere: Raleigh, North Carolina; 11 November 1973
                   North Carolina Music Educator's Association

       Manuscript: Houghton Library:
                     Reproduction of score (SATB); 1973

W49.   The Morning Stars for SATB and orchestra
       revised for piano (1983)
       1978
       Text: Old Testament-Job 38: 1-2, 4, 6-7
       Composed for the Silver Jubilee of the Kentucky Music
       Educators Association

       E. C. Schirmer-# 4359; Not available

       Premiere: Kentucky; 18 March 1978
                   Kentucky All-State Chorus and Orchestra
                   Paul Salamunovich, conductor

       Manuscript: autograph in private hands;
                   only fragment of this score is in the
                   composer's hand; the remainder is in the
                   hand of David Francis Urrows

W50.   Twelve Canticles for SATB and unison voices
        1983
        Dedicated to the Concert Choir of
        Emory and Henry College, Emory, Virginia

        1.   Praise Ye the Lord (Psalm 147:1)
        2.   God Is a Spirit (John 4: 24)
        3.   When Thou Liest Down (Proverbs 3:24)
        4.   My Grace Is Sufficient (II Corinthians 12: 9)
        5.   The Old and the Young (Joel 2: 28)
        6.   I Call to Remembrance (Psalm 77: 6)
        7.   Arise, Shine (Isaiah 60: 1)
        8.   The Path of the Just (Proverbs 4: 18)
        9.   Face Answereth to Face (Proverbs 27: 19)
        10. Fear Thou Not (Zephaniah 3: 16, 17)
        11. Finally, Brethren, Farewell (II Corinthians 13: 11)
        12. Amen

        E. C. Schirmer: 1986
                        No. 1--# 4100
                        Nos. 2 and 3--# 4101
                        No. 4--# 4102
                        Nos. 5 and 6--# 4103
                        Nos. 7 and 8--# 4104
                        Nos. 9 and 10--# 4105
                        Nos. 11 and 12--# 4106

        Premiere: Emory, Virginia; 30 October 1983
                    Concert Choir of Emory and Henry College
                    Charles R. Davis, conductor

        Manuscript: Houghton Library:
                      Uncatalogued
                      Mostly in hand of David Francis Urrows;
                      few illegible sketches in Thompson's hand

W51.   Solstice: A Christmas Song for unison treble voices
        and keyboard
        See W107 for Thompson's original version which was
        written for voice and piano for the Tavern Club
        Christmas Play of 1966

        Text: Robert Lee Wolff; Fearful Symmetry (1966)

        E. C. Schirmer-# 4289; 1988

        Premiere: Christmas 1966

        Manuscript: unknown

W52.   My Master Hath a Garden for SA and piano
       1927; solo song originally written. The optional alto
       part here was added by the editorial staff of E. C.
       Schirmer

       Text: anonymous

       E. C. Schirmer-# 4288; 1989

                              III

                        Stage Works

W53.   Torches for soprano, viola, piano
       Incidental Music for Kenneth Raisbeck's one-act
       "romantic tragedy" Torches. Music consists of prelude
       for viola and piano, and Gismonda's Song to text of
       Raisbeck.
       1920

       Published in: Baker, George P., ed. Plays of the '47'
       Workshop. Second series. New York: Brentano, 1920.

       Premiere: Cambridge, Mass.; 5 February 1920
                  Sanders Theatre
                  Produced by The 47 Workshop

       Manuscript: Lost

W54.   The Grand Street Follies of 1926; for chamber orchestra
       and voices; Musical revue
       1926
       Thompson's songs with lyrics by Agnes Morgan include:
          "Fixed for Life"
          "The Booster's Song of the Far North"
          "Taxi Driver's Lament"
          "My Icy Flow"
          "Ice Mazurka"
          "Beatrice Lillie Ballad"
       Additional songs were contributed by Arthur Schwartz
       and Lily Hyland

       Unpublished

       Premiere. New York, New York; 25 June 1926
                  Neighborhood Playhouse

       Manuscript: Houghton Library:
                    score; "Ice Mazurka"-20 May, 1926

W55.   The Straw Hat for piano; Incidental Music
        1926
        Text: Eugene Labiche; Un Chapeau de paille d'Italie

        Unpublished

        Premiere: New York, New York; 14 October 1926
                   American Laboratory Theater

        Manuscript: Houghton Library
                     Fragments

W56.   Solomon and Balkis, opera in one act
        1942
        Text: Thompson's own adaptation of Rudyard Kipling's
        "The Butterfly that Stamped" from The Just So Stories
        Commissioned by The League of Composers and the
        Columbia Broadcasting System in 1941

        E. C. Schirmer-# 2031; 1942

        Premiere: New York, New York; 29 March 1942
                   CBS Radio broadcast
                   Columbia Concert Orchestra
                   Howard Barlow, conductor
                   Given under the auspices of the Columbia
                   Workshop
                   James H. Fassett, Musical Director

        First Stage Performance:
        Cambridge, Mass.; 14 and 15 April 1942
        Harvard University's Lowell House Dining Hall
        Harvard University Orchestra
        Radcliffe Choral Society
        Malcolm H. Holmes, conductor

        Characters in the opera:
        Solomon--baritone
        Balkis--mezzo, or contralto
        The Butterfly--tenor
        The Butterfly's wife--soprano
        Egyptian Queen--soprano
        The Queens of various countries, representing the 999
        wives of Solomon--sopranos and altos in chorus
        Four Djinns--who neither sing nor speak

        Manuscript: Houghton Library:
                    score; 11 Aug-18 Nov. 1941; Bryn Mawr
                    score; 10 Dec. 1941-19 Feb. 1942; Farmington
                    photocopy of second score above with
                    revisions

W57. The Battle of Dunster Street for piano
      1953

      Unpublished

      Premiere: Unknown

      Manuscript: Houghton Library:
                   score; 19-20 March 1953

W58. The Nativity According to St. Luke: A Musical Drama in
      Seven Scenes SATB, soloists (soprano, mezzo-soprano,
      contralto, 2 tenors, 3 baritones, 2 basses, 2 boys-
      SA), small orchestra
      1961
      Text: New Testament: from first two chapters of the
              Gospel of Saint Luke
              Richard Rowlands: "Upon my lap my sov'reign
              sits" (Scene 6: Mary's Lullaby)
      Composed in honor of the 200th anniversary of the
      dedication of Christ Church, Cambridge, Massaschusetts,
      1761-1961

      1. Zacharias and the Angel
      2. The Annunciation
      3.   The Visitation; contains My Soul doth magnify the
          Lord
      4. The Naming of John
      5. The Apparition
      6. The Adoration; contains Nowell, and Lullaby
      7. The Song of Simeon; contains And the Child Grew

      E. C. Schirmer-# 622 (piano/vocal)
                     # 622A (Chorus part)

                        Nowell (SATB) # 2643
                               (SSAA) # 2567
                               (TTBB) # 2300

                    And the Child Grew (SATB) # 2644

                    Magnificat: My Soul doth magnify the Lord
                                 soprano solo-# 124

                    Lullaby: Upon my lap my sov'reign sits
                          soprano solo-# 125

      Premiere: Cambridge, Mass.; 12 December 1961
                 Christ Church
                 Randall Thompson, conductor

Manuscript: Houghton Library:
               Text
               Zacharias and the Angel-sketches; 5-30
               July 1960; Gstaad
               The Annunciation; 2 November 1960
               The Visitation; 8 January 1961
               The Naming of John; 19 January 1961
               The Naming of John, and The Apparition;
               1961
               The Adoration, and The Song of Simeon; 12-
               29 June 1961
               Master copy for piano and vocal score;
               1961

IV

Orchestral Works

W59.   Pierrot and Cothurnus: Prelude for Orchestra
        1922
        Prelude suggested by the one-act play Aria da Capo
        (1920) by Edna St. Vincent Millay

        Unpublished

        Premiere: Rome; 17 May 1923
                    Augusteo Orchestra
                    Randall Thompson, conductor

        Manuscript: Houghton Library:
                    pencil score; 22 March-2 May 1922

        Sibley Music Library, Eastman School of Music:
           Autograph manuscript: Full score (61 pages)
           Cambridge, Mass.; 1922

W60.   The Piper at the Gates of Dawn: Symphonic Prelude
        1924
        Suggested by a chapter with this title from Kenneth
        Grahames's Wind in the Willows
        Dedicated to Mrs. Felix Lamond

        Unpublished

        Premiere: Rome; 27 May 1924
                    Augusteo Orchestra
                    Randall Thompson, conductor

Manuscript: Houghton Library:
              score; 1-15 May 1924; Rome
              photostat of score; contains annotations
              probably in hand of Serge Koussevitsky
              piano sketch; 24 April-1 May 1924; Rome

Sibley Music Library, Eastman School of Music:
  Autograph manuscript: Full score (42 pages)

W61.   Jazz Poem for piano and orchestra in one movement
       1927

       E. C. Schirmer-# 294; rental only

       Premiere: Rochester, New York; 27 November 1928
                   Rochester Philharmonic Orchestra
                   Howard Hanson, conductor
                   Randall Thompson, piano

       Performance for two pianos:
       Wellesley, Mass.; 18 March 1929
       Blanche Brocklebank and Jean Wilder, pianos

       Manuscript: Houghton Library:
                   preliminary draft; 22 May-14 June 1927
                   score; piano and orchestra; 1927
                   two piano reductions from orchestral part:
                   22 May-14 June 1927; New York, and 27 Jan.
                   1929

W62.   First Symphony
       1929
       Dedicated to Howard Hanson

       Movements
       I.   Allegro brioso
       II.   Poco adagio
       III. Allegro

       Carl Fischer: score and parts-rental
       Birchard: score, 1931

       Premiere: Rochester, New York; 20 February 1930
                   Rochester Philharmonic Orchestra
                   Howard Hanson, conductor

       First New York City Performance; 2 November 1947
       Washington Heights "Y" [M and YWHA] Symphony Orchestra
       Maxim Waldo, conductor

Manuscript: Houghton Library:
             score

original version of first movement, written
in Rome in 1924 and 1925: for mixed chorus
and orchestra; text from Horace's Carmina,
Liber I, XXXII (Poscimur)

original version of the second and third
movement, written in Venice in 1925: for
mixed chorus and orchestra; text from
Horace's Carmina, Liber I, IX (Vides ut
alta)

sketchbook for second and third movements,
1925

W63.   Second Symphony in E minor
       1931
       Dedicated to M. W. T. [Margaret Whitney Thompson]

       Movements
       I.   Allegro
       II.   Largo
       III.   Vivace
       IV.   Andante Moderato: Allegro con spirito

       Carl Fischer: score and parts-rental
       Birchard: score, 1932

       Premiere: Rochester, New York: 24 March 1932
                  American Composers Concert
                  Rochester Philharmonic Orchestra
                  Howard Hanson, conductor

       First European Performance:
       Groningen, The Netherlands; 17 October 1934
       Groningen Orchestral Society
       Kor Kuiler, conductor

       First German Performance:
       Frankfurt, Germany; 31 March 1946
       Frankfurter Stadtische Opernhaus-und Museums Orchester
       Bruno Vondenhoff, conductor

       Manuscript: Houghton Library:
                    sketch;1 July-19 Aug. 1930; Gstaad
                    score; 17 Nov. 1930-24 Feb. 1931; Gstaad

       Sibley Music Library, Eastman School of Music:
          Photolithograph of composer's manuscript

W64.   Third Symphony in A minor
        1949
        Commissioned by the Alice M. Ditson Fund of Columbia
        University

        Movements
        I.   Largo elegiaco
        II.   Allegro appassionato
        III.   Lento tranquillo
        IV.   Allegro vivace

        Carl Fischer: Rental

        Premiere: New York, New York; 15 May 1949
                    CBS Symphony Orchestra
                    Thor Johnson, conductor

        First Performance in the United Kingdom:
        London; 9 June 1950
        BBC Symphony Orchestra
        Sir Adrian Boult, conductor

        Manuscript: Houghton Library:
                     pencil sketches;
                     21 Aug. 1947-19 March 1949

W65.   A Trip to Nahant, Symphonic Fantasy
        1954
        Dedicated to the memory of Serge and Natalie
        Koussevitsky

        Premiere: Philadelphia, Penn.; 18 March 1955
                    Philadelphia Orchestra
                    Eugene Ormandy, conductor

        Carl Fischer: Rental

        Manuscript: Houghton Library:
                    pencil sketch; 7 Aug.-4 Sept. 1953; Gstaad
                    score and printed sheets; ca. 1953; Gstaad

                            V

                    Chamber Works

W66.   Septette for flute, clarinet, string quartet, piano
        1917

        Unpublished

Premiere: 3 June 1917
first movement only

Manuscript: Houghton Library:
             score of first movement; 19 Feb.-31 May
             1917
             score of second movement; 14 July-16 Dec.
             1917

W67. Four Waltzes for two violins and piano
      1918

      Unpublished

      Premiere: Boston, Mass.; 28 March 1918
                 YMCA Building, Bates Hall
                 Pupils of Lillian Shattuck and Laura Webster

      Manuscript: Lost

W68. All on a Summer Eve: Song for violin/cello and piano
      1919 (?)
      Transcription of earlier 1917 song

      Unpublished

      Premiere: unknown

      Manuscript: Houghton Library:
                   score of song with text by Everett Glass;
                   1917 with title page dated 25 Dec. 1919

W69. Scherzino for Flageolet, violin and viola
      1920

      E. C. Schirmer-# 267; 1983

      Premiere: New York, New York; 14 December 1920
                 Leopold D. Mannes, flageolet
                 Leopold Godowski, violin
                 Rieber Johnson, viola

      Manuscript: Houghton Library:
                   score; 14 Dec. 1920; New York
                   parts; 1920

W70.   Quintet for flute, clarinet, viola, cello, piano in
        two movements
        1920
        Dedicated to Leopold Damrosch Mannes
        Winner of the George Arthur Knight Prize at Harvard in
        1920

        Unpublished

        Premiere: unknown

        Manuscript: Houghton Library:
                     score; 3-23 March 1920
                     parts; 1920

W71.   Suite for violin and piano
        1921-22

        Unpublished

        Premiere: unknown

        Manuscript: Lost

W72.   The Wind in the Willows for string quartet
        1924
        Title from Kenneth Grahame's book The Wind in the
        Willows

        1.   River Bank
        2.   Toad, Esq.
        3.   The Wild Wood

        Unpublished

        Premiere: Rome; 15 March 1925
                    Quartetto Venetziano

        American Performances:

        Musical Art Quartet:
        Boston Public Library; 18 December 1927
        Peabody Institute; 17 February 1928
        Columbia University; 29 October 1932

        Durrell Quartet:
        Paine Hall, Harvard University; 8 May 1929

        Boston String Quartet:
        Sanders Theatre, Harvard University; 16 September 1936

        Coolidge Quartet:
        Library of Congress, Washington, D.C.; 11 March 1937

        Stuyvesant Quartet:
        Harvard Club, New York; 9 February 1941

        Pro Arte Quartet:
        University of California at Berkeley; 30 April 1941

        Manuscript: Houghton Library:
                      score: River-bank; 20 Feb. 1924
                      score: Toad, Esq.; 10 March 1924
                      photostat of copied parts; 1924; Rome

W73.   Suite for oboe, clarinet, and viola
        1940
        Dedicated to Bertrand H. Bronson

        E. C. Schirmer: # 2013; complete set; 1941

        Premiere: ? ; 30 March 1940
                     Dorian String Quartet
                     CBS

        Manuscript: unknown

W74.   First String Quartet in D Minor
        1941
        Dedicated to Elizabeth Sprague Coolidge

        Carl Fischer: study score, 1948
                        parts, 1948

        Premiere: Washington, D.C.; 31 October 1941
                   Coolidge Auditorium at Library of Congress
                   Coolidge Quartet

        Manuscript: Library of Congress; Coolidge Collection
                      Washington, D.C.

                      1st movement: 'Kilmarth,' Par, Cornwall '38
                       Devt.-end: Camden, Me. '39
                      2nd movement: Bryn Mawr, June '41
                      3rd movement: Bryn Mawr, July '41
                      4th movement: Bryn Mawr, July-Aug. 4, '41

W75.   Trio for Three Double Basses; Divertimento for Strings
        in four movements. For 3 double basses/cellos/violas
        1949

Dedicated to Serge Koussevitsky

Premiere: Cambridge, Mass.; 1949
           Harvard Club--dinner to honor
           Serge Koussevitsky and members of the Boston
           Symphony Orchestra
Performers: George Moleux, Willis Page, Henry Freeman

E. C. Schirmer: # 1457; published facsimile of score;
                1972

Manuscript: Houghton Library
             Original parts

W76. Second String Quartet in G Major
      1967
      Commissioned by the Harvard Musical Association for its
      130th Anniversary

      I.   Prelude
      II.   Air and Variations
      III. Adagio
      IV.   Allegro con brio

      E. C. Schirmer: study score, 1972--No. 1459
                       parts, 1972--Violin I--No. 1459A
                                    Violin II--No. 1459B
                                    Viola--No. 1459C
                                    Cello--No. 1459D

      Premiere: Cambridge, Mass.; 17 April 1967
                 Harvard Musical Association
                 Brandeis University Quartet

      Manuscript: Houghton Library:
                   sketches; 13 Jan. 1967
                   score; 27 Jan.-12 March 1967

W77. Wedding Music; Suite of Eight Pieces for String Quartet
      1971

      E. C. Schirmer-# 4386 two Amens from these Eight
        Pieces in Collected Amens; # 263

      Premiere: Rome, Villa Aurelia; 1971
                 wedding ceremony of Randall Thompson, Jr.

      Manuscript: Houghton Library:
                   score in Music Book, 1970-1971
                   score in Wedding Music

VI

Keyboard Works

W78. Sonata for piano
      1915
      Lost

W79. In Memoriam, F. C. van Dyck, Jr. for organ
      1916
      Lost

W80. Allegro in D major
      1918

      Unpublished

      Premiere: unknown

      Manuscript: Houghton Library:
                   score; 25-27 May 1918 with annotations in
                   Archibald T. Davison's hand

W81.   Indianola Variations; Seven variations for two pianos;
       Variations nos. 2, 4, and 5 are by Leopold D. Mannes
       1918

       Unpublished

       Premiere: Cambridge, Mass; 18 December 18, 1918
                 Paine Hall
                 Leopold D. Mannes and Randall Thompson

       Manuscript: Houghton Library:
                   score; 4 June 1918 "With printed score of
                   Indianola by S. R. Henry and D. Onivas"
                   score; 1918

       Manuscript copy: Library of the Mannes College
                         of Music; dated 6/11/1918

W82. Scherzo in F major for piano
      1921

      Unpublished

      Premiere: unknown

Manuscript: Houghton Library:
               score; See W83

W83.   Scherzo in G minor for piano
        1921

        Unpublished

        Premiere: unknown

        Manuscript: Houghton Library:
                       score; Jan. 1921; also contains Scherzo in
                       F major; See W82

W84.   Varied Air for piano
        Second movement of an unidentified composition for
        piano; first movement may have been lost
        1921-1922
        Dedicated to Mrs. Frances L Grover

        Unpublished

        Premiere: unknown

        Manuscript: Houghton Library:
                       score; 1921-22
                       score with revisions; ca. 1922

W85.   Piano Sonata in G Minor in one movement; Allegro giusto
        1922

        Unpublished

        Premiere: unknown

        Manuscript: Houghton Library:
                       score; written in Cambridge in 1922,
                       copied in Rome

W86.   Piano Sonata in C Minor
        1922-1923
        Dedicated to Felix Lamond

        Movements
        I.   Lento, moderato, agitato
        II.   Lento, allegretto
        III.   Allegro con brio, maestoso

Unpublished

Premiere: Rome; 15 January 1924
            Marcella Lantenay

American Premiere:
Harvard University; 8 May 1929
Jesús Maria Sanromá, piano

Manuscript: Houghton Library:
             score; 1922-23; Rome

W87.   Suite for piano
       1924
       Dedicated to Leopold D. Mannes because he "wrote 2/3 of
       the subject, and therefore the greater part of this
       suite as well as one of his own--one week in Roma"

       Seven Movements
       I.   Lento
       II.   Allegretto, un poco sostenuto
       III. Larghetto
       IV.   Presto
       V.   Agitato
       VI.   Con moto
       VII. Come prima

       E. C. Schirmer; 1991

       Premiere: Rome; 16 May 1925
                   Randall Thompson

       American Premiere:
       Harvard University; 8 May 1929
       Jesús Maria Sanromá, piano

       Manuscript: Houghton Library:
                    score; 31 Oct.-6 Nov. 1924; with
                    annotations in hand of Mannes
                    score in private hands

W88.   The Boats were Talking for piano
       1925
       Dedicated to Leopold and Edie.
       Title taken from a line in Eleanor Verdery's About
       Ellie at Sandacre (1925)

       E. C. Schirmer-# 255; 1980; Published score dedicated
                                to Leopold D. Mannes

Premiere: unknown

Manuscript: Houghton Library:
                  score; 23 Dec. 1925

W89.   Mazurka for piano
       1926

       Unpublished

       Premiere: unknown

       Manuscript: Houghton Library:
                     score; 20 May 1926

W90.   Larghetto for organ
       c. 1928

       Lost

W91.   Song after Sundown for piano
       1935.   Written in Concord, Mass.

       Carl Fischer, 1936.   In Masters of Our Day: An
       Introduction to Present-Day Music by Living Master-
       Composers, edited by Lazare Saminsky and Isadore Freed

       Reissued by Carl Fischer, 1963. In Masters of Our Day:
       18 Solos in the Contemporary Idiom for the Young
       Pianist

       Premiere: New York, New York; 24 February 1936
                   Harry Compson

       Manuscript: Archives of Carl Fischer ?

W92.   Little Prelude for piano
       1935.   Written in Peace Dale, Rhode Island

       Carl Fischer, 1936.   In Masters of Our Day: An
       Introducton to Present-Day Music by Living Master-
       Composers, edited by Lazare Saminsky and Isadore Freed

       Reissued by Carl Fischer, 1963.   In Masters of Our Day:
       18 Solos in the Contemporary Idiom for the Young
       Pianist

       Premiere: New York, New York; 24 February 1936

Harry Compson

Manuscript: Archives of Carl Fischer ?

W93. The Jabberwocky for piano
1951
Written for his daughter Varney Thompson who
choreographed an informal dance to this music when she
was a student at Jacob's Pillow

Unpublished

Manuscript: Houghton Library:
score; 31 March 1951

W94. Twenty Chorale Preludes, Four Inventions and a Fugue
for Organ
1970

1. Christus, der ist mein Leben (Chorale in Pedal)
2. Aus tiefer Noth
3. Liebster Jesus, wir sind hier
4. Wenn wir in höchsten Nothen sein
5.   Wer nur den lieben Gott lasst walten (Chorale in
     Tenor)
6. Wer nur den lieben Gott lasst walten (Chorale in
     Soprano)
7.   Wer nur den lieben Gott lasst walten (Chorale in
     Bass)
8. Erhalt' uns, Herr, bei deninem Wort
9. Nun sich der Tag geendet hat (a 2)
10. O Ewigkeit, du Donnerwort
11. Herr, ich habe missgehandelt
12. Meine Seele erhebt den Herren (Chorale in Soprano)
13. Meine Seele erhebt den Herren (Chorale in Pedal)
14. Meine Seele erhebt den Herren (Canon at the Octave)
15. Christus, der ist mein Leben (Canon at the Octave)
16. Gott des Himmels und der Erden
17. Jesus, meine Zuversicht
18. Erschienen ist der herrlich' Tag
19. Nun sich der Tag geendet hat (a 4)
20. Jesu, meine Zuversicht
21. Two-part Invention in G major
22. Two-part Invention in A major
23. Three-part Invention in C major
24. Three-part Invention in G major
25. Fugue in C major

E. C. Schirmer-# 1460; 1970

From Preface:
"To stand up in front of a class and write
music is to take one's life into one's hands.
But danger and delight grow on one stock.
The risks pale before the ultimate
satisfaction of creating a piece of music
within the terms of a consistent, beautiful
and expressive style.
All but two of the pieces in this collection
were written in class at the blackboard for
my students in "Tonal Counterpoint." The two
exceptions are my version of the canonic
"Christus, der ist mein Leben (No. 15), an
assignment that proved exceptionally
difficult, and the concluding "Fugue in C"
(No. 25) composed for my students in "Fugue,"
the course that followed.
Normally I worked at the board, in close
collaboration with the class and with my
assistants, thinking aloud while I wrote,
erased, revised again and again, with free
discussion and suggestions at every turn.
As the composition proceeded, one of the
assistants would preserve a copy of what had
been written. In this way, a sizable group
of short compositions was amassed, the source
of the present volume." R. T., 1969

Premiere: in class

Manuscript: Houghton Library:
             Complete manuscript
Note that Thompson's autographs were made on the
blackboard

             University of Virginia Library
             Special Collections/Manuscripts
             Alderman Library: Charlottesville, Va.
             # 17 Erscheinen ist der herrlich tag
             # 18 Jesus meine zuversicht
             Note that these are copies taken down from
             Thompson's work on the blackboard

VII

Songs

Songs are for single voice and piano, except where noted

W95.   Serenade in Seville
       1920
       Text: Robert Cameron Rogers

       Unpublished

       Premiere: Rome; 8 March 1923
                 Flora De Grisogono

       Manuscript: Houghton Library:
                    score; 14 June 1920

W96.   Spring; for high voice
       1920
       Text: William Blake; Songs of Innocence (1789)
       Dedicated to Mrs. William Theodore Richards

       Unpublished

       Premiere: unknown

       Manuscript: Houghton Library:
                    score; 19 May 1920
                    mimeograph copy

W97.   The Ship Starting; for soprano and piano/orchestra
       1922
       Text: Walt Whitman; Leaves of Grass (1855)-from
               Inscriptions

       E. C. Schirmer-# 4493; 1991

       Premiere: Rome; 1923
                  Flora De Grisogono

       Manuscript: Houghton Library:
                    score; 22-31 May 1922; Roxbury
                    score; with score of Tapestry; 4-5 June
                    1925; Rome
                    score; voice with orchestra; 2 June 1922;
                    Roxbury
                    voice part

W98. Tapestry; for mezzo-soprano
      1925
      Text: William Douglas

      E. C. Schirmer-# 172; 1986

      Premiere: 31 October 1934
                 Theodate Johnson

      Manuscript: Houghton Library:
                   score; 4-5 June 1925; Rome

W99. A Ballad; for low voice
      1926
      Text: Elizabeth Ann Moses

      E. C. Schirmer-# 4491; 1991

      Premiere: unknown

      Manuscript: Houghton Library:
                   score; 29 Nov. 1926; New York

W100. Doubts; for low voice
       1926
       Text: Eleanor Dougherty

       E. C. Schirmer-# 4490; 1991

       Premiere: unknown

       Manuscript: Houghton Library:
                    score; 22-28 Aug. 1926; Amherst

W101. Five Songs; for low voice
       1926
       Text: Merle St. Croix Wright

       1. White Moth at Twilight
       2. Drought
       3. Discipleship
       4. Spiritual: I wan' ma friends
       5. The Heavens Declare

       E. C. Schirmer-# 4494; 1991

       Premiere: unknown

>   Manuscript: Houghton Library:
>   score in Five songs; 25 Dec. 1925-3 Feb.
>   1926
>   score; 1925-1926; this score also
>   includes 'Doubts'

W102. Southwind; for low voice
       1926
       Text: Elizabeth Ann Moses

       Unpublished

       Premiere: unknown

       Manuscript: Houghton Library:
                    score; March 1926

W103. New Songs for New Voices; for medium voice
       1927

       1. The Wild Home Pussy (Emma Rounds)
       2. The Echo Child (Mary Ely Baker); Ded. For M. E. B.
       3. My Master Hath a Garden (anon.)
       4. Velvet Shoes (E. H. Wylie)
       5. Some One (Walter de la Mare)

       Harcourt-Brace, 1928

       E. C. Schirmer: Two Songs (My Master Hath a Garden,
                    Velvet Shoes); 1938

       E. C. Schirmer: My Master Hath a Garden-# 113
                    Velvet Shoes-# 114

       Premiere: Velvet Shoes
                  Mannes School of Music; 17 October 1928
                  Greta Torpadie, soprano
                  Leopold D. Mannes, piano

       Manuscript: Houghton Library:
                    score; July 1927; New York; contains each
                    song except The Echo Child
                    3 scores: The Echo Child; 17-18 Aug.
                    1927; Amherst and New York
                    score: The Wild Home Pussy; 12 July 1927
                    score: Velvet Shoes; 18-19 July 1927;
                    New York
                    score: My Master hath . . . : 25 July
                    1927; New York
                    score: Some One: 26 July 1927; New York

W104.   Veritas; for baritone
        1954
        Dedication: Harvard Hymn to the Muses
        Text: Mark Antony DeWolfe Howe

        Published: Harvard Alumni Bulletin 57/3 (23 October
                1954)

        Premiere: Boston, Mass.; 28 January 1954

        Manuscript: Houghton Library:
                score; Jan. 1954
                voice part in Music Book; Jan. 1954

W105.   The Passenger for baritone and piano/chamber orchestra
        Written for Gérard Souzay
        1957
        Text: Mark Antony DeWolfe Howe; Sundown: Earlier and
                Later Selected Poems (1955)

        E. C. Schirmer-# 119 (piano/vocal); 1961

        Premiere: Possible performance before inclusion in
                Five Love Songs. See W23

        Manuscript: Houghton Library:
                vocal/piano score; 18-24 July 1957;
                Gstaad

                The Pierpont Morgan Library:
                New York, New York
                dyeline copy of Houghton Library score

W106.   Siciliano, Love is like the wind upon the water for
        baritone and piano, strings ad lib.
        1952

        Text: Philip H. Rhinelander; The Gorgonzola

        Later incorporated into Five Love Songs (1978)
        See W23

        E. C. Schirmer-# 162; 1980

        Premiere: Boston, Mass.; Christmas 1952
                Tavern Club

        Manuscript: Probably in the Tavern Club Archives now
                in the Massachusetts Historical Society

W107.   Solstice; for medium voice
         1966
         Text: Robert Lee Wolff; <u>Fearful Symmetry</u>

         E. C. Schirmer-# 171; 1986

         Premiere: Boston, Mass.; Christmas 1966
                    Tavern Club

         Manuscript: Massachusetts Historical Society

VIII

<u>Unpublished Solo Instrumental Works</u>

W108.   Fuga a tre for unspecified instrument
         1977

         Manuscript: Houghton Library

W109.   Katie's Dance
         1969

         Unpublished

         Manuscript: Houghton Library
                      score; 22-28 Aug. 1969

W110.   Canon a three for equal voices: I will lift mine
         eyes
         ?

         Manuscript: Houghton Library

IX

<u>Arrangements</u>

W111.   <u>A Book of Songs by Erskine Wood with Accompaniments</u>
         <u>for Piano by Randall Thompson</u>
         Voice and Piano

         G. Schirmer; 1922

         Contents:
         The White Seal's Lullaby (Rudyard Kipling)

O Mistress Mine (Shakespeare)
Ariel's Fairy Song (Shakespeare)
Ariel's Sea Dirge (Shakespeare)
Sigh No More, Ladies (Shakespeare)
A Summer Lullaby
An Indian Lullaby
Ballades des dames des temps jadis (Francois Villon)
Love, Ere Love Flies beyond Recall (Justin Huntly
McCarthy)
Gunga Din (Rudyard Kipling)
Little Erskine's Baby Song

Premiere: Probably private

Manuscript: unknown

W112.   The Lark in Morn SATB arrangement of English
folksong 1938
From Cecil Sharp's Folk Songs from Somerset (1904-08)
Written for the University of California Chorus

E. C. Schirmer-# 1782 (with piano reduction); 1940
?   SA; arrangement made by E. C. Schirmer's
                editorial staff

Premiere: Berkeley, California; 2 December 1938
           University of California Chorus
           Randall Thompson, conductor

Manuscript: Houghton Library: October 1938

W113.   Ave Caelorum Domina by Josquin des Prez, for TTBB
Year: Unknown, but prepared while at the University
of Virginia

E. C. Schirmer-# 2332; 1986

Premiere: Probably in class

Manuscript: Photocopy; University of Virginia's
            Alderman Library; Charlottesville, Va.

W114.   Jefferson's March (1801)
[James Hewitt (1770-1827); composed in honor of
Jefferson's Inauguration for Grand Procession in
Philadelphia 4 March 1801]
April 1943
Band arrangement

Premiere: Charlottesville, Va.; 13 April 1943
Cabell Hall, University of Virginia
Jefferson Bicentennial Concert

Manuscript: University of Virginia; Alderman Library
             Special Collections
             Accession No. of Collection 4008; Box CF
             Autograph conductor's score and parts
             Gift of the composer: 25 September 1952

W115.   Song Arrangements relating to Thomas Jefferson
        March and April 1943

        1. Song by Maria Cosway: "Tacite ombre orrende larve"
           [Maria Cosway was a friend of Thomas Jefferson]

        2. Hail, Liberty, the Sweetest Bliss! [A Quick Step
           to the New President's March; written to be paired
           with Jefferson's March; March 1801]. Work
           mentions Thomas Jefferson throughout.
           Thompson arranged both numbers 1 and 2 for two-
           part women's voices--the Glee Club while at the
           University of Virginia in March 1943

        3. Lovely Peggy. Unison Women's Voices
           Arrangement made with students in harmony class
           30 March and 2 April 1943

        Manuscript: University of Virginia; Alderman Library
                     Special Collections
                     Accession No. of Collection 1914; Box 1
                     Autograph scores; March 1943

W116.   The Place Where Johnny Dwells
        n. d.; made while at the University of Virginia

        Manuscript: University of Virginia
                    Glee Club and University Singers Library
                    (uncatalogued)

W117.   Cold on the Mountain for tenor and TBB
        1952
        Carol [words and music] by P. H. R. [Philip H.
        Rhinelander]

        Unpublished

        Manuscript: Houghton Library:
        Reproduction of manuscript; 1952

X

Tavern Club Plays to Which Thompson Contributed

The archives of the Tavern Club of Boston are housed in the
Massachusetts Historical Society, 1154 Boylston Street,
Boston, Mass. 02215 (Tel. 617/536-1608)

W118.   The Millionaire. Words and Lyrics by Philip H.
         Rhinelander
         1951. Revised/1953; Revived
         Two songs by Thompson: Prairie Home and Aria pensée

W119.   The Gorgonzola.   Words and Lyrics by P. H.
         Rhinelander
         1952
         Siciliano for baritone and piano by Thompson; this
         was incorporated into the Five Love Songs (1978)
         See W23

W120.   Fearful Symmetry. Robert Lee Wolff
         1966
         Two songs by Thompson: Solstice and Chanson gourmand

W121.   Promotion, Oh, Promotion. D. Sargent
         1975

Writings by Thompson

T1.   --------. "The Bartered Cow." <u>Modern Music</u>
            IX/1 (November-December 1931), <u>31-33</u>.

Thompson reviewed the premiere of Louis Gruenberg's <u>Jack</u>
<u>and the Beanstalk: A Fairy Opera for the Childlike</u> given by
students at the Juilliard School of Music on 19 November
1931. The performance was conducted by Albert Stoessel.
Thompson found the prose of John Erskine's libretto to be
elucidating. Gruenberg's music had the mystery necessary to
hold Thompson's attention. The Cow dominates the story with
"her seasoned knowledge of life." Thompson would have
preferred a contralto rather than a male voice in the role of
the Cow.

T2.   -------. with Howard Hinners, J. B. Munn,
            Jeffrey Mark. <u>Catalogue of the College</u>
            <u>Music Set</u>. New York: G. Schirmer, 1933.

Two catalogs of records and scores: alphabetical by name
of composer, and classified according to form and medium of
performance; two catalogs of books on music: alphabetical by
name of author, and by subject; supplementary bibliography,
and index. Thompson wrote the Preface.

T3.   --------. <u>College Music: An Investigation for</u>
            <u>the Association of American Colleges</u>. New
            York: The Macmillan Company, 1935.

As the Dirctor of this study sponsored by the Carnegie
Corporation, Thompson spent the academic year of 1932-33
traveling about the United States visiting the music
departments of thirty liberal arts colleges and universities
asking the question, "What should a college attempt to do in
music?" He asked this question and many others of
presidents, deans, faculty, as well as students. After

gathering his materials, Thompson worked most closely with
Ernest H. Wilkilns, Robert L. Kelly and Douglas Moore of the
eighteen-member Sponsoring Committee in setting forth his
findings in printed form.   Today this work is valuable
historically for showing the primitive state of music study
in the early thirties in this country.   "Music does not yet
stand in suitable relation to other subjects in the
curriculum or thought of any American university."   At that
time, music had about it an aura left over from the
"irrational heritage from the Romantic era."   Not yet a
scientific study, music study, of course, quite quickly
picked up its pace and some of those early pathfinders, such
as Otto Kinkeldey and Oscar Sonneck, who liberated the study
of music from the Romantic aura, are mentioned here.

T4.   --------.   "College Music in the Post-War
               World." On General and Liberal Education:
               A Symposium.   Bulletin No. 1 of the
               Association for General and Liberal
               Education. Washington, D. C. (June 1945),
               52-56.

     Thompson was Professor of Music at the University of
Virginia when he wrote this article.   He discusses the most
important question facing the Liberal Arts college and the
graduate school of Arts and Sciences: is music being taught
as a Liberal Art?
     He points to the enormous growth of interest in music in
colleges during the 1940s and discusses the three factors
that produced the change leading to this growth:
improvements in the music programs of secondary schools,
radio and recordings which made music more available and
wide-spread, and the rise of musical scholarship and its need
seen for music departments.
     In the 1940s music "appreciation" grew naturally and
departments did not need to champion it.   Appreciation, in
fact, was really giving way to courses in History and
Literature of Music; these disciplines, Thompson felt, were
the backbone of the college's music program.
     Thompson further comments on the field of musicology with
its virtues of "accuracy and thoroughness" and as well its
dangers: "dullness and pedantry."   Every music department
should have a musicologist with a "creative touch," that is,
a scholar who has a real association with the performance of
music.
     For Thompson, there is no place for sight singing and ear
training on the college level.   These endeavors should be
handled in the secondary schools.
     On the subject of theory, he points to the appearance of a
number of excellent textbooks that can be used.   And finally,
on the subject of applied music: every music major in a

Liberal Arts college will be required to play the piano adequately but should not be given credit toward a degree for this ability.

T5.   --------. "The Contemporary Scene in American
            Music." The Musical Quarterly XVIII/1
            (January 1932), 9-17.

Thompson summed up the American scene by pointing to five major tendencies with regard to American composers and by pointing to several absurdities in American musical life. He divides composers into the Nationalists which include Gershwin, Copland, Antheil, Goldmark, Douglas Moore and William Grant Still; their work is full of jazz. The Eclectics include Daniel Gregory Mason, Edward Burlingham Hill (Thompson's own teacher), Leo Sowerby, Howard Hanson, Mark Wessel; their music in often programatic. The Esoterics include Varèse, Ornstein, Salzedo, Ives, Rudhyar, Ruggles, and Cowell; a listenser has to be among the initiated to understand their music. The Eccentrics include Virgil Thomson who is unique but not alone in having a "side-show complex." Thomson is also among the Nationalists by virtue of his Symphony on a Hymn-tune. Among the Innovators is Henry Cowell because of his experiments in new sonorities for the piano.

Thompson summed up his succinct remarks by pointing to two important facts, and one moral. Fact one: the U. S. leads the world with the small orchestra of musical comedy, and the ballroom. Fact two: after the war, America begins to influence European music, especially with regard to the influence of American jazz. The moral: Thompson thought American should stop trying to spot similarities in composers's music, and simply hear it as an individual's voice. Leave similarity-spotting to the musicologists. Further, Thompson pointed to the real need to get over comparing American music to European music, or finding European influences on American music.

Note: This article was reprinted as "The Vivid Contemporary Scene in American Music." Musical America LII (10 April 1932), 8.

T6.   --------. "Mannes, David." Dictionary of
            American Biography. Supplement Six: 1956-
            1960, edited by John A. Garraty. New York:
            Charles Scribner's Sons, 1980.

Thompson's article on David Mannes (1866-1959), founder of the Mannes Music School with his wife Clara Damrosch Mannes, and father of his friend Leopold Damrosch Mannes.

T7.   --------.   "The Emperor at the Opera." Modern
               Music X/2 (January-February 1933), 109-10.

Thompson noted that Louis Gruenberg's The Emperor Jones
(based on Eugene O'Neill's play) had proved that "we have the
technic to create American opera."   The use of drums
throughout was quite effective. Thompson noted the work's
immediate success and hoped it would continue to have a
"series of triumphs."

T8.   Essays on Music in Honor of Archibald Thompson
               Davison by his Associates. Foreword by
               Randall Thompson. Cambridge, Department of
               Music, Harvard University, 1957.

In this volume, Davison's forty-one years of teaching are
celebrated as well as the marking of his seventieth birthday
on 11 October 1953. The contributors to this volume were
confined to "his past and present musical colleagues at
Harvard and to those who had received advanced degrees under
his instruction." Thompson, in addition to writing the
foreword, was on the publication committee. All periods of
music's history are explored in this volume with
contributions by Ralph Kirkpatrick, Willi Apel, Otto
Kindeldey, William Austin, Donald J. Grout, Walter Piston,
Lincoln B. Spies and Curt Sachs. There is also a bibliography
of Davison's works by J. M. Coopersmith.

T9.   --------.   "American Composers V.   George
               Antheil." Modern Music VIII/4 (May-June
               1931), 17-28.

In Thompson's contribution to this series on American
composers, he makes a "dispassionate appraisal of the man"
many had labled the 'Bad Boy of Music.' Antheil had
experienced a failed concert in Carnegie Hall in 1927 but
people kept returning to his music despite the ridicule
heaped upon him; Thompson concluded that something must be
there.
     Thompson liked his First Symphony, Zingareska, which was
performed in Berlin and against which Krenek protested
because it was symphonic work with jazz in it. Thompson
liked Antheil's jazz.
     Ezra Pound's book on Antheil did little to advance the
composer's cause.
     On Ballet Mechanique: Thompson called it the
"quintessence of industrialism." Ferdinand Léger made a film
to be shown in synchronization with the music at its first
performance in 1926, but a later performance in New York
omitted the showing of the film.

On _Transatlantic_: Thompson saw the first production in Frankfurt in May of 1930. No American critic was there to see this excellent production. The work has a "rough and ready, American style. . . . A rough style dictated by real content is better than an impeccable style revealing no content at all. And like it nor not, we will some day perhaps by brave enough to admit that this roughness is a family characteristic of ours."

T10.   --------. "Jacobi's Quartet and Sessions' Sonata." _Modern Music_ XII/3 (March-April 1935), 135-38.

Thompson reviewed the two works in question after he heard them at a League of Composers concert at the French Institute in New York on 18 February 1935. The Pro Arte Quartet played Jacobi's Quartet and John Duke's performance of the Sessions Piano Sonata was notable for its "incisiveness and insight." Thompson found Jacobi's work most interesting when he gave himself over to being "daring" and did not follow fashion. Thompson felt this was an "important entry in Jacobi's catalogue of works," but probably a transitional one in the overall development of the composer. Sessions's Sonata, which had its first New York performance at this concert, was already a legendary work and rightly so as Thompson found it "highly disciplined" and full of integrity. "The work is, if anything, overcharged with thought, tightened beyond the point of freedom in its own expression, condensed in its incisiveness to a point where its communicativeness is hampered rather than helped." Thompson found its one drawback was its difficulty which will keep it from being heard as often as he would like to hear it.

T11.   --------. [Letters to Douglas Moore] _Letters of Composers: An Anthology_, edited and compiled by Gertrude Norman and Miriam Lubell Shrifte. New York: Grosset and Dunlap, 1946.

Two letters from Thompson to Douglas Moore; both are in private hands. The first letter, from Concord, Mass., was written on 22 April 1936 in response to Moore's comments on hearing _The Peaceable Kingdom_. Thompson takes his critics to task for their muddled remarks on the work. The second letter is addressed to Moore and his wife Emily. Written on vacation in Encampment, Wyoming on 22 July 1940, Thompson tells of hearing the first performance of his _Alleluia_ at the opening exercises at the Berkshire Music Center.

T12.   --------.   "Modal Counterpoint in the Liberal
                Arts Curriculum." The College Music
                Association.   Third Annual Meeting.
                Cleveland, Ohio, 1950.

Thompson loved counterpoint and solving puzzles. For more
than ten years he had tried his hand at the puzzle cannon
that serves as the colophon to the first volume of Padre
Martini's Esemplare and the cannon that Neukomm wrote for
Haydn's epitaph.   For a long time Thompson had no progress.
He wanted to get to heaven with a solution in hand.
     Hans T. David pointed out that it could not be solved as
it appeared in Grove, as it was incorrectly reproduced.   Karl
Geiringer sent Thompson a copy of the correct cannon and it
was reproduced in Musik in Geschichte und Gegenwart.
     Padre Martini's ten rules for counterpoint in his
Fundamental and Practical Essay on Counterpoint (Bologna
1774-75) are a valuable adjunct to teaching counterpoint.
Thompson found Fux's Gradus ad Parnassum equally valuable.
The tone of their teaching is important.
     Thompson felt that in teaching counterpoint "kindness,
patience, and helpfulness are essential and the only road to
success."
     Teacher of modal counterpoint must be able to work at the
board in front of the class, thinking out loud as he works.
Teacher must be able to compose a motet at the blackboard.
Thompson told of wrting his "Now I lay me down to sleep" on 8
May 1947.   Quoting Horace, Thompson commented on the student
of modal counterpoint: he must not simply follow rigid
rules.   "The avoidance of error can lead to wrong, when there
is a lack of art."
     The study of theory is the study of musical composition
and the study of modal counteroint is essentially the study
of the art of choral composition, learning to write for
voices.   What is singable is most important.
     This entry also appears in B133 and B212.

T13.   ------- et al. "Neglected Works: A Symposium."
                Modern Music XXIII/1 (Winter 1946), 3-12.

Thompson joined Cecil Michener Smith, Carlos Chavez,
Robert Palmer, Lou Harrison, Aaron Copland, Harold Shapero,
Paul Rosenfeld, Leonard Bernstein, and Ingolf Dahl to answer
the question: what are the ten most neglected contemporary
works? Thompson's list:
     Hindemith's Mathis der Mahler, Berg's Lulu, Bartók's
     The Palace of Prince Bluebeard, Sessions's First
     Symphony, Satie's Socrate, Ives's Fourth Symphony,
     Malipiero's The Crucifixion, Virgil Thomson's Four
     Saints in Three Acts, Shostokovich's Fourth Symphony,
     and Stravinsky's Renard and Mavra.

T14.   --------.   "The New Music Library." Harvard
                    Alumni Bulletin LVII/16 (4 June 1955), 659.

Remarks on the forthcoming building and opening of the Eda
Kuhn Loeb Music Library, built under the chairmanship of
Thompson.

T15.   -------.   "Requiem--Notes by the Composer."
                    American Choral Review XVI/4 (October
                    1974), 16-32.

Thompson wrote his Requiem upon the inspiration of
Frederick S. Pratt II, a choral conductor who died young.
Pratt did not live to put something back into music after all
he had received from it. Thompson promised to do this and
the Requiem is the embodiment of that promise.
Written between 20 November 1957 and 21 March 1958,
Thompson described how he set up the work using double
chorus. This was the influence of the Age of Golden
Polyphony on him. He gives five reasons why the double
chorus has advantages over the usual four-part chorus and
also discusses technical problems that arise in composing an
extended a cappella work for chorus:

1. Equality of the two choruses.
2. Unity; keeping to a tonal plan in mind, especially where
there is no unifying motive or motto used.
3. Form; formal contrast was in mind as Thompson composed
three fugues.
4. Tempi; tempo contrasts were considered when texts were
laid out.
He chose texts from throughout the Bible, although the work
is not a litugical one. His idea was a dramatic conflict,
between life and death. One chorus represents souls of the
faithful, and the other the mourners.
Thompson especially concentrated on the nature of the
final movement, "a four-voiced fugue for Chorus II in which
the episodes are largely replaced by the interpolation of a
more homophonic and wholly independent Alleluia, sung first
by Chorus I, then by both choruses together." These episodes
were originally interludes for the piano in his song The
Passenger
This entry also appears in B133.

T16.   --------.   "The Second Year at Yaddo." Modern
                    Music XI/1 (November-December 1933), 40-42.

The second year of the Yaddo Festival had lost the spirit
of its first year and had gone into an "emotional old age."
Thompson felt there was an unfortunate lack of attention to

the subject of esthetics in the discussions of the modern composer's problems and music in the United States. Many are "selling" American music but this could be dangerous, if the music is not good.

T17.   --------. "The Story of an Alleluia." American
               Choral Review. Special issued compiled by
               David Francis Urrows. XXII/2 (April 1980),
               24-27.

Thompson was asked by Mark Anthony DeWolfe Howe, chairman of the board of trustees of the Boston Symphony, to write a choral composition in celebration of the opening of the Berkshire Music Center in the summer of 1940. Thompson did not feel up to writing a fanfare type of composition in view of the War in Europe at the time. Instead, "Alleluia," written in the space of five days in July, was the fulfillment of this request. It had one rehearsal and its premiere on 8 July. Written for four-part mixed chorus and having become popular, there were efforts at making various arrangements of it. Thompson felt that none of these were successful as they changed the original intent of the composition. Thompson decided to ask Doc [Archibald] Davison for his opinion on arranging it for men's voices. He too found that "as it stands it just defies you tamper with it."
    Davison died in 1961 and seven years later Thompson was still wrestling with the "Alleluia" problem. He finally solved its mystery by discovering "that many of the passages in 'Alleluia' had been written, unintentionally, in four-part invertible counterpoint. The voices that would have to be literally transposed from the original, whether for men's or women's voices, and which yielded a tessitura too high or too low, proved readily invertible, in one way or another. Note by note, the inversion of the voices could be chosen to preserve the original melodies and harmonies."
    Thompson acknowledges his debt to Doc Davison, and regrets that he never knew the published versions for men's and for women's voices alone.
    This entry also appears in B133.

T18.   --------, Archibald T. Davison, John H. Finley,
               Jr., Kenneth B. Murdock. [Tribute to
               Stephen Davidson Tuttle] Harvard
               University Gazette. 15 January 1955.

    This tribute by his fellow faculty members at Harvard University followed the sudden death of Stephen D. Tuttle (1907-1954). He had been one of Harvard's most illustrious students, completing his doctorate in 1941 with his dissertation "The Keyboard Works of William Byrd." Thompson

had known Tuttle earlier at the University of Virginia where
Tuttle had been Instructor in Music, Assistant Professor, and
finaly Chairman of the Music Department.   While at Virginia,
Thompson and Tuttle worked together with the Glee Club.

T19.   --------.   "Writing for the Amateur Chorus: A
                  Chance and a Challenge."   American Choral
                  Review.   Special issue compiled by David
                  Francis Urrows.   XXII/2 (April 1980), 5-15.

     Thompson begins by quoting some remarks he had made
earlier at a meeting of the Intercollegiate Music Council at
Yale University in May of 1959.   He asked all those in the
audience who were not passionately fond of choral music to
leave the room, because he wanted to speak only to those who
were fanatics about choral music.
     Thompson pointed out the large numbers of amateur choruses
found throughout the U. S. but how the contemporary composer
grumbles about not having a place to sell and hear his music.
Thompson feels these composers should heed the cry from these
amateur choruses for new literature.   These choruses want a
cappella music.   Since there is a great proliferation of
mixed choruses in the twentieth century, there ought to be a
real "school of choral composers."   There is not, and
Thompson gives several reasons for this lack of a "School of
Choral Composers."   First of all the idea that absolute music
is supreme has hindered choral music considerably.   Thompson
feels good absolute music cannot be achieved by a composer
before he writes good choral music.   The second reason for
this lack of a "School of Choral Composers" lies in the
"difficulty of applying contemporary compositional techniques
to writing for chorus.   For example dissonance, irregular
rhythm simply do not fit choral writing.
     This entry also appears under B133 and B212.

T20.   -------- and Philip Hofer.   "The Yonghy Bonghy
                  Bo."   Harvard Library Bulletin XV/3 (July
                  1967).

     Thompson, in what he called "my only sally into the field
of musicology," discussed Edward Lear's own music for his
poem "The Yonghy Bonghy Bo," and the refinement of the music
executed by one Professor Pomè, who apparently took down the
melody from Lear's singing.   Thompson discusses the nature of
the tune, in relation to the nineteenth-century ballad
tradition, Pomè's "corrections," and the effects of Pomè's
harmonization upon Lear's original.   Hofer discusses the
text.

Reviews By Thompson

The six reviews Thompson wrote for the Saturday Review of Literature are presented here together chronologically.

T21.   --------. "The Old Songs." Review of Read 'em and Weep, The Songs You Forgot to Remember by Sigmund Spaeth (New York: Doubleday, Page & Co., 1926). Saturday Review of Literature III/20 (11 December 1926), 418.

Thompson quite liked Spaeth's selection of old songs, especially the humorous ones. While he was not moved to weep over the humorous ones, it could well have been the "sad" ones that could bring a tear. These sad songs "will prove the most laughable of all. . . ." The book is layed out both chronologically and topically and any faults that Thompson saw with the book were well outweighed by "the richness of the material," including the running comments and footnotes by Spaeth.

T22.   --------. "Adorer of Women." Review of The Prodigious Lover by Louis Barthou (New York: Duffield & Co., 1927). Saturday Review of Literature III/46 (11 June 1927), 894.

Thompson's review of the French ex-Premier's "erotical biography" of Wagner and his relationship with the three women who ruled his life: Minna Planer, Mathilde Wesendonck and Cosima von Bülow. This work is a translation from the French by Henry Irving; it is fluent but not without its flaws. Thompson tells his reader that Barthou paints Wagner with his warts and claims his music is a "direct outcome of his character and behavior." Thompson asserts that the work "is Wagner without his music."

T23.   --------. "A Mirror Up to Music." Review of Words and Music by Sigmund Spaeth (New York: Simon & Schuster, 1926). Saturday Review of Literature III/51 (16 July 1927), 974.

Spaeth's book carries the subtitle "A Book of Burlesques" and is divided into four "lively" chapters, each satirizing the great composers and their music. Spaeth's "running commentary is indeed rich and subtle musical observation.

Here there are flashes of insight, the cream of a wealthy
musical intelligence, revealing the weaknesuss, faults, and
eccentricities of great composers."

T24.   --------. "Miscellaneous" [Reviews].   Review
              of Bronx Ballads by Robert A. Simon (New
              York: Simon & Schuster, 1927). Saturday
              Review of Literature IV/5 (27 August 1927),
              76.

    This article is not signed by Thompson. Simon's book is a
collection of eleven songs with prefatory notes. Simon was
music critic of the New Yorker. The book is illustrated,
Thompson reports, with " 'gag-line' cartoons." Its "chief
characteristic is its vulgarity--in this case, as often, a
virtue. . . . Readers would be more readily convulsed with
laughter if they were more accustomed to long Hebrew names
and the use of Yiddish--or if both performers and listeners
had the good fortune to be, say, three sheets to the wind."

T25.   --------. "Ars Lyrica." Review of Terpander,
              or Music and the Future by Edward J. Dent
              (New York: E. P. Dutton & Company, 1927).
              Saturday Review of Literature IV/15 (5
              November 1927), 282.

    Thompson feels Dent is qualified to write on current
musical trends because he is not a composer. Dent was the
"generalissimo of the annual International Modern Music
Festivals," and in this position used his "tact and
linguistic versatility" to mollify clashes between various
musical factions at these events. Dent's work is "an
interpretation of the future of music by means of the nature
and ultimate significance of all music." Dent avoids
sensationalism and thus his work has "that classicism and
universality, ever grateful but, alas, infrequently achieved
either in sytle or in content by musical commentators. It is
not for one time only; it will apply as forcefully and as
suitably to the music that is new in 1950 or a hundred years
hence."

T26.   --------. "Exploration of Counterpoint."
              Review of Steps to Parnasuss by Johann
              Joseph Fux, translated and edited by Alfred
              Mann (New York: W. W. Norton, 1943).
              Saturday Review of Literature XXVII/4 (22
              January 1944), 33.

Thompson reviews Alfred Mann's English translation (for

the first time) of Fux's classic 1775 Gradus ad Parnassum.
"With the virtue of a fluent translation Mr. Mann combines
the grace of true scholarship. A book is fortunate indeed to
be well translated by one whose knowledge of its subject
matter enables him at the same time to edit it, and
supplement its contents, with skills and insight." Thompson
hopes that the work will be widely used in the classroom in
both music history and analytical courses.

T27.   --------. "Contemporary Music." Review of
                    Music Ho! A Study of Music in Decline by
                    Constant Lambert (New York: Charles
                    Scribner's Sons, 1934). Christendom, A
                    Quarterly Review I/5 (Autumn 1936), 887-89.

Thompson reviews the "racy and provocative study of the
contemporary musical scene," written by Lambert and a work
with which Thompson felt a special affinity. Lambert traced
all the then-current isms in music to their sources, examined
them, "weighed [them] and (for the most part) found [them]
wanting." Stravinsky was the center of the controversy of
the taste of newness for the sake of newness. Thompson
noted: "we now have the delicous spectacle of old
revolutionaries chiding youth for its consonance and its good
manners." Sibelius, the one "bridge builder" of twentieth-
century music, comes through the discussion with praise.

T28.   --------. [Book Reviews] Review of Sixty Odd:
                    A Personal History by Ruth Huntington
                    Sessions (Brattleboro, Vermont: Stephen
                    Daye Press, 1936). The New England
                    Quarterly XI/1 (March 1938), 210-11.

Written while Thompson was at the University of California
at Berkeley, he notes that Mrs. Sessions's life as the
daughter of Frederic Huntington (Plummer Professor of
Christian Morals at Harvard College and later Bishop of
Syracuse) might have well been prosaic, but no, her "simple
history is rich and meaningful." As an amatuer musician
herself who once studied in Europe, she saw the "fulfillment
of her dreams in music" in her distinguished son, Roger
Sessions.

T29.   --------. [Book Reviews] Review of
                    Contributions to the Art of Music in
                    America by the Music Industries of Boston:
                    1640-1936 by Christine Merrick Ayars (New
                    York: The H. W. Wilson Company, 1936).

The New England Quarterly XI/1 (March 1938), 208-09.

Thompson found this work highly valuable for its many facts about music in Boston. The work is divided into three sections: the first on Boston's publication of music and musical journals, the second on music engraving and printing, and the third on the making of musical instruments in the city.

T30.   --------. "Music Then and Now." Review of Music in Western Civilization by Paul Henry Lang (New York: W. W. Norton, 1941) and Our New Music by Aaron Copland (New York: Whittlesey House, 1941). The Virginia Quarterly Review 18/1 (Winter 1942), 155-60.

Thompson called Lang's now-classic history "probably the most complete and provocative single-volume history of occidental music in the English tongue." Copland's Our New Music gave Thompson considerable pause for thought as he found Copland's thinking on contemporary music vacillated between espousing a return to eighteenth-century principles of composition on the one hand, and an endorsement of writing "music for the masses" and spreading this music through the use of radio on the other hand. Constant Lambert's Music Ho! and John Tasker Howard's Our Contemporary Composers were, according to Thompson, both more comprehensive in their reviews of the current American musical scene than this work, which was really a "full-length portrait of Aaron Copland, and this is valuable in view of his prominence in present-day music."

Speeches Presented By Thompson

T31.   --------. "College and Conservatory." Concord Summer School of Music. Concord, Massachusetts. 4 July 1935. Manuscript not in the Houghton Library; unknown.

T32.   --------. "Music, A Fill." 1934. Manuscript not in the Houghton Library; unknown.

T33.   --------.   "Music: A Palm Tree."   1934.
              Manuscript not in the Houghton Library;
              unknown.

T34.   --------.   "Orpheus in College."   n. d.
              Manuscript in Scrapbook box at the Houghton
              Library.

T35.   --------.   "Music and the University."   1936.
              Manuscript in storage box # 207 at the
              Houghton Library.

T36.   --------.   "A Short Historical Account of Music
              at Harvard."   Harvard Tercentenary
              Broadcast.   Symphony Hall, Boston, Mass.;
              16 September 1936.   Manuscript at the
              Houghton Library.

T37.   --------.   "Henry Lee Higginson: Fellow of
              Harvard College and Member of the Class of
              1855." Harvard Tercentenary Broadcast.   17
              September 1936. Manuscript at the Houghton
              Library.

T38.   --------.   "The Harvard Glee Club."   Harvard
              Tercentenary Broadcast.   ? September 1936.
              Manuscript at the Houghton Library.

T39.   ---------.   "An Evaluation of our Musical Life."
              Bennington College, Bennington, Vermont.
              30 April 1937.   Manuscript at the Houghton
              Library.

T40.   --------.   "Musicology and Education."   Radio
              broadcast to the International Congress of
              the American Musicological Society, meeting
              in New York City.   15 September 1939.
              Manuscript at the Curtis Institute in
              Philadelphia, Pa.

T41.   --------.   "American Music Writers."   Town Hall,
              New York City.   19 January 1940.
              Manuscript at the Houghton Library.

T42.   --------.   "Music, A Mirror."   Princeton
            University, Princeton, New Jersey.   22 May
            1946.   Manuscript at the Houghton Library.

T43.   --------.   Remarks at the dedication ceremonies
            of the Eda Kuhn Loeb Music Library, Harvard
            University.   7, 8, 9 December 1956.
            Manuscript at the Houghton Library.

T44.   --------.   Talk before the Harvard Club of New
            York, on the Harvard University Music
            Department.   30 April 1959.   Manuscript at
            the Houghton Library.

T45.   --------.   "Music as a Way of Life: A Tribute
            to Henry S. Drinker."   Haverford College,
            Haverford, Pennsylvania.   7 January 1962.
            Manuscript at the Houghton Library.

T46.   --------.   Remarks at dedication of the Stephen
            Davidson Tuttle Memorial Harpsichord.
            Cabell Hall, University of Virginia,
            Charlottesville, Va.   5 November 1963.
            Holograph manuscript in the Special
            Collections Department of the Alderman
            Library.   University of Virginia.   Gift of
            Thompson; 20 November 1963.

T47.   --------.   "Contemporary Religious Music."
            Religious Association Forum.   Smith
            College, Northampton, Massachusetts.   3
            February 1964.   Manuscript at the Houghton
            Library.

T48.   --------.   Convocation Speech.   University of
            Tennessee, Knoxville, Tennessee.   1966.
            Manuscript at the Houghton Library.

T49.   --------.   Sixth Annual Scottish Rite Chair
            Convocation Speech.   North Carolina (?)   6
            May 1966.   Manuscript at the Houghton
            Library.

T50.   --------.   Remarks at dedication of Daniels
                Hall.   Radcliffe College, Cambridge,
                Massachusetts.   17 November 1966.
                Manuscript at the Houghton Library.

T51.   --------.   "How to teach and write music at the
                same time." Kansas Co-operative Composers
                Project.   8 April 1968.   Manuscript at the
                Houghton Library.

Bibliography

B1.   [Unsigned] "Activities of Musicians." The New
            York Times (29 March 1936), Sect. 10, 7.

American compositions were stressed at the concerts of the
San Francisco Federal Music Project. A recent concert
featured works of Ernst Bacon (supervisor of the San
Francisco Federal Music Project), Robert McBride, Frederick
Preston Search, Mark Wessel and Randall Thompson.

B2.   [Unsigned] "Activities of Musicians Here, Afield."
            The New York Times (11 March 1934), Sect. 10,
            6.

Mrs. Eugene Meyer spoke for the League of Composers in
announcing that it intended to commission works for the next
season, give composers more opportunities to be played under
"laboratory conditions" and undertake the recording of new
works. Thompson was on the list of those who would possibly
be commissioned.

B3.   [Unsigned] "Anthem Profiles." Church Music Digest
            1/3 (January/February 1985), 71.

Brief review and comments on Thompson's Alleluia. "This
piece is a complete musical and spiritual experience."

B4.   [Unsigned] "Appointed Director of Curtis Institute
            of Music." The New York Times (22 March 1939),
            Sect. 0, 4.

Mary Louise Curtis Bok announced that Thompson would be
the successor of Joseph Hofmann in the directorship of the
Curtis Institute. Thompson was being released from his

position in the Department of Music at the University of California.

B5.   Armstrong, Donald Jan. A Study of Some Important Twentieth Century Secular Compositions for Women's Chorus with a Preliminary Discussion of Secular Choral Music from a Historical and Philosophical Viewpoint. DMA. University of Texas. Austin, Texas. 1969.

Central focus is not on Thompson's work. Rosemary is mentioned as a piece of "entertainment" which does not require an intellectual response and American Mercury as exemplifying a composer's good use of prose.

B6.   Bacon, Elmore. "American Music Sparkles in Fine Bill at Severance." Cleveland News (22 February 1946).

Review of Thompson's Second Symphony performed by the Cleveland Orchestra under Rudolph Ringwall. "Here is American music that lives, breathes and in shouting brass proclaims America. It is syncopative to the nth degree. Its forthright rhythms, its catchy tunes--one of them an idealized 'Old Man River'--its brilliance and its flashing color were all realized in the Ringwall reading." Bacon liked the Symphony's "freshness and . . . musical integrity that takes it right up to the top of the list of music for America."

B7.   --------. "Cheer Gingold and Szell for Artistry in Paganini Music." Cleveland News (24 March 1950).

Review of the first performance of Thompson's Third Symphony by the Cleveland Orchestra under George Szell in Severance Hall on 23 March 1950. The reviewer found the work "colorful, brilliant and melodious. While it is at times rather despairing in mood, almost tragic in its implications, it rounds into a dazzling Scherzo and a close that has its enthusiastic heights and a concluding atmosphere of warmth and happiness."

B8.   ---------. "Rubinstein, Leinsdorf in Star Roles at Severance." Cleveland News (3 December 1943).

Thompson was unfortunately not in attendance on 2 December 1943 when Erich Leinsdorf led the Cleveland Orchestra in its first performance of his Second Symphony. He missed the wildly enthusiastic rounds of applause that greeted this performance. Bacon finds this Symphony "a thoroughly American work that has melody, brilliance, a clever style and fetching rhythmic ingenuity. Throughout it smacks of the folk tune. And it has about as beautiful a largo as we have heard. Some of its sonorities and melodic fancies are reminiscent of Bloch, others of Gershwin, but only in style. It is entirely original."

Bacon finds this work could be used for a movie setting, "although the composer declares it has no program either literary or spiritual."

B9.   ----------. "Stern and Ringwall Score in Notable
           Severance Bill." Cleveland News (6 January
           1950).

Ringwall directed the Cleveland Orchestra in its third performance on 5 January 1950 of Thompson's Second Symphony. This rehearing reaffirmed Bacon's earlier opinion "that it is one of the finest symphonic works that we have heard by an American composer.

Director Ringwall brought out all of its clever tonal colorations and pointed up artistically all of its clever design, its beautiful melodic line and its vivid rhythmic patterns. The slow movement in particular found the strings singing a summer song in the sunlight. . . ."

B10.   Bantu, Lorene. "Choral Works of Randall Thompson."
           The American Organist 44 (September 1961), 24.

Review of a performance at Trinity Church in Boston on 18 June. Thompson conducted the first performance for mixed voices of his The Gate of Heaven, the Sanctus from his Mass of the Holy Spirit, Alleluia, and The Peaceable Kingdom. The Gate of Heaven presented the "most unusual and arresting music beautifully interpreted."

B11.   Barzun, Jacques. Music in American Life.
           Bloomington, Indiana: Indiana University
           Press, 1956.

While at Columbia University, Barzun served on the musicology committee of the American Council of Learned Societies and for his own thoughts in this work, he draws heavily on his friends who gave lectures under this organization's aegis. Here he quotes from Thompson's lecture "Education for the Professional Musician" given at the Conference on Music in Contemporary American Civilization

sponsored by the American Council of Learned Societies at the
Library of Congress in December 1951:

> Sad is the picture of the composer whose narrow and
> misguided esthetic judgments prevent him from setting
> any words to music because he glories in the fancied
> superiority of his 'absolute' or 'pure' music (in
> contradistinction to that low form, vocal or choral
> music employing words).   How the 'absolute music'
> fallacy ever started exercising its sinister influence
> in this country is hard to understand.   It still
> persists, though it is losing its grip; which is well,
> since much of the most beautiful music employs words,
> and many a sublime page owes its inspiration to the
> lyric theater, a medium which the purist wholly rejects
> on smug esthetic grounds.

B12.   --------. "Randall Thompson." Proceedings of the
          American Academy and Institute of Arts and
          Letters. 2nd Series/3. New York, 1986.

A tribute to Thompson written and read by his long-time
friend Barzun at the Institute Dinner Meeting on 1 April
1986.   Barzun notes that no member of the music section of
the American Academy prepared "an authoritative memorial
tribute" to Thompson and so he, Barzun from literature,
apologizes for the shortcomings of his tribute. He says that
Thompson was a composer loved by American audiences for whom
he loved writing music, more than he was loved by his fellow
composers.

B13.   Beatty, Gerald. "Nine Composers Pen New Works for
          Event." Berkeley Gazette (11 April 1958).

To display "its new treasures," the University of
California at Berkeley dedicated its new May T. Morrison
Music Building, Hertz Hall, Edmond O'Neill Memorial Organ and
the Ansley Salz Collection of instruments by commissioning
compositions from nine composers, among them was Randall
Thompson.   His Requiem was written for the occasion.
Others: Ernest Bloch, Darius Milhaud, Roger Sessions, Sir
Arthur Bliss, Andrew Imbrie, William Denny, William O. Smith
and Arnold Elston.   List of events for the weeks-long
festival is given.

B14.   Bernstein, Leonard. Findings. New York: Simon
          and Schuster, 1982.

Bernstein gave tribute to Thompson in the New York

Philharmonic Young People's Concert "A Tribute To Teachers" performed on 2 November 1963 and later telecast on the 29th of November. Bernstein and the New York Philharmonic played the third movement of Thompson's Second Symphony. "This movement is a wonderful sort of jazzy scherzo; and I'll never forget what a challenge it was to conduct it at the age of 21, (and it my first public concert!)--because the rhythms in it are so tricky."

B15.   B. H. "Vesper Service." Wellesley College News
            36/31 (25 June 1928), 6.

   Review of the bacclaureate vesper service held on a Sunday evening in the chapel. It was "one of the most beautiful of the year." Thompson played Bach's Pastorale in F, conducted the choir in Pergolesi's Stabat Mater, and closed in playing Franck's A minor Chorale.

B16.   Blitzstein, Marc. "Talk-Music-Dance." Modern
            Music XI/1 (November-December 1933), 34-40.

   "There is no point in discussing Randall Thompson's Symphony No. 2 (Philharmonic 3 Nov.) as though it were a serious or profound essay. The wish was to write a lightweight, untroubling work. Considered as such, it is banal, poor music, more or less well-dressed, unentertaining in its stale sequences, flatted sevenths, canned yearnings. The material lacks taste, fervor, thought, or original thought. . . . It is too bad. He is much better than this tawdry music implies."

B17.   Blodgett, Walter, "Leinsdorf Returns with Exciting
            Musical Treat." Cleveland Press (3 December
            1943).

   Reviewer found this program "the most exciting of any Leinsdorf" had given his audience. Thompson's Second Symphony opened the evening in its Cleveland Orchestra premiere. "The symphony is an ingratiating work. It is not particularly profound, and, thank heaven, it does not begin with a searching significance it cannot live up to. The music is sincere. Its effects are created by logical progressions, conceived in counterpoint and dedicated to the proposition that all keys are equal." Blodgett enjoyed its "simplicity and lack of fuss."

B18.   Bloomfield, Arthur.   "Between Earthly, Heavenly
                Choir." California Bulletin (26 May 1958).

     Reviewer found it difficult to wait to get to his
typewriter after hearing Thompson's Requiem in its first
performance at the May T. Morrison Festival on the Berkeley
campus.   Like Stravinsky's Symphony of Psalms and Honegger's
King David, Thompson's work is "one of the choral
masterpieces of the century."
     Before the dress rehearsal Bloomfield talked with
Thompson about his choral writing.   Thompson:

     Some American composers have simply aped European
     musical styles--25 years behind the times.   The latest
     thing to ape is the music of Anton Webern of the 12-
     tone school.
     . . . this imitating has spelled failure for the
     composer.   Lots of the music emerges as what I call
     forcible feeble.   The composer should not slavishly
     imitate.   He should assimilate into a personal style
     the elements from older music he likes best.   And he
     should think first of the emotion he wants to express.
     He should communicate to the audience.

B19.   Boissevain, Hedy.   "Help Wanted: Choral Songs;
                Amateur Chorus Lacks Thems."   Palo Alto Times
                (7 August 1963).

     Review of Thompson's lecture in the Tuesday Evening
Series at Stanford University where he was in residence for
eleven days and conducted his A Feast of Praise, commissioned
by Stanford.   Thompson told his audience that the U. S. is
full of amateur groups "thirsty for good new music to
perform."   There is not this new music for these groups
because of what Thompson calls the "tyranny of absolute
music. . . . The idea persists among 'neo-highbrows' that
music is not pure if it has words. . . .   The idea is
damaging to all music. . . .   An instrumental style can
become turgid and lose touch with the human spirit. . . .
[W]riting for voices has a 'purifying and refining effect' on
any composer's work.
     "Writing for voices also shows up shortcomings in a
composer's technique, . . . and most of our young composers
haven't acquired sufficient technique."   Choral music makes
"terrifyingly simple demands."   Thompson believes that "good
texts for choral music must be based on universality of
appeal.   The would-be choral composer must memorize lots of
poetry and be familiar with the Bible.   After chosing a text,
then sing it a thousand ways to yourself until you latch on
to a tune.   Let the tune and the words develop the form."
When the composition is complete "sing every part yourself.

If you can't sing it yourself, there's something wrong."

B20.   Borgman, George Allan. Nationalism in Contemporary
                 American Music.   M. M. Degree.   Indiana
                 University. 1953.

   Borgman listened to 170 American works on record and
consulted the scores for these works to determine if the
works were indeed nationalistic according to his definition.
Nationalistic implies some extramusical or programmatc
element. Two of these works were Thompson's: String Quartet
No. 1 in D minor and the Alleluia, both of which he concluded
are not nationalistic.

B21.   Briggs, John. Leonard Bernstein: The Man, His Work
                 and His World. Cleveland, Ohio: The World
                 Publishing Co., 1961.

   Thompson taught Bernstein orchestration at the Curtis
Institute, where, Bernstein admits, he was not happy. Both
student and teacher were fond of "abstruse puzzles found in
British newspapers. At lessons, Thompson would begin the
two-hour session by sneaking out of his desk the latest issue
of the London Times. Only when they had worked the puzzle
would they turn to orchestration."

B22.   Brookhart, Charles Edward. The Choral Music of
                 Aaron Copland, Roy Harris, and Randall
                 Thompson. Ph.D. diss. George Peabody College
                 for Teachers. 1960.

   After reviewing the Odes of Horace, Americana, Mass of the
Holy Spirit, Requiem, The Last Words of David, Now I Lay Me
Down to Sleep, Tarantella, and The Testament of Freedom,
Brookhart summarizes the characteristics of Thompson's
general style which shows an admiration for the choral style
of the Renaissance, the Baroque, and especially for Handel.
Thompson's melodic writing shows a strong preference for
diatonic and modal lines, which are strongly influenced by
text. The harmonic idiom of the choral music is quite
conservative. Thompson uses many word painting devices, both
literal and subjective. These devices often produce an
unsatisfying interruption in the musical flow of some
compositions. Craftsmanship is Thompson's forte, probably
due to his strong grounding in academic techniques and to his
experiences as a choral conductor.

B23.   Cameron, Susan.   "Famous Composer Performs in
                 Concert at E & H. Today." Bristol [Va.] Herald
                 Courier (30 October 1983), 3B.

Thompson was in attendance at the premiere of his Twelve
Canticles performed by the Emory and Henry Concert Choirs,
under Charles R. Davis, on 30 October 1983.   The work was
sparked by his visit in 1981 when he gave a lecture on campus
in the Reynolds Lecture Series.
"What was originally only a longing turned into
fulfillment.   I couldn't resist writing something for these
people.   I've felt a love for them since my first visit, but
my love for Virginia is the background for this," Thompson
said.   Thompson was greatly influenced by an early professor
who bubbled over with enthusiasm for music.   "This enthusiasm
was infectious and bore fruit."

B24.   "Campus Critic: An Hour of Music," Wellesley
                 College News 36/30 (31 May 1928), 5.

Unsigned review of Thompson's organ recital in the chapel
on the Wellesley campus.   He played Bach's "Toccata and
Fugue" in D minor, Handel's "Andante Maestoso," Brahms's
Three Chorales, Franck's Chorale, and Widor's "Toccata."
"There is constant broad motion in this masterpiece [Widor's
Toccata] and Mr. Thompson's performance was excellent."

B25.   "Choir Concert in New York wins Highly Favorable
                 Recognition." Wellesley College News 37/14 (17
                 January 1929), 6.

"Unqualified success attended the choir's first venture
abroad in singing at the Town Hall in New York City on
December twenty-second." The reviewer (unsigned) quotes from
N. Y.'s Morning Telegraph, and prints a letter that Thompson
received from Gerald Reynolds, conductor of the Women's
University Glee Club of New York City.
From Mr. Reynolds:

   Your concert last night in town Hall was so enjoyable
   and so significant that it compels serious attention
   from everyone.   What they and you are doing is most
   important if the enormous gifts of American youth are
   to mature towards an adequate expression.   The next
   generation already gives promise of such resource that
   one is almost fearful at being a part in its guidance.
   The more comfort for us then when we hear such a
   program sung so well by the Wellesley Choir.

B26.   "Choir School of St. Thomas has Golden
            Anniversary." The Diapason 60/5 (April 1969),
            1.

    Unsigned review of the 2 March 1969 anniversary concert of
the Choir School of St. Thomas Church in New York City for
which Thompson wrote The Place of the Blest.   Thompson was
not able to fly from Switzerland for the concert because of
bronchitis.   George Bragg of the Texas Boys Choir led the
premiere performance at the evensong festival service.

B27.   "Choir will assist Mr. Thompson at Harvard."   The
            Wellesley College News 36/18 (23 February
            1928), 1.

    Unsigned notice of Thompson's organ recital on 28 February
1928 in the Appleton Chapel at Harvard.   He played his own
"Larghetto" and the Wellesley College Choir sang his
antiphonal anthem Pueri Hebraeorum.

B28.   [Unsigned]   "Chorus and Chorale will present
            Stanford concert Sunday afternoon."   Palo Alto
            Times (15 November 1963).

    Announcement of concert with Thompson's A Feast of Praise
on 17 November.   It had been commissioned by Harold Schmidt,
conductor of the Stanford University Chorus.

B29.   Cohn, Arthur.   Recorded Classical Music.   A
            Critical Guide to Compositions and
            Performances.   New York: Schirmer Books, 1981.

    As professional music critic, music publisher, and music
librarian, Cohn sets forth his ideas about the best
recordings of certain works, and what works are worthy of
hearing.   The Second Symphony "prompts the thought that
Randall Thompson is to American music what Vaughan Williams
is to English music."

B30.   [Unsigned]   "Composer Randall Thompson, 85; known
            for his choral works." The Philadelphia
            Inquirer (10 July 1984).

    Obituary in which a glimpse into Thompson's private world
reveals that he did not "favor forcing them [his children] to
practice or even to listen to music."   He wanted them to
discover music on their own and guided them only if they
needed it.

B31.   [Unsigned]   "Composer to Conduct Workshop." The
            Cleveland Plain Dealer (4 January 1976), V-8.

Thompson's residency in Cleveland was sponsored by the
Epworth-Euclid United Methodist Church and the Cleveland
Chapter of the American Guild of Organists. He conducted an
open workshop-rehearsal, featuring The Peaceable Kingdom. On
Sunday of his stay, he conducted the Epworth-Euclid Chancel
Choir in a concert of his music, including the Cleveland
premiere of "The Gift Outright" from A Concord Cantata.

B32.   [Unsigned]   "Composer to Direct Premiere of Work."
            Palo Alto Times (29 July 1963).

Notice of Thompson's eleven-day stay at Stanford where he
will conduct the premiere of his then-unnamed work on 11
August in Dinkelspiel Auditorium. Featured in Stanford's
Tuesday Evening Series, Thompson spoke on "Composing for
College Choruses: A Chance and a Challenge." He last
visited Stanford in the spring of 1958 when the Stanford
Chorus and Orchestra gave the West Coast premiere of his Ode
to the Virginian Voyage.

B33.   [Unsigned]   "Composer Talks on Music Today." The
            Daily Californian (20 May 1958), 5.

Thompson spoke on the University of California campus at
Berkeley at noon in Dwinelle Hall. The title of his talk:
"Music, amen."

B34.   Copland, Aaron. "American's Young Men of Promise."
            Modern Music III/3 (March-April 1926), 13-20.

Thompson was among the seventeen young American composers
Copland singled out for recognition.

B35.   --------. Music and Imagination. Cambridge,
            Mass.: Harvard University Press, 1953.

Copland gave six Charles Eliot Norton Lectures at Harvard
during the 1951-1952 academic year; these lectures were
accompanied by six very short concerts as illustration of his
lectures. On 19 March 1952, Thompson's Americana was
performed by the New England Conservatory Alumni Chorus with
Lorna Cooke DeVaron, conductor and Elizabeth Davidson,
accompanist.

B36.   --------. Our New Music: Leading Composers in
            Europe and America. New York: Whittlesey
            House, 1941.

Copland's review of the state of contemporary music. He
mentions Thompson in his remarks on the recording of works by
American composers (he does not tell which work/s) and he
quotes figures on the use of the phonograph in the classroom
from Thompson's 1933 survey in College Music. Note that
Thompson reviewed Copland's 1941 work for The Virginia
Quarterly Review.

B37.   --------. "Our Younger Generation--Ten Years
            Later." Modern Music XIII/4 (May-June 1936),
            3-11.

Copland takes up ten years after his first discussion of
seventeen talented young American composers. Here he
reconsiders "these composers in the light of a decade of
activity on their part. . . ." He introduces a new list of
young composers to watch. Did those original 17 represent "a
real generation of American composers?" Copland thinks so;
they represented the "most important generation of composers
America had yet produced."
Copland finds it curious to see that Thompson, a man of
scholarly and academic background, should have made a "bid
for popular appeal, as in his Second Symphony. Thompson has
the audience very much in mind when he composes. This
attitude is not without its dangers, particularly when the
composer gives us the impression . . . that he has been
concentrating on the sonorous effect rather the musical
thought behind it."

B38.   ---------. "Scores and Records." Modern Music
            XIV/2 (January-February 1937), 98-101.

Samuel Barber's Scene from Shelly recalls the early work
of Thompson.

B39.   Copland, Aaron and Vivian Perlis. Copland: 1900
            Through 1942. New York: St. Martin's/Marek,
            1984.

Thompson figures as a fellow contemporary American
composer--sharing the scene at the 1932 Yaddo Festival and
serving on the Central Music Committee with Richard Donovan,
Robert Russell Bennett, Wallingford Riegger, and Aaron
Copland for the Second Festival in 1933.

B40.   Cowell, Henry. "Current Chronicle." The Musical
               Quarterly XXXV/3 (July 1949), 448-65.

   "Randall Thompson's Third Symphony offers moments of
delight: there is real freshness and ease in his handling of
folk-like material in the last two movements. . . .   The
first two movements, however, are of a quite different nature
from the last two, so that in spite of certain technical
resemblances in the elements of the first and last movements,
the Symphony seems to split apart in the middle.   The last
half clearly wins out over the first half in interest and
charm."
   Cowell points out that Thompson builds his music "through
expansion and development of short motifs."   But he doesn't
use right techniques to help him through long works. Cowell
feels that Thompson is better in handling folk elements in
music.   (Note: Thompson's Symphony is discussed on pages
463-65 of this "Current Chronicle.")

B41.   Creigh, Robert Hugh. Stylistic Characteristics of
               Randall Thompson's Choral Music.   Degree of
               Master of Education.   Central Washington State
               College.   July 1970.

   A study of Thompson's traits should be undertaken by the
choral director who wants to perform Thompson's music.
Creigh covers Alleluia, Americana, A Feast of Praise, The
Gate of Heaven, The Last Words of David, Odes of Horace, The
Peaceable Kingdom, and the Requiem.   Thompson writes music
that "will reach and move the hearts of his listeners in his
own day."   For this reason, he did not follow esoteric,
intricate techniques and styles and forms.   His music is
marked by "economy, simplicity of means, and nobility of
expression."

B42.   Crowder, Charles. "Festival Celebrates Founding of
               Jamestown." Musical America 77/8 (July 1957),
               5.

   Review of Ode to the Virginian Voyage's first performance
on 1 April 1957.   ". . . of distinctive and memorable beauty
is the portion of the poem extolling the wonders of Virginia,
set to a flowing melody of charm and dignity.   Four stanzas
are sung in unison, each in turn by the separate sections of
the choir, and in a fifth stanza, by all.   This new work has
many moments of captivating charm. . . .   It is an occasion
piece of considerable merit and fine taste."

B43.   Crutchfield, Will. "Randall Thompson, Teacher;
            Composed Works for Chorus." The New York Times
            (10 July 1984), B-6.

Obituary in which Crutchfield calls Thompson "music's
Norman Rockwell."

B44.   Davis, Peter G. "America's Senior Composers--Why
            Was Their Impact Profound?" The New York Times
            (28 September 1980), Sect. II, 25.

Otto Luening, William Schuman, Aaron Copland, and Samuel
Barber were honored on their 70th birthdays. "How many
American composers under the age of 70 are likely to be so
honored when they attain 'grand old man' status?" Thompson
is listed as one of many of Copland's contemporaries who had
an impact on that particular generation. Davis says that
"today's generation of composers under 60 are simply not
making an equivalent impact. The reasons for this state of
affairs involve a complex interaction of esthetic, social,
and economic developments since 1945." He examines the
generation of 1890-1910 through recordings to see what were
the vital signs of those days. Thompson, according to Davis,
had a preoccupation with trying to be an American composer,
especially in his First Symphony, which "scales few heights
perhaps, but by the same token it has a fresh, eager-to-
please, confident personality and exercises a winning
appeal."

B45.   Davis, Ronald L. A History of Music in American
            Life, 3 vols. Vol. 3: The Modern Era, 1920-
            Present. Malabar, Florida: Robert Krieger
            Publishing Co., 1981.

Reviews high points of Thompson's oeuvre. "Noted most for
his choral works, Thompson has an amazing proficiency for
accenting words and setting them in a tempo appropriate to
their meaning. He knows how to achieve a dramatic climax,
startling contrasts, and create singable music."

B46.   [Unsigned] "December 22 Scheduled for Choir
            Concert in New York." Wellesley College News
            37/13 (20 December 1928), 1.

Announcement of upcoming Town Hall concert in New York
City of the 90-member Wellesley Glee Club under Thompson's
direction. Pueri Hebraeorum was on the program as well as
16th c. madrigals, Purcell's "Sound the Trumpet," and works
by D. G. Mason and Leopold Mannes.

B47.   [Unsigned]   "Dessoff Choirs Rehearsing."   Musical
                Courier (7 November 1931).

Thompson is "engaged as guest conductor for the season and
programs have already been completed."

B48.   Downes, Olin.   "Boston Symphony Opens Season Here;
                Carnegie Hall is Packed."   The New York Times
                (24 November 1939), 28.

Thompson's Second Symphony was heard on a program--one of
two by the Boston Symphony--with Arthur Foote's E Major Suite
for String orchestra, Walter Piston's Concertino for Piano
and Orchestra and Roy Harris's Third Symphony.   Downes
reviewed the efforts of Serge Koussevitsky and the Boston
Symphony to give American music a chance to be heard.   One
hundred twenty-six compositions by forty-seven American
composers had been performed by Koussevitsky during his
tenure as head of the Boston Symphony Orchestra.

B49.   --------.   "Chadwick Work Played at Festival: 'Rip
                Van Winkle' Overture well received at Eastman
                School Event."   The New York Times (22 May
                1931), 28.

Review of the third concert of American music held in
observance of the tenth anniversay of the Eastman School of
Music.   Howard Hanson led the Rochester Philharmonic
Orchestra in Kilbourn Hall on 21 May.   On the program were
George Chadwick's Rip Van Winkel Overture, Leo Sowerby's
Medieval Poem for organ and orchestra (composer at organ),
Edward Royce's Far Ocean, Bernard Wagenaar's Divertimento,
and Thompson's First Symphony.
The program placed "in juxtaposition and in strong and
striking contrasts the figures of four young Americans, each
experimenting in his own way to perfect an individual style."
Downes labled Thompson a modernist.   "The Thompson work is in
three movements, based upon a single theme.   It is earnestly
composed.   It has what may be called unity on paper, and,
when all else fails, the composer beats his drum and blows
his brass wildly, but the difference between theory and
result is well demonstrated here. . . .
The finale is the gayest, the most supple and spontaneous
of the three sections, but the symphony is too much worked
over and in spite of the carefully arranged scheme, it
fusses, hobbles and halts in its progress. . . ."
Downes hears the voices of Stravinsky, Debussy, and
Moussorgsky in Thompsons's Symphony and felt that it was, at
best, a "formative work."

B50.   ---------.   "Music: Thompson Work in Local Bow;
            Eugene Ormandy Leads 'Trip to Nahant'."   The
            New York Times (20 April 1955), 39.

Ormandy led the Philadelphia Orchestra in the New York
premiere of Thompson's work in the final concert of the
season at Carnegie Hall. Downes found that the work "has a
story, an imaginary program, which, shocking to relate, is of
a sentimental and romantic sort." This symphonic poem has
two outstanding musical ideas: the music of the New England
barn dance and the music of the love duet, in which horn and
oboe are involved. His chief criticism is that the score is
too long; he would like to hear a "more concentrated version
of the music" with the love-duet music cut down and made
contributory to the other music.

B51.   ---------.   "New Trends in Composition: Thompson's
            'Testament of Freedom' seen as an Expression
            of Our National Traditions and Spirit." The New
            York Times (22 April 1945), Sect. X, 4.

Review of Serge Koussevitsky's conducting of the Boston
Symphony with the Harvard Glee Club in Carnegie Hall in a
concert dedicated to the spirit of President Roosevelt who
had just died. Roosevelt lived for the ideals that Jefferson
had represented. The work was significant "because of its
indication of a certain trend now perceptible in American
music." Thompson was writing for his fellow men and the
great ideas which had united them. "It is neither surprising
nor inappropriate that the score should have the pomp of
ceremonial in the proper places and the flavor of ritual in
others."
    At a dinner at Koussevitsky's, Thompson's Alleluia was
performed; it "surpassed all the other music of the evening.
It did not matter that other music on the program was written
in advanced harmonic idioms, while Mr. Thompson's procedure
could have been termed conventional or old-fashioned."

B52.   ---------.   "Thompson Leads Dessoff Choirs." The New
            York Times (17 December 1931), 26.

In Margarethe Dessoff's absence, Thompson led the Dessoff
Choirs on 16 December in a Town Hall concert. The evening
began with Michael Bach's motet "'Unser Leben ist ein
Schatten,' . . . a beautiful work for double chorus." Four
16th-century motets by Vittoria, Gallus, Lassus and Aichinger
comprised the second group of works. "Mr. Thompson's short
but excellent notes drew attention to the analogy between the
arts of Vittoria and El Greco."

Also on the program were a series of seven choruses
"Unserer lieben Frau," by Franz Philipp, Thompson's own Tiger
Joy ("Mr. Thompson has done much to meet the mood of the
poet. . . .   The music found favor with the audience.), and
several pieces of Peter Warlock, the nom-de-plume of Philip
Heseltine "who killed himself under exceptionally tragic
circumstances just year ago today."   Heseltine's The Full
Heart, "dedicated to 'The immortal memory of the Prince of
Venosa'(that very Gesualdo, composer and criminal of the
Renaissance, whose biography Philip Heseltine wrote in
collaboration with Cecil Gray)," had its American premiere.

B53.   --------.   "Two American Scores: Werner Josten's
              'Concerto Sacro' and Thompson's Symphony
              Rewarding."   The New York Times (12 November
              1933), Sect. 9, 6.

Downes reviewed the New York premiere of Thompson's Second
Symphony in which Bruno Walter conducted the New York
Philharmonic-Society Orchestra.   Downes felt that both Josten
and Thompson were content "to create music rather than
talking about themselves . . . " and that they had "produced
compositions of "indubitable inspiration, sincerity and a
high grade of workmanship. This has been done without waving
the flag or apostrophizing the eagle."   Further on Thompson's
work: "His symphony . . . is not a work of complete balance
and sustained inspiration. But it is a very fine effort by a
creative musician of indisputable talent . . . " who wrote
this "music with admirable frankness and esprit, and a very
clear technic and a pervading sense of style."   Downes
further felt that the work as a whole showed promise of
things to come, and thus he hoped other composers might have
a look at what Thompson was doing, not by imitating Thompson,
but simply by "getting in touch with life about them."

B54.   Dox, Thurston J.   American Oratorios and Cantatas:
              A Catalogue of Works Written in the United
              States from Colonial Times to 1985,   2 vols.
              Metuchen, New Jersey: Scarecrow Press, Inc.,
              1986.

Dox gives for each score the location of the manuscript,
publisher, specification of voices and orchestra, performance
time, and information on the premiere.   In Vol. I Dox places
The Passion According to St. Luke under the heading of
Oratorio, and quotes from Thompson's own program notes on the
work:

But in one or two important details apart from using

the chorus as narrator, the present setting differs
from other Passions which I happen to know.   It
contains no interpolations of contemporary religious
poetry.   Seventeenth-and eightennth-century settings
often used such poetry, of not a very high order
perhaps, for the very purpose of introducing soprano
and alto solos for variety. This I preferred not to do
because good religious poetry is rather scarce these
days and partly because little if any religious poetry
could behold its place beside the ineffable beauty of
Luke's prose.   And second, unlike any other oratorio
setting of the Passion which I know, the present one
opens with the triumphal entry into Jerusalem. . . .

In Vol. II under the heading of Cantata: A Feast of
Praise, The Place of the Blest, A Psalm of Thanksgiving.

B55.   Dumm, Robert. "Holidays Marked by Randall Thompson
            Work." Music Magazine 164 (February 1962),
            26.

Reviewer welcomes Thompson's Nativity According to St.
Luke.   "It is written in an idiom of welcome sanity and
offers pageant-hungry churches something palatable and
enduring."

B56.   Durgin, Cyrus W. "Adieux, Charles Munch." Musical
            America LXXXII/5 (May 1962), 11.

"Randall Thompson has a way of writing for chorus with a
polish and subtlety I believe unequalled by any composer
living today.   Those gifts were again evident when Thompson
conducted the first performance of his Frostiana at Jordan
Hall on 21 March.   These are choral settings of seven poems
by Robert Frost, which Thompson set in a lyrical manner and
harmonic vocabulary not unlike that of Brahms.   The effect
was of grace which enriches without obscuring the lines of
Frost."

B57.   ----------. "Totting Up Accounts of the 64th Boston
            Symphony Season." Boston Globe (6 May 1945).

Durgin reviews the Boston Symphony's season under Serge
Koussevitsky.   "There seems to have been no one new work that
stands above all others and promises to endure as a
masterwork."   Noting that The Testament of Freedom has
"received some harsh flippancies," he found it "music of
integrity, aspiration and more than a little achievement."

B58.   Edwards, Arthur C. and W. Thomas Marrocco. Music
                 in the United States. Dubuque, Iowa: Wm. C.
                 Brown, 1968.

Thompson is placed under "neo-classic tendencies." His
"musical texture is a sympathetic blend of sixteenth-and
seventeenth-century contrapuntal techniques with homophony; a
typical treatment shows the dissonance (tension) of
contrapuntal movement resolved into chordal cadences. But
there is never any feeling of complexity, regardless of the
kind of texture. [He] unashamedly uses the triad and all its
tonal involvements."

B59.   E. F. P. "Vespers." Wellesley College News 37/31
                 (20 June 1929), 6.

Review of Baccalaureate Vespers service on 16 June at
which Thompson conducted a performance, "which was probably
the first in America" of Handel's 1748 oratorio Saul. This
was Thompson's last appearance before a Wellesley audience.
"It is to be regretted that the choir will no longer have the
inspiration of Mr. Thompson's able training and leading."

B60.   Elwell, Herbert. "Randall Thompson Symphony to
                 Have First Performance by Orchestra at
                 Severance." The Cleveland Plain Dealer (28
                 November 1943).

Erich Leinsdorf introduced Thompson's Second Symphony to
the Severance Hall audience. The work "ranks as one of the
most popular symphonies by an American composer."
Thompson was Elwell's "senior by one year at the American
Academy in Rome. A more likeable and more talented companion
[the author had] never known. Socially and artistically he
was a leader among the fellows at the academy, and it is
gratifying to see that he has won his well deserved place as
a leader in American music. In his outlook were vitality and
optimism and a fine sense of proportion. Something of this
gets into his music to make it one of the healthiest
contributions we have had to the American 'school'."

B61.   --------. "Ringwall Scores with U. S. Music." The
                 Cleveland Plain Dealer (22 February 1946), 22.

Rudolph Ringwall, the associate conductor of the Cleveland
Orchestra, conducted the second performance of Thompson's
Second Symphony by the Cleveland Orchestra. Thompson's work

was programmed with Arthur Foote's Suite in E major, and Edward Burlingame Hill's "Lilacs," Poem for Orchestra, After Amy Lowell. "The second hearing of the Thompson Symphony was especially welcome, as the performance seemed to bring out important features in the work not fully appreciated before. One was more than ever aware how this gifted composer, though preserving classic lines for clarity, had not given in to academic formulae, but had infused his structure with vitality and given his material a truly indigenous flavor."

Elwell lamented the fact that members of the orchestra did not always follow Ringwall's gestures, and thus shading was often missing in Thompson's work. Ringwall was praised for being "close to the heart of the American scene."

B62.   ---------. "Stern Is Agile in Violin Concerto."
             The Cleveland Plain Dealer (6 January 1950).

Review of Thompson's Second Symphony "which Ringwall has given us on other occasions. It is probably worth playing again, but we suggest that he now look around for something new."

B63.   -------. "Gingold Brilliant in Violin Concerto."
             The Cleveland Plain Dealer (24 March 1950), 15.

Review of the first performance by the Cleveland Orchestra of Thompson's Third Symphony under George Szell. The Symphony is "a work entirely free from the 1925 jazz implications which have caused his Second Symphony to become somewhat dated. The Third was given a performance which undoubtedly would have delighted the composer, and the work was cordially received.

This symphony, due perhaps to a certain complacent formality, may not live forever, but . . . [it] is living music of the present, music that sings its way freely, simply, sincerely and with the traditional consciousness of symphony deriving from song. Above all, it is excellent writing. Everything sounds, flows and reaches mature emotional fulfillment." Elwell feels that this symphony "ranks as one of the finest American symphonies yet penned."

B64.   Emerson, Paul. "Composer Visiting at Stanford Says
             Conservatories Shallow." Palo Alto Times (3
             August 1963).

Upon arrival at Stanford for a visit to conduct his then-unnamed composition (A Feast of Praise), Thompson held a press conference at which he commented on the failure of

American music conservatories to "produce top-rate musicians." Juilliard, Curtis, and Eastman, he noted, have "squelched the intellectual growth their students need to mature into first-rate artists, teachers, or composers." Students do not need to be solely musicians. "You have to have an education and this is where the conservatories fail . . . . A great percentage of conservatory graduates, I find, just can't think."

He also commented on composers of electronic music. The composers "think their music has intellectual content. But it stimulates only those who can follow higher mathematics. It's unemotional and intellectually boring." For Thompson the art of music is based on the ability to communicate. "Many modern composers have thrown away all the rules and thrown together sounds. These composers are just a noisy tribe."

B65.   [Unsigned] "Emory & Henry Concert Choir Hosts a
          World Premiere." Emory and Henry Today II/1
          (October 1983).

Premiere of Thompson's Twelve Canticles with the Emory and Henry Concert Choir under Charles R. Davis. This premiere was one of the highlights in this choir's 25-year history. Thompson had visited the school in 1981 and promised to complete a composition for the Concert Choir. Davis thought Thompson was just being polite, "so I was a little surprised when Mr. Thompson called in late August to tell me the compositions were completed and he was ready for the E & H. Concert Choir to give the premiere!" Thompson, his son, and his daughter-in-law attended the performance.

B66.   Ericson, Raymond. "Handel and Haydn Society Turns
          150 in Full Voice." The New York Times (29
          March 1965), 44.

Edward Gilday, conductor of the Society for six years, led the group in the premiere of Thompson's Passion According to St. Luke in Symphony Hall in Boston.

Ericson felt the decision to commission this work from Thompson a very wise one as "the 65-year-old Harvard professor is among the best composers of choral music today with a superb flair for setting the English language."

His style is rooted in the music of "Holst and Vaughan Williams, modality, even some jazzy syncopation. . . . Practically every note for singers and instrumentalists counts. The long passages for chorus are set with a suppleness and sensitivity that keeps its music from becoming repetitious. . . . It is a score that may well prove more durable than others with more striking ideas. Certainly it is worth the attention of any sizable choral group."

B67.   Ellsworth, Ray. "Americans on Microgroove--Part
            II: A Discography." HiFi 6 (August 1956), 60-
            66.

   Ellsworth places Thompson with his "orthodox" composers,
and states that he should be known more widely. His Second
Symphony shows modernity chiefly in its sparse
instrumentation and economy of means; otherwise it is
traditional, and has a beautiful second movement built on a
Deep River kind of theme. Review of the Second Symphony and
The Testament of Freedom on Mercury Recording MG 40000 and
the String Quartet in D Minor on Concert Hall 1092.

B68.   Ericson, Raymond. "Oratorio Society Gives Thompson
            Premiere." Musical America LXXX (June 1960),
            38-39.

   Review of the first New York performance of Thompson's Ode
to the Virginian Voyage with the Oratorio Society of New York
under T. Charles Lee, conductor at Carnegie Hall on 3 May
1960. "The composer invokes the styles of Purcell and Handel
and dance forms such as the hornpipe to set off the Drayton
poem, but there is also a pretty folk-like melody for the
tribute to Virginia. . . . Thompson writes for chorus and
orchestra with the utmost fastidiousness and tact; he knows
the value of brevity and how to relate each section of the
work to the whole. Although an occasional piece, it is a
useful and valuable addition to the choral repertoire."

B69.   Ewen, David. Composers Since 1900: A Biographical
            and Critical Guide. New York: The H. W.
            Wilson Co., 1969.

   A well-written, concise review of Thompson's
contributions. Especially noteworthy here are Ewen's notes
on the extensive performances of the Second Symphony, which
in addition to its numerous American performances, was played
in England, Italy, and Germany. "Within a decade it received
over five hundred performances." Photo.

B70.   Forbes, Elliot. "Americana." American Choral
            Review   XVI/4 (October 1974), 40-55.

   Thompson's writing of choral music since 1928 has been a
great service to his countrymen. All of Thompson's music has
been written with the thought that "the audience has to

understand every word." He writes music that is "consistently singable and suited to the text at hand." Forbes discusses, with musical examples, the high points of Thompson's choral-writing career, as well as presenting some background on Thompson's Scottish heritage, which proved to have some influence on the themes he used.

Thompson's study with Bloch led to his experimental works such as the Piano Sonata and the Suite for Piano. Pianist John Powell in the early 1930s introduced Thompson to the music of the Sacred Harp Singers. Thompson later acquired several editions of the Original Sacred Harp, whose influence appears in The Peaceable Kingdom.

This entry also appears in B133.

B71.   --------, compiler. "List of Choral works by
           Randall Thompson. American Choral Review
           XVI/4 (October 1974), 56-61.

List of Thompson's choral works through 1973; works are divided into Secular and Sacred. This list does not contain unpublished works.

This entry also appears in B133.

B72.   ---------. A History of Music at Harvard to 1972.
           Department of Music: Harvard University, 1988.

While this work focuses primarily on John Knowles Paine, Walter Raymond Spalding and A. Tillman Merritt and their contributions to music at Harvard, Thompson figures prominently both as student and later professor and chairman of the department. In a 1979 letter to David E. Knauss, we find Thompson's remarks on his teacher William C. Heilman whose opinion Thompson sought on his youthful compositions.

In 1935 Thompson was a member of a visiting committee on curriculum at Harvard. With Davison, Merritt, Piston, Woodworth, Thompson presented "A Proposed Revision of the Music Curriculum" which resulted in a survey Music 1, The History of Music, taught by Davison.

Forbes outlines the details of the development of the Walter Bigelow Rosen Professorship of Music established in 1951 in memory of W. B. Rosen, class of 1937. Thompson was named the first Rosen Professor.

From 1952 to 1957 Thompson's chairmanship of the department saw the reshaping of the music concentration curriculum, the building of the Eda Kuhn Loeb Music Library, and the appointment of Nino Pirrotta to head this Library. In addition, Thompson developed a new course for himself: Choral Composition. Forbes draws on Thompson's annual reports in which he points to the activities and progress of the department to the dean and we are hereby given a view of

Thompson's positive administrative hand.

Notable among activities during Thompson's tenure as chairman was a two-day conference, "The American Composer and Choral Music" sponsored by the department and the summer school on the 10th and 11th of August 1953. Thompson moderated the session, "The Need for New Church Music." A concert, conducted by Harold C. Schmidt and Virgil Thomson, of works by Thompson, Thomson, Elliott Carter and Irving Fine ended the conference.

B73.   --------. "The Music of Randall Thompson." The
             Musical Quarterly XXXV/1 (January 1949), 1-23.

The earliest serious study of Thompson's music, complete with musical examples and a photo of the composer. Many of Thompson's lesser-known works (pre-1945) are given careful consideration, including his early Piano Sonata in C minor, The Piper at the Gates of Dawn, The Last Invocation, and Solomon and Balkis. Forbes treats Thompson's harmonic language and style and notes the influences of the past upon his work. Most valuable here is the discussion of the evolution of Thompson's First Symphony from its genesis as a choral work with orchestra in Rome and Venice in 1924 and 1925. To be noted is a page from the Second Symphony in the composer's autograph, printed courtesy of the Eastman School of Music where the autograph was housed for many years. It is the choral music, however, which most attracted Forbes. "The Peaceable Kingdom is [according to Forbes] the most inspired work by the composer. . . . The remarkable quality about this piece is its simplicity of means and consequent clarity." [Forbes was teaching at Princeton University when he wrote this article; later he became a colleague of Thompson's at Harvard.]

B74.   ---------. "Thompson, Randall." The New Grove
             Dictionary of Music and Musicians, 20 volumes,
             edited by Stanley Sadie. London: Macmillan,
             1980. Vol. XVIII, 784-85.

As early as 1924 in his Five Odes of Horace, Thompson "established the qualities of vocal writing which distinguish all his music written for this medium: lines which by their shape are grateful and rewarding to sing, individual choral colours to serve the successive word sounds, care for the natural rhythm of the spoken word and an exquisite sensitivity to literary organization reflected in his musical phraseology."

B75.   Frankenstein, Alfred. "From a Biblical Prophecy, A
              Modern Masterpiece." High Fidelity 11/2
              (February 1961), 59.

Review of the recording made on Fellowship of the Singing
City of Philadelphia under Elaine Brown of Thompson's The
Peaceable Kingdom. Thompson was not the first composer to be
inspired by a painting, and in his case it was a cycle of
more than one hundred "peaceable kingdom" paintings done by
Edward Hicks.

B76.   --------. "Grand Music Festival is Set at UC."
              San Francisco Chronicle (1 December 1957), 4.

A detailed account of the activities that were being made
for the May T. Morrison Festival of Music on the Berkeley
campus of the University of California in April and May of
1958.   Thompson, as a former faculty member and founder of
the University Chorus, was commissioned along with several
other composers to write works for this occasion dedicating
the new music buildings. Frankenstein gives particulars on
the new Morrrison Hall, the Hertz Hall, the Ansley Salz
Collection of string instruments and the new Edmond O'Neill
Memorial organ—all to be dedicated. David Boyden, chairman
of the music department, led the press on a tour of the new
buildings. Frankenstein describes the library, practice
rooms, etc.

B77.   --------. "Musicians Should Help Design Music
              Halls." San Francisco Chronicle (28 May 1958).

After the five-week May T. Morrison Festival, Frankenstein
made conclusions. Of the five new works performed during
this Festival, he numbered Thompson's Requiem as one of the
outstanding works heard. He noted that the newly-dedicated
Hertz Hall, at which much of the Festival took place, is
itself a fine "musical instrument" and the "only auditorium
in the Bay Region of which that can be said."

B78.   --------. "Randall Thompson Work Premiered." San
              Francisco Chronicle (24 May 1958), 16.

Review of the premiere of Thompson's Requiem commissioned
by the University of California at Berkeley for the May T.
Morrison Festival. Frankenstein felt it is a work "likely to
have a considerable number of performances in the coming
years" as it is one of the composer's "most inventive and
philosophical, and one in which his genius for choral writing
reaches something of a climax."

The performance of the Requiem was "superbly handled by
the University Chorus under [Edward] Lawton's direction, and
with that fresh, vivid, crystal quality that is so
characteristic of Lawton's work."

B79.   --------. "Records in Review." High Fidelity I
            (Spring 1952), 55-56.

Thompson's influence on Samuel Barber's Piano Sonata.

B80.   Fuller, Donald. "Forecast and Review: Russian and
            American Season, 1945." Modern Music XXII/4
            (May-June 1945), 255-56.

"'The Testament of Freedom', a choral-orchestral opus on
strangely chosen words by Thomas Jefferson, appeared first at
a Boston Symphony concert. The sequences with suspensions,
cribbed from some harmony textbook, are just a few of the
pinpricks in this drab texture. When Thompson fails to get
inspiration from a hymn tune, he falls back on an alma mater
or bluntly patriotic song. His battle picture would suit
some child's game with toy soldiers."

B81.   Gessler, Clifford. "Thompson Requiem Closes U. C.
            Morrison Music Festival." Oakland Tribune (23
            May 1958).

Review of premiere of commissioned Requiem for the May T.
Morrison Festival at the University of California at
Berkeley. In this work for double mixed chorus the emphasis
is on "peace, joy and praise."
". . . one chorus sings the lamenting lines, the other the
joyful or consolatory ones. When the two choruses joined in
climaxes, it sounded like the pealing of many bells."
Reviewer notes that 15 lines were omitted in the
performance probably because there is much repetition of the
text. The chorus accompanist provided the chorus with
"support at the piano with soft chords and basic melodies,"
although it is an unaccompanied work.

B82.   Gilman, Lawrence. "A New American Symphony
            Performed by the Philharmonic." New York
            Herald Tribune (3 November 1933), 13.

Thompson's Second Symphony was performed by the
Philharmonic Society under Bruno Walter at Carnegie Hall on
the 2nd of November. Thompson was present and "was acclaimed

by the audience with a fervor that is seldom bestowed upon an
American composer--unless, of course, he happens to be Mr.
Gershwin."
   Gilman thinks "[Thompson] has made use of popular idioms,
melodic and rhythmic, and his manipulation of these is
civilized and craftsmanlike. He has not hesitated at times
to be obvious; he has not strained, he has not restricted his
fancy and his feeling; he has not been afraid to sound quite
different from Schönberg. His music has humor, and warmth,
and pleasantness; many will find it agreeable and solacing."
   Photo of the 34-year-old composer.

B83.   Glackin, William C.   "A Happy Song for Death."
           Valley Leisure from the Sacramento Bee (31 May
           1958), L-23.

   A detailed review of the music of Thompson's Requiem
premiered by the University of California-Berkely Chorus
under Edward Lawton. Glackin points to Thompson's "musical
attitude" as one of "peace and hope." The work is "charged
with the spirit of praising the Lord for His everlasting
light. This Requiem, ultimately, is a song of joy at the
prospect of eternal life."
   Glackin found that the work "had not quite enough change
of pace, but this may reflect the fact that last Friday's
performance omitted a sizeable part of the fourth section."

B84.   Gleason, Harold and Warren Becker.   Twentieth
           Century American Composers,   2nd edition.
           Music Literature Outlines-Series IV.
           Bloomington, Indiana: Frangipani Press, 1980.

   Chronology of career and compositions, outline of style
(techniques and devices), and bibliography.

B85.   G. M. S.   "All-American Concert."   Christian
           Science Monitor (7 October 1939).

   Serge Koussevitsky, that champion of the American
composer, conducted two programs in Symphony Hall, playing
works of American composers. Thompson's Second Symphony on
the second program brought cheers from the audience. "The
work is rhythmic and at times percussive, yet by adroit
orchestration the composer sounds the trumpet of the newer
idiom without becoming banal. . . . He has not yet
perfected his technique, but he reveals a vision. Whereas
for some, the 'big city' and its turmoil represent America,
Mr. Thompson looks about him and discovers an America, which
is both imaginative and contemplative, and he is not

reluctant to give a picture of what he sees."

B86.   Haar, James.   "Randall Thompson and the Music of
             the Past." American Choral Review XVI/4
             (October 1974), 7-15.

    Haar studied choral composition with Thompson as a
graduate student in the mid-1950s when Thompson was working
on the Mass of the Holy Spirit. The work serves as an
example of the sound advice he gave his students. Haar shows
Thompson to be close to sixteenth-century musical practices,
steeped as he was in the music of Lasso and Palestria.
    This entry also appears in B133.

B87.   Haber, James E.   [Notes on Activities of Glee
             Club]. Harvard Glee Club Foundation Bulletin
             23 (June 1965).

    On the 23rd of April, Thompson conducted the Harvard Glee
Club, Radcliffe Choral Society and Harvard-Radcliffe
Orchestra in a program of his own works. "This was a rare
opportunity to perform very singable music as the composer
intended, and was regarded by all as a very fitting and
memorable close to Mr. Thompson's career at Harvard."

B88.   Hall, David.   [Record Review]. Stereo Review 42/4
             (April 1979), 152.

    Review of the 1978 recording of the First Symphony and The
Testament of Freedom with Utah Symphony Orchestra and
Chorale. "Thompson's The Testament can be--when performed
by, say, Serge Koussevitsky with the Harvard Glee Club and
the Boston Symphony Orchestra (I remember those 78-rpm discs)
or the Eastman School of Music forces under Howard Hanson--a
splendidly stirring piece of civic music. . . . Regrettably,
however, Maurice Abravanel simply fails to give the music the
rhythmic vitality it needs." Hall briefly discusses the
history of the First Symphony.

B89.   [Unsigned] "Harvard Glee Club Foundation Medal."
             Harvard Glee Club Foundation Bulletin 14 (May
             1957).

    On 22 March 1957 Thompson became the sixth recipient of
the Harvard Glee Club Medal, presented "in recognition of
[his] association with and interest in the Harvard Glee Club,
and his long devotion to the field of choral music." His Mass
of the Holy Spirit was given its first complete performance.

B90.   [Unsigned] "Harvard Post to Thompson." The New
              York Times (16 May 1948), 65.

Brief announcement made by the provost of Harvard, Paul H.
Buck, that Thompson, starting 1 July, has been named
Professor of Music at Harvard. He leaves his teaching post
at Princeton to accept the Harvard position.

B91.   Hepner, Arthur. "Choral group does fine with
              'Boston Composers Concert'." The Boston Globe
              (16 March 1990).

Review of the Newton Choral Society's concert featuring
composers from Boston. Under the direction of David Carrier
at the First Baptist Church of Newton, Thompson's Five Odes
of Horace opened the program and was joined by "choral" works
of Daniel Pinkham, and Alan Fletcher.

B92.   Howard, John Tasker. Our American Music; A
              Comprehensive History from 1620 to the Present,
              4th edition. New York: T. Y. Crowell Co.,
              1965.

Howard quotes from Lawrence Gilman's review of Thompson's
Second Symphony in the New York Herald Tribune on 3 November
1933. He further notes that Thompson, along with Benjamin
Britten and Alexandre Tansman, received the Coolidge Medal
for distinguished service to chamber music.

B93.   Hughes, David G., Leon Kirchner and Elliot Forbes.
              "Faculty of Arts & Sciences--Memorial Minute:
              Randall Thompson." Harvard Gazette (4 October
              1985), 4.

Tribute to Thompson placed on the records at faculty of
Arts and Sciences meeting of 21 May 1985. Photo of Thompson.

B94.   Hume, Paul. "The Record Player." Washington Post
              (23 June 1946).

Review of Koussevitsky's conducting of the Boston Symphony
Orchestra and the Harvard Glee Club on the Victor 1054
recording of The Testament of Freedom. Hume was especially
taken with the "repeated statements of the proposition: 'The
God who gave us life gave us liberty at the same time; the
hand of force may destroy but cannot disjoin them.'" On the
music to which this text is set: "It is a beautiful tune
which has haunted me for days. Later portions of work

achieve an unusually high level of emotional and musical
quality."   Hume wonders whether there is "at beginning of
second section," a "suggestion of undue theatricalism. . . .
It is my feeling, finding a lump in my throat each time I
play it, that this combines some of our greatest American
tradition in writing with some of the finest music written
recently."

B95.   Hussey, Dyneley. "Music: An American Symphony."
             The   Spectator 166/5873 (17 January 1941), 60.

   Music has been the last of the arts to exhibit truly
American traits. Thompson's Second Symphony was played at a
recent Saturday Royal Philharmonic concert and it showed a
"new, authentic note that one could recognize as American--
something taut and steely, devoid for the most part of
conventional frills and informed with a dry, incisive humor
that, like American jokes asks for a quick wit in the hearer
. . . . The symphony is not by absolute standards a great
work."   On the final movement: "someone without [the]
composer's authority in the program notes had labled the
movement with the grandiose title of 'Celebration of
Democracy,' which inevitably raised expectations of a flight
into regions where even Beethoven himself was not entirely
successful in maintaining altitude."

B96.   Jacobs, Arthur, ed. Choral Music. Baltimore:
             Penguin Books, 1963.

   Discusssion of Alleluia, The Peaceable Kingdom, and
Americana.
   " [Thompson] is essentially modern and technically
adventurous in spirit, [and] is essentially a Romantic
(although he would probably die rather than admit it)."

B97.   Jenkins, Gwendolyn N. The Choral Style of Randall
             Thompson. M. M. Eastman School of Music of the
             University of Rochester. 1955.

   Unavailable

B98.   Johe, Edward H. "Hymn Anthem and Prelude
             Literature." The Hymn 16/3 (July 1965), 92-93.

   Review of "Nowell" and "The Lord is My Shepherd."
   " [Nowell] is a carol from the composer's The Nativity
According to St. Luke available in three settings: mixed
voices, women's voices and men's voices.

This might be called the Christmas counterpart to Thompson's famous Alleluia, in that the one word Nowell is sung for 10 pages of never-flagging zeal."
On "The Lord is My Shepherd": "Simply beautiful! For 11 pages it flows through 12/8 and 4/4 meters in harmonic style and in a vocal range coductive to projecting the feeling of this psalm."

B99.   J. S. D. "New Issues for the Choir." The Diapason
           42/7 (1 June 1951), 22.

Brief notice of the publication of The Last Words of David. "There are no extraordinary difficulties, but a full chorus is required."

B100.   J. W. "Arnold Foster Choir and Orchestra." The
           Musical Times 99 (April 1958), 209.

Review of hefty concert given at St. Pancras Town Hall on 13 February 1958. Thompson's Ode to the Virginian Voyage was in company with Mendelssohn's Calm Sea and Prosperous Voyage, Glazounov's Symphony No. 6, Samuel Wesley's In Exitu Israel, Rubbra's Festival Gloria, Falla's Nights in the Gardens of Spain, and a Pastoral Suite by Lars-Erik Larsson. Thompson's work "excited the keenest expectations. . . . It was an excellent idea on the composer's part . . . to use the forms and styles of English music of the seventeenth and eighteenth centuries, with Handel apparently predominating. But why the introduction of pseudo-Parry ('Jerusalem'. . . ?"

B101.   Keiser, Tucker. "Randall Thompson's Music; Noted
           Composer's Work Impressive." The Boston Post
           (1 November 1953), 42.

Review of the Framingham Community Chorus's performance of The Peaceable Kingdom, and comments on Thompson's choral output, including Alleluia, Americana, Rosemary, as well as the solo "Velvet Shoes," and his arrangement of "The Lark in Morn." "Unlike many of his colleagues, he thinks in vocal terms, knows what is grateful for the human voice, and never pushes it into instrumental ranges of expression. He realizes that the singer . . . has to hear his next pitch before he can produce it. His choruses, consequently, are masterpieces in logical part-writing."

B102.   Kingman, Daniel. American Music: A Panorama. New
               York: Schirmer Books, 1979.

   In the chapter entitled "Music with Film, Dance, Drama,
and Poetry," Kingman recommends to students as an
"introduction to American choral music of the last half
century": Thompson's The Peaceable Kingdom and Roger
Sessions's When Lilacs Last in the Dooryard Bloom'd.

B103.   [Unsigned] "Kipling & Thompson Opera." Time 39 (6
               April 1942), 59-60.

   In Thompson's one-act, three-quarter hour opera the
"climax came at the earth-shaking but quite inaudible stamp
of the butterfly." Thompson's work was the first work to be
performed under the 'Composers' Theater' plan, a joint-
venture of CBS and the League of Composers. The plan was to
pull U. S. opera out of the doldrums by getting native
composers to write operas that are simple and inexpensive,
and then get schools and colleges to produce them. Thompson
had earlier hoped to collaborate with Thornton Wilder on this
particular opera. After that fell through, he realized he
could use "Kipling's dialogue word for word." This reviewer
found the score "fresh, unaffected, . . . packed with
singable melody." He heard "conventional harmonies, the
archaic touches, the occasional flavor of Handel's music,   .
. ." and decided that the music was a turning to the past.
   When the reviewer noted that Thompson had written only on
commission for the past ten years, Thompson commented: "A
musician is like an architect; nobody is going to draw plans
until someone is ready to put up a building."

B104.   Kolodin, Irving. "Recordings in Review." Saturday
               Review 53/13 (28 March 1970), 62.

   Review of recording of Thompson's Second Symphony,
conducted by Leonard Bernstein with the New York Philharmonic
on Columbia stereo recording (MS-7392). This was the first
work the young Bernstein conducted in public as a student at
Tanglewood in 1940. Kolodin finds that this work startled
American audiences with its simplicity at a time when most
American composers were opting for complexity. This
simplicity makes the work as warming today as it was in the
thirties.

B105.   --------. "Yaddo Festival Brings Hearing of Native
               Works." Musical America LII/9 (10 May 1932),
               3; 6.

Kolodin's report on the conference of composers and critics at the Trask mansion on the Yaddo estate in Saratoga Springs, New York.   Kolodin was representing the New York Sun, and the only other "critic" in attendance was Alfred H. Meyer of the Boston Transcript.   Kolodin gives careful attention to reviewing a number of compositions; it was the twenty-three-year-old Israel Citkowitz's String Quartet that made the greatest impression.   Thompson was at the Festival; a group photo shows Thompson seated between Wallingford Riegger and Russell Bennett.   Most interesting are Kolodin's remarks on Copland's exhortation to critics and his view of the ideal critic: "one who cultivates a lively curiosity in what native composers are doing, who would go out of his way to inquire about their new works, [and] how their ideas are shaping themselves."

B106.   --------.   "Yaddo Reaps Fruits Sown in Rebellion."
The [Spokane, Washington] Spokesman-Review (14
September 1952), 6 x.

While Kolodin does not mention Thompson's role in earlier Yaddo Festivals, he does point to the Festival's twentieth anniversary at Saratoga Springs, New York in 1952.   He remembers the "epoch-making statement by Aaron Copland . . . in which he noted the scant newspaper coverage of the event and vowed that more attention was paid by the American press to a modern-music premiere in Wuertemburg, Germany, than to a whole festival of premieres in Saratoga."
Copland was incorrectly quoted by the press who reported that Copland said: "Frankly, I consider newspaper criticism a menace.   We would be better off without it."   The press had a field day with its error in reporting and American music gained attention.   "From this occasion dated a new trend in American music and its dissemination."

B107.   Kristoffersen, Kaj.   "Morrison Festival of Music to
Feature Concert Series."   The Daily Californian
(28 March 1958), 10.

Summary of forthcoming six-weeks May T. Morrison Music Festival at the University of California at Berkeley at which dedication of new music facilities will take place.   Thompson was commissioned, as a former faculty member, to write a work; his Requiem was premiered.   Other composers with connections to the Berkeley campus--Darius Milhaud, Roger Sessions, and Ernest Bloch--were also commissioned to write music for this occasion.

B108.   Krummel, Donald W., Jean Geil, Doris J. Dyer, and

Deane   L.   Root.   Resources of American Music History: A Directory of Source Materials from Colonial Times to World War II.   Urbana, Ill: University of Illinois Press, 1981.

Guide to ten U. S. archival sources in which Thompson materials may be found.

See also materials in the Vienna Historical Society, Vienna, Maine 04360 and the Massachusetts Historical Society, 1154 Boylston Street, Boston, Mass. 02215 for archival sources pertaining to Thompson but not listed in Krummel's 1981 publication.

B109.   Kummer, Randolph Frederick.   An Analysis of the Compositional Techniques employed in the 'Requiem' by Randall Thompson.   Masters Thesis, University of Wisconsin.   1966.

An analysis of the Requiem with regard to its treatment of the text, the contrapuntal and harmonic devices used, its treatment of dissonance and how it treats the forces of multiple choruses.

B110.   Kyle, Marguerite Kelly. "AmerAllegro-The 1955 Year: Premieres, Performances, Publications, Recordings."   Pan Pipes of Signma Alpha Iota 48/2 (January 1956), 33-42; 46-77.

Report on Thompson's musical hearings in New York, Philadelphia, Boston, and Washington.   Most notable was a performance of The Peaceable Kingdom heard during the Twelfth American Music Festival at the National Gallery of Art in Washington; it was performed by the choir of St. John's Church, Georgetown.

B111.   [Unsigned].   "Laboratory Theatre Gives 'The Straw Hat'."   The New York Times (15 October 1926), 20.

Review of Labiche's French farce The Straw Hat, adapted to English by Paul Tulande and Agnes Hamilton James.   The work "furnished an artless and fairly mad evening, chiefly interesting for some good tunes supplied by Randall Thompson, who owes, one suspects, more than a passing bow to Sir Arthur Sullivan."   The reviewer reported that the lyrics were unintelligible.

B112.   Laciar, Samuel L.   "Music; The Guild Singers." The
         Philadelphia Evening Public Ledger   (7
         December 1939).

Thompson was present to hear Isador Freed conduct the
Guild Singers in The Peaceable Kingdom among other works, in
the foyer of the Academy of Music. Mr. Freed paid "great
attention to the dynamics and gave an excellent performance."

B113.   Lange, Art.   [Record Review].   American Record
         Guide 42/6 (April 1979), 41.

Review of Thompson's First Symphony and The Testament of
Freedom with the Utah Chorale and the Utah Symphony under
Maurice Abravanel on Angel S-37315.   "[The Testament] became
an immediately popular work; today, however, it is difficult
to explain why such a white elephant of a work should be so
winningly received.   The text . . . is prosaic and, unlike
poetry which enjoys clearly defined rhythmic cadences,
defeats any attempt at melodic versification. . . .   The
Utah Chorus doesn't help matters any by sounding listless and
anemic in its articulation."
The First Symphony "is an improvement. . . .   [It]
contains a number of joyous, serene, and highly lyrical
moments packed into a comparatively consonant harmonic idiom
à la early Harris, Piston, Copland. . . .   Conductor
Abravanel's pacing makes even the occasionally rambling
rhetoric sound convincing, and Angel's engineering is better
than I have heard on any of their recent issues."

B114.   Lawrence, Vera Brodsky.   Music for Patriots,
         Politicians, and Presidents: Harmonies and
         Discords of the First Hundred Years. New York:
         Macmillan Publishing Co., 1975.

G. Willig's imprint of the Jefferson March for flute or
violin and piano is here reproduced. This march was written
to honor the newly inaugurated President Thomas Jefferson at
the Grand Procession in Philadelphia on 4 March 1801.
Thompson made an arrangement of this March about the time he
composed The Testament of Freedom while at the University of
Virginia.

B115.   Leavitt, Donald L.   "Secular Choral Music: A
         Survey." MLA Notes 13/4 (1960-61), 659.

Frostiana "embodies most of the virtues of the composer's
choral writing, without being among his best works. . . .
[It is] not in the same class with The Peaceable Kingdom."

B116.   Lee, Bruce.   "Chorus Gives First Concert of
         Semester." The Daily Californian (5 December
         1938), 3.

The University Chorus appeared in their first concert,
under Thompson's direction, in the Gymnasium for Men on the
Berkeley campus on the 2nd of December. The chorus displayed
"an amazing aptitude in their break-offs and in their volume,
control and tone color. And since the chorus is composed of
technically untrained singers who have practiced as a group
for only a semester, their performance was even more
remarkable and enjoyable." The Peaceable Kingdom was
featured.

B117.   Lee, Grant.   "Nothing but the News." Musical
         Courier 155/7 (May 1957), 6.

Brief notice of the premiere performance of the Ode to the
Virginian Voyage by the Norfolk Symphony Orchestra, College
of William and Mary Choir, and the Norfolk Civic Chorus in
the new Phi Beta Kappa Hall at the College of William and
Mary on 1 April 1957.

B118.   Leichtentritt, Hugo. Music of the Western Nations,
         edited and amplified by Nicolas Slonimsky.
         Cambridge: Harvard University Press, 1956.

In this somewhat curious, unfinished work which Slonimsky
pulled together, Thompson's Second Symphony is called "a fine
work exhaling an optimistic mood." Based on Jefferson's
texts, The Testament of Freedom forms "an impressive edifice
in a neo-Handelian manner."

B119.   --------. Serge Koussevitsky, the Boston Symphony
         Orchestra and the New American Music.
         Cambridge: Harvard University Press, 1947.

Leichtentritt devotes attention to Thompson's Second
Symphony, Alleluia, and The Testament of Freedom.
"Thompson's symphonic style is akin to Hill's in that it
maintains the symphonic classical tradition, [and] is not
intent on a dazzling display of radical modernism. . . .
The advocates of sensational modernism will not likely be
satisfied with this type of music. Yet, though not
revolutionary in spirit, it has an evolutionary value."
Thompson's Alleluia is "a modern work of art, representing
a renaissance of the classic vocal art."
In the Testament, Leichtentritt finds that Thompson has
achieved much "with few means--a sign of mastery. Yet one

might question whether still more might not have been
achieved with a more plentiful dose of imagination."

B120.   Levinger, Henry W. "The New York Concert and Opera
              Beat." Musical Courier 151/8 (June 1955), 44.

Review of the 19 April 1955 concert by the Philadelphia
Orchestra under Eugene Ormandy. Thompson's A Trip to Nahant
received its New York premiere. "The work is similar to
Smetana's 'Moldava,' insofar as it is a travelogue, though
one intermingled with a love story. . . . It was, because of
its melodiousness, a surefire hit with the audience, and the
composer acknowledged the audience's approval with many bows
from the stage."

B121.   Levy, Alan Howard. Musical Nationalism: American
              Composers' Search for Identity. Westport, Ct.:
              Greenwood Press, 1983.

Early in his study, Levy mistakenly lists Thompson along
with about two dozen other Americans who went to Paris to
study in the twenties. Later Levy takes up Leo Sowerby and
Thompson as examples of two composers who went to Rome,
rather than Paris, and therefore they remained more
conservative than their counterparts who took part in the
avant-garde climate of Paris.

B122.   Loesser, Arthur. "Ringwall, Violinist Stern Share
              Honors." Cleveland Press (6 January 1950).

Review of Thompson's Second Symphony, "a work heard here
several times before. . . . Its ideas are often humorous,
sometimes clever, and occasionally cheap."

B123.   ----------. "Thompson Symphony, Gingold Share
              Honors." Cleveland Press (24 March 1950).

Review of first performance of Thompson's Third Symphony
by the Cleveland Symphony under Szell. Loesser calls it "a
readily acceptable work. Its four movements represent a
well-understood sequence of moods, their patterns are
transparently clear; the Symphony speaks a commonly familiar
grammar and syntax, ...
Thompson is no man's imitator, yet he is a traditional
thinker at heart, tying himself to the train of the 19th
Century symphonists. Let this not be regarded as a reproach,
now that we are spelling 'progress' with a small 'p.'
Puzzling an audience is very old hat these days."

B124.   Loessi, John.   The Choral Works of Randall
             Thompson.   M. M. thesis, Cincinnati
             Conservatory of Music.   June 1955.

Loessi interviewed Thompson in December of 1954 to discuss
his philosophy of composition.

Thompson told Loessi that he had been influenced by Handel
in using a good combination of homophonic and polyphonic
texture.   Models in his works also figure in the music of
Monteverdi, DesPres, and Orlando di Lassus.   A cappella music
is the highest form of musical art, according to Thompson.

Loessi quotes from a speech Thompson made in Cleveland to
the College Music Association on 27 February 1950.   Thompson
told of writing "Now I lay me down to sleep" in a modal
counterpoint class:

> Because they (the students) voiced a complaint about
> having to use Latin texts.   I explained to them that
> the use of Latin texts was one of the real advantages
> of studying modal counterpoint; but, at the same time,
> I saw no reason to insist.   During the next two
> meetings, I wrote the following motet on the board,
> with a text they could all understand: "Now I lay me
> down to sleep."   To this I added an 'alleluia' as a
> closing.   Naturally they were all familiar with that
> word, though I confess I did not venture to ask them
> what it meant.

Loessi thinks Thompson should be placed with Carl
Sandburg, Frank Lloyd Wright, Norman Rockwell, and John
Steinbeck.

B125.   E. J. L. [Lorenz, Ellen Jane].   "Campus Critic:
             Dartmouth-Wellesley Concert."   Wellesley
             College News 37/29 (23 May 1929), 5.

Review of Dartmouth Glee Club and Wellesley College Choir
which shared a program.   Reviewer proclaimed Dartmouth group
the best that had shared with Wellesley.   Many felt the
Wellesley Choir had strayed too far from its usual
programming; it eschewed the serious side for "music in a
light vein."   This included Theodate Johnson's singing of
Thompson's children's songs.   "Mr. Thompson is to be
congratulated on his compositions and also on finding for
them as artistic and sympathetic an interpreter as Miss
Johnson."   For this reviewer this group was the most
enjoyable part of the program.

B126.   Lowens, Irving.   "Recent Music."   Musicology 2/4
           (July 1949), 431.

Thompson's First String Quartet in D minor was issued as
the first string quartet in the newly inaugurated Carl
Fischer Study Score Series. Brief history of its commission,
first performance and winning of the Coolidge Award for
Chamber Music, "a well-merited honor." Thompson has stuck by
his credo of writing music to "reach and move the hearts of
his listeners in his own day. . . . Thompson's music falls
easily on the ear, but despite its deceptive simplicty and
open frankness, it has a depth and power which many works of
considerably greater grandiloquence lack."

B127.   --------. Music in America and American Music.
           Brooklyn: Institute for Studies in American
           Music, 1978.

Thompson's music is "American music." He is one of those
who was a true American composer of "'American music,' that
is, of music sprung from national roots, and it is these
composers who speak to us today most eloquently and most
meaningfully, perhaps because we are so eager for a spiritual
home."

B128.   Lupo, Gloria Nell.   Expressiveness in Musical
           Setting of Poems by Robert Frost.   M. A.
           thesis, University of North Carolina. 1963.

Thompson is one of about a dozen composers Lupo discusses
in relation to Robert Frost's poetry. Thompson's setting of
seven poems entitled Frostiana are studied. Both Frost's
poetry and Thompson's music have a close affinity to folk-
art. Appendix contains a list of songs that are settings of
poems by Frost.

B129.   Machlis, Joseph.   Introduction to Contemporary
           Music, 2nd edition. New York: W. W. Norton,
           1979.

Very brief review of Thompson's work. List of Thompson's
students drawn from throughout the text: Samuel Adler, Karl
Kohn, Leo Kraft, and Donald Macinnis.

B130.   A. M. [Mann, Alfred].   "Choral Performances."
           American Choral Review 10/2 (Winter 1968), 69-
           71.

Report from Boston on the first performance of Thompson's
Psalm of Thanksgiving on 15 November 1968. The composer led
the chorus of the New England Conservatory of Music at this
Centennial Concert which was part of a three-day symposium,
"The Conservatory Redefined." The event included the
inauguration of Gunter Schuller as the Conservatory's new
president.
Thompson wrote the work for the Conservatory's chorus
which was prepared by Lorna Cooke DeVaron. Thompson drew
upon The Psalter and the King James version of Psalm 107 for
his text for the work for mixed chorus and children's voices.
Musical examples.

B131.   --------.   "Madrigals."   American Choral Review
             XXIX/1 (Winter 1987), 24-26.

Mann recalls his student days at the Curtis Institute when
Thompson was the director.   In 1939 Thompson organized the
"Institute Chorus, consisting of all Curtis students, and he
invited Samuel Barber, then a new member of the faculty, to
direct a madrigal group."   Curtis students were not
accustomed to music-making in such an ensemble. Thompson
chose Handel's Utrecht Jubilate and had Fritz Reiner lead the
performance. This brief appearance of choral activity
unfortunately quickly disappeared.

B132.   --------.   "Psalm and Gospel Settings." American
             Choral Review XVI/4 (October 1974), 33-39.

These are Mann's editorials on three occasions when the
American Choral Review featured Thompson's work during the
1960s.   Each of the three works discussed, The Nativity
According to St. Luke, The Passion According to St. Luke, and
A Psalm of Thanksgiving were based on scriptural texts and
written on commission.
This article also appears in B133.

B133.   --------, ed.   Randall Thompson: A Choral Legacy
             Studies, Reflections, Tributes. Boston, Mass.:
             E. C. Schirmer Music Company, 1983.

Individual articles found in this collection are annotated
elsewhere. See B70, B71, B86, B132, B209, T12, T15, T17, T19

B134.   Martin, George. The Damrosch Dynasty: America's
             First Family of Music. Boston: Houghton
             Mifflin Co., 1983.

Thompson was interviewed by Martin. As well, a number of
his letters were used to draw portraits of the numerous
members of the Damrosch, Mannes and other families as they
are drawn in this work. Thompson comments on Frank
Damrosch's abilities as a choral conductor. Thompson's close
friendship with Leopold Damrosch Mannes, both at Harvard and
later, is given attention from the musical as well as
personal standpoint. Mannes played the American premiere of
Thompson's Piano Suite on the 16th of November 1925 at the
Mannes School in New York.

B135.   Mason, Daniel Gregory. Music in My Time and Other
            Reminiscences. New York: The Macmillan Co.,
            1938. Reprint. Westport, Ct.: Greenwood
            Press, 1970.

Mason remembered the Beethoven Association which met in
its first home in West Forty-Fourth Street and those who
enjoyed each other's fellowship. Among those he remembered
were Randall Thompson along with Leopold Mannes, Carl
Bricken, William Dinsmore, Quinto Maganini, Wolfe Wolfinsohn.
Mason mentioned having heard Thompson's Jazz Piece, a
"brilliant tour de force, which appeals to me much less than
his songs."
The important point of the fellowship of all those
mentioned by Mason was their banding together against the
forces of chaos, and to further their sense of a calling
toward music. Mason pointed out several of the group who
"wandered or strayed" from the calling of music. At that
point in America's music life, strong commitments were
treasured.
Mason suggested Thompson's Symphony [the Second] to the
conductor Autori who had it performed. Thompson wrote to
Mason in November of 1935 to thank him for this kindness.
Some time later Mason wrote Thompson about the Symphony
after hearing it performed under the W. P. A. conductor,
Alexander Thiede of Boston:

    I must tell you once more how beautiful I find your
    symphony, and how happy I am about it. After all the
    times I have dragged myself to concerts in the hope of
    liking the music of my fellow-countrymen, sat through a
    long evening, and gone home with a headache, it is such
    a joy just to savor something, without an afterthought
    or analysis. . . . [I]t is satisfying to hear
    something that could not have been written anywhere but
    in 'these States'."

B136.   Mason, Jack. "News and Comment About Art and
            Artists, Music and the Dance." Oakland Tribune

(10 April 1938).

Notice of the first joint concert of the University of
California Symphony Orchestra and the University Chorus. The
Chorus was under the direction of Thompson who had joined the
faculty in the fall of 1937.   Thompson conducted his
Americana, and Albert I. Elkus conducted Thompson's symphonic
prelude The Piper at the Gates of Dawn.

B137.   Maxwell, Jerome C. An Investigation of the Musical
             Devices used by Randall Thompson to Compose
             Works on the Text of Robert Frost.   M. A.
             thesis, The Ohio State University. 1966.

The complete score of Frostiana is bound with this
thesis. Maxwell gives the background of the commission,
composition, and premiere of Frostiana, and brief picture of
Frost. Purpose of study: to analyze the musical setting of
Thompson's seven Frost poems. These poems were studied to
provide the conductor of this work an understanding essential
to a performance. Maxwell asked: What is the meaning of the
poem? Does the musical setting seem to be appropriate to this
meaning? What kinds of compositional devices has the composer
used to enhance the text?   What problems regarding
interpretation are evident from study of the score?   What
technical problems are involved in the performance of the
compositions? Maxwell chose Thompson, Frost and these works
because of their appeal to students.

B138.   McGilvray, B. W.   The Choral Music of Randall
             Thompson, an American Eclectic.   D. M. A.
             Diss. University of Missouri. Kansas City,
             Missouri. 1979.

Through interviews with the composer and his colleagues
and students, McGilvray fashioned this study which consists
of a "short biographical sketch of the composer, an
investigation of his philosophies on music and composition,
texts, and teaching, the influence modal and tonal
counterpoint and American music had on his compositions, and
a descriptive analysis of the major choral works."
One of the reasons Thompson went to study at Harvard was
because of the presence of George Herbert Palmer, who made
the greatest impression on the young Thompson. Palmer was
editor of the poetry of George Herbert, and translator of the
Odyssey. Thompson repeatedly stresses the need for a strong
liberal arts education.
Thompson speaks of the Rite-of-Spring Syndrome: a
composer tries to write complex music that will cause riot;
it appeals to only a few. "It is far better to write a good

piece of light music than a bad piece of heavy music. And a
good piece of light music is not easy to write."
     Thompson is a "nationalistic American composer. His
compositions are for American audiences, use American texts,
and are influenced by American sounds. This characteristic
is by design, not by accident. He is not an innovator. His
music language was established early and has changed little,
if any, during his productive life."

B139.   [Unsigned] "M. C. Taylor Gives Fund to Composers."
          The New York Times (9 April 1931), 27.

     Myron C. Taylor gave a site on the French Riviera, on the
Grand Corniche, to the Department of Musical Composition of
the American Academy at Rome. Mr. Taylor set up the Anabel
Taylor Foundation, in honor of his wife, to oversee the "the
extending of the work of the academy in musical compositions.
It is Mr. Taylor's purpose that American composers of merit
shall hereafter receive the same practical encourgement that
many European composers have in the past received through
wealthy patrons." Thompson is noted as having been one of
the Fellows of the American Academy in Rome who had obtained
the Grand Prix in music.

B140.   Mueller, John Henry. The American Symphony
          Orchestra: A Social History of Musical Taste.
          Bloomington, Indiana: Indiana University Press,
          1951.

     Several charts deal with American Orchestras and American
composers. A feeble attempt to show how popular Thompson,
among others, really is.

B141.   M. L. "Radcliffe-Wellesley Concert." Wellesley
          College News 37/12 (13 December 1928).

     Review of concert which featured the Radcliffe Choral
Society and the Wellesley College Choir. The Wellesley Choir
sang Thompson's Pueri Hebraeorum. This reviewer felt the
choir did not do justice to Thompson's music.

B142.   Morgenstern, Sam, ed. Composers on Music. New
          York: Greenwood Press, 1969.

     Virgil Thomson on "the completely steady crescendo" which
is "natural to American musical thought" in his article
"Americanisms" 27 January 1946:

The music of Barber and Schuman and Piston and Hanson
and Copland and Harris and Bernstein and Gershwin and
Cowell and Sowerby and Randall Thompson and William
Grant Still is full of crescendos. It is also full of
rhythmic and metrical irregularities. But none of it
is romantic music in the European sense, because the
crescendos and the rhythmic irregularities are not two
aspects of the same device.

B143.   [Unsigned) "A Music Master's 50 Yrs." San
         Francisco Examiner (5 August 1963), 49.

   Thompson told the press that he had been a true boy
soprano in his youth. After his voice changed, he was
terribly hurt when he was turned down by the Harvard Glee
Club. "I decided then and there that if I couldn't sing for
them, I would write music for them to sing--and I did!"
   Thompson gave his views on contemporary composition ("Some
feel that if you can't compose for a backward-playing tape
recorder you haven't arrived"), folk singers and
hootenannies, and on the difficulty of creating in a troubled
age. His advice to aspiring musicians: "Go to college and
get a good education first. Learn how to write and how to
think. Then you can compose and perform with intelligence."

B144.   [Unsigned] "Music by Thompson Featured for
         Concert." The Daily Californian (24 April
         1940), 2.

   "One of the compositions by Randall Thompson . . . will be
played at the annual spring concert of Alpha Mu . . . today
in International House auditorium." The program was
conducted by University [Berkeley] students.

B145.   [Unsigned] "Musical Vespers to Honor Alumnae
         Graduate Council." Wellesley College News
         36/16 (2 February 1928), 1.

   Notice of a Musical Vespers. Thompson had just completed
his Pueri Hebraeorum and had dedicated it to the Choir; it
was on this program.

B146.   Nicholas, Louis. Thor Johnson: American
         Conductor. Ephraim, Wis.: The Music Festival
         Committee of the Peninsula Arts Association,
         1982.

Thor Johnson was at the University of North Carolina where

he had his Carolina Salon Ensemble, an extra-curricular activity, play for Randall Thompson when he visited there for a symphony rehearsal.

B147.   Nichols, Dorothy.   "Choral Concert Rich, Distinctive."   Palo Alto Times (18 November 1963).

Harold Schmidt conducted the 150-voice chorus in Thompson's A Feast of Praise as part of the Stanford Chorus's autumn, 1963, concert; this was after Thompson had conducted the premiere of this work in the preceeding August.

B148.   --------.   "Chorus Packs House."   Palo Alto Times (12 August 1963).

Review of Thompson's conducting program of his own music; among the works was the premiere of A Feast of Praise. Thompson conducted the Stanford University Chorus in the Dinkelspiel Auditorium on 11 August 1963.
Thompson's works on the program "reveal a somewhat lulling sameness. Thompson's is a gentle soul who is fond of the die away, velvet-voiced ending."

B149.   [Unsigned]   "Overtones."   [Publication of the Curtis Institute of Music] (April 1939), 32-33.

Announcement by the Curtis Institute of Thompson's appointment as Director of the Institute. In addition to the usual educational and teaching background, the courses he taught while at the University of California at Berkeley are listed: Choral Literature, the String Quartets of Beethoven, the Operas of Mozart, and a graduate course in Choral Composition. Further, Thompson points to the fact that he follows in a long line of tradition in which a composer heads a conservatory. Thompson was also scheduled to teach in addition to directing the Institute.

B150.   [Unsigned]   "Paris Conservatoire Orchestra Gives All-American Program."   Musical America LIX/8 (25 April 1939), 11.

Isidor Philipp requested an all-American program to be given at the Sorbonne. Charles Munch conducted the Société des Concerts du Conservatoire. Thompson's Second Symphony was on this program given 29 March 1939 in the amphitheatre of the Sorbonne.

B151.   Parker, Henry Taylor.   "[Unknown]"   Boston
          Transcript. 29 February 1928.

Review of Thompson's direction of the Wellesley College
Choir at Appleton Chapel at Harvard and a report on
Thompson's playing of his own Larghetto.

B152.   H. T. P. [Parker, Henry Taylor].   "Mr. Thompson and
          the Choir Win Distinction." Wellesley College
          News 36/20 (8 March 1928), 1; 7.

Review of Thompson's direction of the Wellesley College
Choir at Appleton Chapel at Harvard. Thompson led the choir
from the organ and played his own "Larghetto"; the choir sang
his Pueri Hebraeorum. Mr. Parker [unknown here to the
reader] quotes his own "serious criticism" found earlier in
the Boston Transcript: "The qualities that the singing of
Mr. Thompson's choir reflects are also the qualities of his
writing--energy, fervor, the vigors that shall leave no room
for sweetness and sentiment, even if harshness be now and
then the price. Elsewhere than in two college chapels, this
Pueri Hebraeorum deserves a hearing."

B153.   Phemister, William.   American Piano Concertos: A
          Bibliography.   Bibliographies in American
          Music, Number Nine.   Published for the College
          Music Society.   Detroit: Information
          Coordinators, Inc., 1985.

Thompson's 1927 Jazz Poem is listed. Stewart B. Sabin's
Rochester Democrat and Chronicle review of the premiere, in
which Thompson himself played the solo, is quoted. Sabin
liked its jazz which he calls "clever, tuneful, trickily
rhythmic, and quite what this young composer should write if
he finds it the means to express his thought."

B154.   Pincus, Andrew L.   Scenes From Tanglewood.   Boston,
          Mass.: Northeastern University Press, 1989.

Pincus's personal view, as a "practicing journalist," of
Tanglewood. His remarks here on Thompson's Alleluia first
appeared in Berkshires Week. See below.

B155.   ---------.   "Tanglewood from the Inside."
          Berkshires Week from The Berkshire [Pittsfield,
          Mass.] Eagle (28 June-4 July 1985), 30.

The tradition of performing Thompson's Alleluia at the

opening ceremonies at Tanglewood continues. "The piece never fails to produce a reverential effect, like a benediciton at the end of a sermon."   So once again at the end of the opening concert the director of vocal music, John Oliver, led the students, who had arrived from various points and who "will not have known the Alleluia before their arrival, and will be hardly more aware of its significance. . . ."

B156.   Piro, Richard J.   "Not white, not rich, not different." Music Educators Journal 54/2 (October 1967), 52-54; 103.

Students from two culturally disparate schools in Somerset and Swansea, near Boston, came together to learn Thompson's A Testament of Freedom under Paul Gayzagian and then performed the work for a group of poor, disadvantaged students who took the bus from the Harry S. Eiseman, Jr. High School in Brooklyn.   These Brooklyn students had never left their home environment and the experience of being house guests with the Boston students and their families, as well as sharing Thompson's music, was a completely new adventure.   After the Brooklyn students had heard the Testament of Freedom, they too wanted to learn it.   Despite their lack of musical training, they struggled with the text and music, eventualy being able to present a performance, accompanied by a host of visual aids especially for the benefit of their local audience.   In performing this work, the children's confidence in their ability, their view of themselves and their self-esteem rose immeasurably.   "The Testament of Freedom was taught to the children for its worth and for the students' own aesthetic growth."

B157.   Pisciotta, Louis Vincent. Texture in the Choral Works of Selected Contemporary Composers. Ph.D. diss. Indiana University. 1967.

Thompson is one of ten composers covered in Pisciotta's study in which he examines Thompson's works from the twenties to the time of this study.   In summary, the choral works of Thompson show a strong connection between their texture and musical form.   In all the works examined, texture is closely related to one or more structural functions such as the introduction or opening phrase, developmental passage, climax, bridge or transition, sectional frame, cadence, coda, or closing section.   This seems to be one of the principal ways in which it exerts formal influence.

B158.   Pleasants, Henry. "Philadelphia Greets Thompson."
             Modern Music XVII/1 (November-December 1939),
             48-49.

Pleasants found the performance of Thompson's Second
Symphony by Ormandy and the Philadelphia Orchestra a kind of
official welcome to Thompson in his new position as Director
of the Curtis Institute. It was the only new music the
orchestra had introduced all season and the Symphony was
already eight years old at the time.
Pleasants found it "expertly and resourcefully scored,
compactly made and endowed with a full measure of native
flavor." The weakest movement, he found, was the scherzo
which had a "static affect."
While Pleasants found that there was much "life and
invention" in the work, it was a little "too ordered" and
lacked the real fire of "artistic imagination" needed in a
great work. He did not find it academic or pedantic, and yet
he could not "go all out for this symphony."

B159.   Porter, Quincy. "American Composers, XVIII:
             Randall Thompson." Modern Music XIX/4 (May-
             June 1942), 237.

Porter points to Thompson's interest in writing for
listeners; he has no interest in startling through
experimentation but in pleasing, through simplicity, and
superb craftsmanship.
An example from Americana points up Thompson's ability to
set words so that they are understood easily. His rhythmic
patterns are clearly defined as shown by two examples from
his Second Symphony, and an example from his recent String
Quartet [First], and his "lyric sense" is shown by an example
from the slow movement of his Second Symphony. The Suite for
oboe, clarinet, and viola is touched on here.
Thompson liked to quote Thomas Carlyle: "Create, create!
Be it the pitifullest, most infinitessimal product, it is the
best that is in you. Out with it, then!"
A drawing of Thompson by John Canaday accompanies this
article.

B160.   --------. "Solomon and Balkis in Cambridge."
             Modern Music XIX/4 (May-June 1942), 266.

The premiere of Thompson's Solomon and Balkis had taken
place on CBS radio a few weeks earlier on 29 March, but
Porter reviewed the performances of 14 and 15 April in 1942
in Cambridge. Philip Stolar, tenor, sang the role of the
Butterfly, with Malcolm Holmes conducting. Leonard Kent was
the dramatic director of the production. This "practical

work" was encouraged by the League of Composers and CBS and can be "effectively presented by amateurs." Porter felt it the work of a "fine craftsman" and that Thompson had accepted the direct influences from Handel, Monteverdi, and Wagner. Porter had a feeling of let-down near the end because Thompson had concentrated his efforts in the first two-thirds of the work.

B161.   [Unsigned]   "Premiere Concert Slated at Emory." Bristol [Va.] Herald Courier (23 October 1983).

Announcement of Thompson's presence on the campus of Emory and Henry College. His Twelve Canticles were slated for premiere by the College's concert Choir. When he visited the College in 1981 he brought with him sketches of three compositions that he had the choir sing at that time. "Thompson was so delighted with the quality of that performance that he stood at intermission to tell the audience of his intention to complete the three pieces as well as nine others planned in the series, with all to be dedicated to Emory and Henry."

B162.   [Unsigned]   "Present New Songs." Musical America XLVIII/28 (27 October 1928), 12.

Reviewers, singers and teachers were invited to the David Mannes Music School on 17 October 1928 to hear Greta Torpadie, soprano, and Leopold Damrosch Mannes, piano, perform the 25 songs that were written expressly for the newly published collection New Songs for New Voices. Thompson's Velvet Shoes is in this collection.

B163.   [Unsigned]   "Progress Story Inspiration for 'Testament of Freedom'." The Charlottesville Daily Progress (3 May 1962).

Article written to announce performance of the Testament of Freedom at the Memorial Gymnasium in which the University of Virginia Glee Club and the National Gallery Orchestra played Thompson's work as the highlight of Charlottesville's 200th Anniversary concert. Thompson found the "text of the fourth and last chorus in a short story published April 13, 1942, in The Charlottesville Daily Progress." While looking for further Jefferson texts to set, Thompson mentioned his problem to Bernard Mayo, who at that time was proofing his Jefferson Himself. Mayo lent Thompson the proofs and Thompson compiled further texts for his setting. Thompson composed the work "between Jan. 24 and March 23 in the choir room at the back of the University of Virginia chapel within sight of the Rotunda."   Further history of performances of the work are mentioned.

B164.   Reis, Claire. Composers in America: Biographical Sketches of Living Composers with a Record of their Works 1912-1937. New York: The Macmillan Co., 1938.

One of the earliest biographical sketches of Thompson; it appeared while he was in Berkeley.

B165.   --------. Composers, Conductors, Critics. New York: Oxford University Press, 1955.

As one of the founding members and executive chairman for twenty-five years of the League of Composers, Reis took an active interest in the promotion of new American music. She helped in commissioning new compositions and in promoting their performances. Arthur Judson, manager of the New York Philharmonic wanted to promote competitions for new works, complaining that commissioned works may have only a single performance. Reis countered his remarks with a letter from Thompson to her. He reported on the fate of his League of Composers work The Peaceable Kingdom: in one year 762 copies of the score and 669 copies of individual choruses had been sold.

B166.   Renzelman, Gary Eugene. A Stylistic Analysis and Comparison of the A Cappella Choral Music for Mixed Voices by Three Contemporary American Composers: Aaron Copland, William Schuman, Randall Thompson. M. A. thesis, University of California at Los Angeles. 1960.

Renzelman discusses Thompson's Alleluia, Glory to God in the Highest, his arrangement for mixed voices of the folk song The Lark in Morn, the Mass of the Holy Spirit, Odes of Horace (only Vitas hinnuleo . . . and Montium custos . . . of the original five Odes, and the much later Felices ter), The Peaceable Kingdom, and the Requiem.
On the Mass: "For the purposes of a religous service, Thompson's Mass might be successful in creating a deeply devotional attitude for the worshippers, but the musical worth of the experience would be doubtful."

B167.   [Unsigned] "Resigns as Director, Curtis Institute of Music." The New York Times (21 February 1941), 16.

The resignations of Randall Thompson, Director of the Curtis Institute and Fritz Reiner, head of its orchestra department were announced and accepted with deep regret by Mrs. Mary L. C. Bok, founder and president of the Institute. Although the resignations came within a few hours of each other there was no relation between the two. Thompson said his resignation resulted from "differences of opinion between myself and the board of directors concerning fundamental issues in music education." Thompson did not elaborate upon his remarks, but it was reported that these issues involved a "conflict between musicianship and academic education."

B168.   Restine, James Harold. The Choral Idiom of Randall Thompson. M. A. thesis, West Texas State College. 1959.

An organized, succinct study that set out to discover Thompson's means of achieving "idiomatic expression" in his choral compositions. Restine studied Thompson's idiomatic writing by considering "(1) the implements used to gain this end and (2) the limitations placed upon the composer by use of the vocal instrument." Restine concluded his work with an appendix that lists Thompson's compositions, choral and otherwise, with copyright and completion date, first performance, and publisher. Appendix C lists seven recordings of his choral music.

B169.   Rich, Alan. "Current Chronicle." The Musical Quarterly XLIV/3 (July 1958), 367-70.

Rich writes from Berkeley, California where he reviews the festivities that accompanied the opening of new classroom and concert-giving facilities at the Music Department of the University of California.
There was a six-weeks festival which featured six major works commissioned for the new facilities and given their premieres. These were by men whose careers had at one time brought them to Berkeley: Ernest Bloch, Sir Arthur Bliss, William O. Smith, Darius Milhaud, Roger Sessions, and Randall Thompson.
There were also premieres of uncommissioned works by the music faculty. The entire Festival was broadcast on KPFA-FM.
Thompson's seventy-minute Requiem concluded the Festival. "To offer a work of these proportions to a university chorus is to flirt with danger, and it is likely that a supporting piano will be needed frequently and importantly, as it was in Berkeley, whenever the piece is sung. Within its conservative framework the work has many moments of simple and poignant beauty. . . .   It cannot, however, be proclaimed a composition completely devoid of tedium."

B170.   Rogers, Harold.   "St. Luke Passion Premiere."
          Christian Science Monitor (1 April 1965), 14.

Edward Gilday led the Handel and Haydn Society in the
world premiere of Thompson's The Passion According to Saint
Luke at Boston's Symphony Hall, in celebration of the
Society's 150th anniversary. The Society commissioned this
work and it was only the second time it had done so.   To
celebrate the Society's 100th anniversary, it had
commissioned Horatio Parker's Morven and the Grail.
"One might describe the basic style of the entire work as
verismo da chiesa--as if a Puccini had turned away from earth
to heaven. . . .   Both he and Puccini employed old
techniques, tested by time for dramatic power. The ascending
or descending movement of parallel thirds and sixths over a
pedal point . . . is always a winner. And Dr. Thompson
achieved a thematic unity by just such a device in the
narrative portions by the chorus." Thompson was present for
the performance.

B171.   Rosenwald, Hans. "Speaking of Music." Music News
          43/4 (April 1951), 10-11.

Short summary of Thompson's work, along with a number of
his contemporaries. Rosenwald quotes Lawrence Gilman on what
is wrong with Thompson's music.   There is mention of the
Second Symphony, Jazz Poem, Peaceable Kingdom, Testament of
Freedom, and Salomon and Balkis ("rather anemic and provided
at best good entertainment").

B172.   Sabin, Robert. "Twentieth-Century Americans."
          Choral Music: A Symposium, edited by Arthur
          Jacobs.   Baltimore: Penguin Books, 1963.

"No American composer has written for voices with more
ease and effectiveness than Randall Thompson. His brief
Alleluia (1940) for unaccompanied chorus is a model of its
kind, and proves that one can be a traditionalist and still
write fresh, powerful, inspiring music."

B173.   Sabin, Stewart B. "American Composers' Concert."
          Rochester [New York] Democrat and Chronicle (21
          February 1930).

Review of the first performance on 20 February of
Thompson's First Symphony in Kilbourn Hall. Howard Hanson
led the orchestra in the sixteenth concert in the Eastman
School American Composers series. Thompson's work "appealed
to the writer for what one might call cardinal virtues; it

was built on a framework; its three movements correlate;
there is in it much excellent instrumentation that challenges
and holds attention. The opening bids for attention with
percussion, but makes progress to something solid; following
this progress is not always easy in the fist movement in
which there seem to be lapses from the flow of the writer's
imaginative architecture; at times there are passages which
seemed more resultant from impulsive imagination than
adherence to the logical conclusion of the matter."

B174.   Sablosky, Irving. American Music. The Chicago
          History of American Civilization, edited by
          Daniel J. Boorstin. Chicago: The University
          of Chicago Press, 1969.

    Ernest Bloch came to the United States in 1916, and was
one of the first foreigners to teach Americans on their own
soil.   "It is hard to know whether he or Nadia Boulanger
taught the greater number of major American composers. Roger
Sessions, Douglas Moore, Bernard Rogers, Quincy Porter,
Randall Thompson all came to Bloch in Cleveland [sic] in the
1920s."

B175.   Saminsky, Lazare and Isadore Freed. Masters of Our
          Day: An Introduction to Present-Day Music by
          Living Master-Composers. New York: Carl
          Fischer, 1936.

    Thompson's Song After Sundown ("To be played as a singer
might sing it") and Little Prelude ("A fine example of neo-
classic writing") join piano pieces by fourteen of Thompson's
contemporaries (among whom are Aaron Copland, Howard Hanson,
Deems Taylor, Frederick Jacobi, and Roger Sessions) in this
collection designed for the "average American child . . .
growing up without any knowledge of the profound changes that
have taken place in music since the turn of the century."
Note that eighteen of these solos, including Thompson's, were
reissued in 1963.

B176.   Sargeant, Winthrop. "Musical Events." New Yorker
          36 (14 May 1960), 191-92.

    Review of the Ode to the Virginian Voyage. Sargeant found
it a "pleasant, and at times even stirring affair, expertly
scored for chorus and orchestra and containing a robust
theme--to the words 'Virginia Earth's only Paradise'--that I
would unhesitatingly recommend to Virginians as a state song.
The musical idiom used in this work is popular . . . [and]
unabashedly Handelian." That, Sargeant concludes, is not bad
as the work managed to hold the audience's attention.

B177.   Schwerké, Irving. "Paris Pays More Heed to Jazz
           than List of Serious Americana." Musical
           Courier (1 May 1939), 6.

Thompson's Second Symphony was performed on 29 March under
Charles Munch's baton at the Sorbonne. The hall was half
full due to insufficient advertising. A few days later, Duke
Ellington played to a packed house at the Palais Chaillot.

B178.   Seaton, Lorraine. "Clear Call for More." The Hong
           Kong Standard (12 June 1990).

Review of Thompson's The Peaceable Kingdom ("a joy, and as
the voices warmed up, the words of these texts from the Bible
really came across.") and Alleluia as sung by the Hong Kong
Bach Choir under the direction of David Francis Urrows.

B179.   Sessions, Roger. "American Musical Culture."
           Review of College Music by Randall Thompson
           (New York: The Macmillan Company, 1935).
           Saturday Review of Literature XIII/24 (11 April
           1936), 16-17.

Sessions found Thompson's work was "written with humor and
insight which makes it a pleasure to read in spite of the
statistical nature of its contents." Thompson's "arguments
. . . are presented with sincerity and feeling, and one far
superior in cogency, as well as in tone, to those of his
critics. . . . "
Thompson's "guiding principle is his thesis that
instruction in music itself, and not techniques of
performance, should be the basis of the university
curriculum."

B180.   Shackelford, Rudy. "The Yaddo Festivals of
           American Music, 1932-1952." Perspectives of
           New Music (Fall/Winter 1978), 92-125.

A chronicle of the Yaddo Festivals in Saratoga Springs,
New York. Thompson was on the Central Music Committee which
planned the Second Yaddo Festival of 1933. Thompson wrote
the only "general assessment" covering the 1933 Festival in
Modern Music; here he "deplored the lack of adventure and a
certain stolid self-importance that seemed to have settled
in."
Thompson had a composition [Velvet Shoes] performed and
recorded at one of the four concerts held on the 18th and
19th of September in 1937.

B181.   Shull, Carl N.   The Development of an Annotated
             Guide to Music by Distinguished Composers for
             Children's Voices.   U. S. Department of Health,
             Education, and Welfare.   Office of Education;
             Bureau of Research.   25 October 1970.
             Elizabethtown College, Elizabethtown, Penn.

Thompson is one of 136 contemporary composers represented
in this annotated guide to children's vocal literature.
Shull rates the works from easy to most difficult after
giving information on text, publisher, date of composition,
and a description of the music harmonically, rhythmically,
texturally. A valuable guide but unfortunately not in print.

B182.   Slonimsky, Nicolas.   Supplement to Music since
             1900.   New York: Charles Scribner's Sons,
             1986.

Under entry which notes Thompson's passing on 9 July 1984:
"Randall Thompson, American composer who took pride in
writing music in a euphonious traditional manner without
being seduced by modern innovations, whose choral work The
Testament of Freedom to words by Thomas Jefferson became a
national classic. . . .
On The Testament of Freedom: ". . . conceived in the
spirit of simplicity, leaving not a discord untamed in its
prevalent C major. . . . "

B183.   Smedley, Bruce Robert.   Contemporary Sacred Chamber
             Opera: A Medieval Form in the Twentieth
             Century.   Ph.D. diss.   George Peabody College
             for Teachers, 1977.

Thompson's 90-minute opera Nativity According to Saint
Luke; A Musical Drama in Seven Scenes portrays the Nativity
in the context of the prophecy contemporary with it. Both
staging and costuming are simple. The work is a singer's
opera; voices are in the most prominent position.
    For Smedley the work is more "a devotional celebration"
than a "dramatic reenactment."
    Thompson wrote to Smedley in August of 1976 about the
work, calling it "a series of altar paintings or stained-
glass windows." He wanted the result to be "simple and
unostentatious."
    In addition to the premiere in Cambridge in December 1961,
there have been a few foreign performances including a
Japanese translation used at the United Christian Churches of
Japan's annual Christmas celebration at Osaka on 20 December
1965.

B184.   Sneller, Joseph.   "Randall Thompson Work Conducted
             by Ormandy."   Musical America LXXV/7 (May
             1955), 23.

Thompson's A Trip to Nahant was given its first New York
performance in Carnegie Hall on 19 April 1955 by the
Philadelphia Orchestra under Ormandy. It is "a work of real
distinction. Although long, it is not tedious. This is due
to Thompson's distinguished melodic gift and the remarkable
skill in which he varies the manner of the introduction of
his themes. The music is geniunely evocative and American in
spirit, and although two of its subjects derive from a
square-dance pattern and the shaped-note phrases of early
American hymn-singing, it is by no means a pastiche. . . .
Mr. Ormandy conducted the score with tremendous brio and
clarity."

B185.   Solow, Linda I., editor, Mary Wallace Davidson,
             Brenda Chasen Goldman, Geraldine Ostrove,
             associate editors.   The Boston Composers
             Project: A Bibliography of Contemporary
             Music/Boston Area Music Libraries.   Cambridge,
             Mass: MIT Press, 1983.

The aim of the editors "is to list every composition,
published or unpublished, by every art music and jazz
composer resident in the greater Boston area during the
latter half of the 1970s." Works are listed alphabetically
under composer. In most cases the instrumentation of
Thompson's orchestral scores is given. This is a valuable
guide to the contents of both the Houghton Library and the
Eda Kuhn Loeb Music Library at Harvard University with regard
to Thompson's manuscripts and personal papers.

B186.   Spalding, Walter Raymond.   Music at Harvard: A
             Historical Review of Men and Events. New York:
             Coward-McCann, 1935. Reprint. New York:
             DaCapo Press, 1977.

Spalding gives a good idea of the kind of atmosphere and
tradition in which Thompson found himself as a student when
he entered Harvard in 1916 and as a professor from 1948 to
1965 when he retired. Thompson is specifically mentioned as
the recipient of a fellowship to the American Academy in Rome
in 1927.

B187.   Sparger, A. Dennis. A Study of Selected Choral
             Works of Randall Thompson. M. A. thesis,
             Eastern Illinois University. 1965.

     The seclected works are those for mixed chorus, chosen
because they are in the most typical choral grouping, provide
the richest choral color, and are chronologically
representative of Thompson's style.

B188.   Stanley, Hildegard Jo. The Major Choral Works of
             Randall Thompson with Particular Emphasis on
             the Analyses of the 'Testament of Freedom'.
             Master of Church Music. Southwestern Baptist
             Theological Seminary, School of Church Music
             [James McKinney, Dean]. 1962.

     Thompson composes to be heard and not just in Carnegie
Hall but "in a Baptist Church Choir in the panhandle
country." "Thompson," according to Stanley, "is a present-
day American composer who takes devices from the past periods
of music history and treats them in a modern idiom. He does
not use combinations of tones which are unpleasant to the
average listener, nor is he so conservative that he cannot
capture the interest of the trained musician." Stanley
choses the term "neo-classicist" to describe Thompson.

B189.   Stevenson, Robert. Protestant Church Music in
             America. New York: W. W. Norton & Co., 1966.

     Stevenson labels much present-day church music "concert
music set to religious text. "Thompson's Mass of the Holy
Spirit, written for the Episcopal Communion Service, uses
"learned devices." Comments on The Peaceable Kingdom: "The
anomaly of Hicks's patronage is the more keenly felt when the
Quaker antipathy to all art-music is remembered. Hicks, a
fanatic, deplored even his multiple-copy paintings, such as
the peaceable kingdoms, as pomps of Satan." On The Nativity
According to St. Luke: Thompson chose an older poet, Richard
Rowlands, rather than a contemporary one.
     "In 1958, [Leo] Sowerby--after surveying the American
scene from the organ bench of the Episcopal cathedral in
Chicago (where he then served)--awarded merit ribbons" to
Randall Thompson and other native-born Americans.

B190.   [Unsigned] "Sproul Names New Director;
             Reorganization of University Choral Groups
             Planned by Music Leader." The Daily
             Californian (19 August 1937), 2.

Thompson was appointed to a new professorship in an effort to stimulate interest in University choral groups at Berkeley. Thompson's main work was in reorganizing and directing these groups. He was also to be active in connection with the University Symphony orchestra.

B191.   S. S. "Obituary" [Thompson]. The Musical Times CXXV/1699 (September 1984), 524.

Sadie sums up Thompson's life, but does not mention Thompson's Harvard education.

B192.   [Unsigned] "Stanford 150 Voice Choir Plans Concert." [Albany, Calif.] Thousand Oaks Times (13 November 1963).

Announcement of 17 November performance by the Stanford University Chorus under Harold Schmidt's direction; Thompson's A Feast of Praise on the program.

B193.   [Unsigned] "Stanford to Present Rare Haydn Work." San Francisco Chronicle (11 November 1963), 51.

Announcement of concert of 17 November presenting Haydn's "Salve Regina" and Thompson's A Feast of Praise, which was commissioned by Harold Schmidt.

B194.   Strassburg, Robert. Ernest Bloch, Voice in the Wilderness: A Biographical Study. Los Angeles: The Trident Shop, 1977.

Thompson studied composition privately with Bloch for one year while in New York City. Here one gets a glimpse of the music Bloch stressed in his teaching. He transmitted his love of polyphonic choral music to all of his private composition students who, in addition to Thompson, included George Antheil, Quincy Porter, Roger Sessions, Bernard Rogers, Herbert Elwell, and Theodore Chanler.

B195.   [Unsigned] "St. Thomas Church Choir School celebrates 50 Years." The American Organist 52/5 (May 1969), 27.

On 2 March 1969 there were two services in the St. Thomas Church in New York City to celebrate the 50th anniversary of the boys choir school. Thompson's Alleluia was performed as the evening's offering anthem. George Bragg, founder and director of the Texas Boys Choir, filled in as conductor of Thompson's commissioned work <u>The Place of the Blest</u> in Thompson's absence due to illness.

B196.   [Unsigned]   "Suite by Randall Thompson for an
              Unusual Combination."   <u>Musical America</u> LXI/12
              (July 1941), 32.

    Announcement of the publication of the Suite for Oboe, Clarinet, and Viola by E. C. Schirmer Music Co.   Remarks on each of the movements: "The most exhilarating movement is the third, a short Allegro of unbottoned jollity, with a suggestion of the Negroid idiom woven into the spirit of a country break-down. . . . [It is] is a notably rewarding work for three instruments that are rarely found hobnobbing free of the participation of other members of their families."

B197.   [Unsigned]   "Symphony and Chorus at U. of C.
              Sunday." <u>Emeryville [Calif.] Herald</u> (8 April
              1938).

    Announcement of joint concert of the Berkeley Symphony and Chorus.   Thompson's <u>The Piper at the Gates of Dawn</u> and <u>Americana</u> were scheduled. <u>Americana</u>". . . though one of his most recent productions, has been performed in many cities throughout the country and has evoked enthusiastic comments. It evidences, in addition to Mr. Thompson's mastery of both the orchestral and choral idioms, a sense of broad and delicate humor."

B198.   Tawa, Nicholas E.   <u>Serenading the Relectant Eagle:</u>
              <u>American Musical Life, 1925-1945</u>.   New York:
              Schirmer Books, 1984.

    Tawa mentions the folowing Thompson compositions in his discussion of this era: <u>Alleluia</u>, <u>Americana</u>, <u>Jazz Poem</u>, <u>The Peaceable Kingdom</u>, String Quartet, <u>Solomon and Balkis</u>, Suite for Oboe, Clarinet and Viola, Symphony No. 1 ("easy-to-enjoy-nationalism"), Symphony No. 2,   Symphony No. 3 and <u>The Testament of Freedom</u>.   Tawa quotes a number of comments by and about Thompson that have appeared elsewhere in this bibliography.

B199.   --------. <u>Art Music in the American Society: The</u>
              <u>Condition of Art Music in the Late Twentieth</u>
              <u>Century</u>.   Metuchen, New Jersey: Scarecrow
              Press, 1987.

This work is not about "composers," Tawa tells us, nor "musical styles and compositions," but rather about the state of art music this country.

"By the year 1985, the aggressive modernism that characterized so much of the art music written in the twentieth-century had begun to seem outmoded. The sort of melody and harmony with which the general audience has always identified seemed to be returning to its former favorable position. Twentieth-century American composers whose works conserved some of music's traditional values were less apt to be dismissed as irrelevant to contemporary concerns." Thompson, along with many of his contemporaries, began to be discussed and performed "with greater understanding and sympathy than had a been the case in the first three decades of the post-World War II years."

B200.   --------. A Most Wondrous Babble: American Art
           Composers, Their Music, and the American Scene,
           1950-1985. Westport, Ct.: Greenwood Press,
           1987.

Tawa's discussion of the "traditionalists," (among whom Thompson figures), is peppered with terms such as "death" and "alienation," and the issue of the split between the composer and audience is covered. That Tawa does not mention Thompson's name in this work, although the composer was actively working on the scene during the thirty-five-year period under review, is not surprising considering Thompson's music had no association with these terms, and his relation with his audience had no split.

B201.   [Unsigned] "Thompson Here to Lecture, Conduct."
           Stanford University Weekly (1 August 1963).

Short notice of Thompson's presence on Stanford's campus to participate in Stanford's Workshop in Choral Music which was designed for directors of school, college, church, and community choral organizations. Thompson was slated to give a Tuesday evening lecture: "Composing for College Choruses: A Chance and a Challenge" and to direct the premiere of his 12-minute then-unnamed work (A Feast of Praise) for mixed chorus and brass choir.

B202.   Thomson, Virgil. American Music Since 1910. New
           York: Holt, Rinehart, and Winston, 1972.

Thomson outlines Thompson's life and accomplishments under "106 American composers." He characterizes Thompson as the "author of a most effective Symphony, No. 2, and one of our most indigenous-sounding string quartets."

B203.   --------.   The Art of Judging Music.   New York: Alfred A. Knopf, 1948.

Thomson reviewed the Guilet Quartet's 17 April 1945 performance of Thompson's First String Quartet in the Times Town Hall for the New York Herald Tribune. "Each rehearing brings it closer to my heart, not only for its touching Appalachian Mountain Americanism but for its broader musical interest as well. It is one of the lovely pieces our country has produced, that any country, indeed, has produced in our century. And its reading last night by Mr. Guilet and his teammates--Louis Gralitzer, Frank Brieff, and Lucien K. Laporte--was a dream of sweetness and of poetry."

B204.   -------.   "The Musical Scene."   New York Herald Tribune (15 May 1949).

Review of Thompson's Third Symphony which Thomson found "both grateful and gracious to the ear."

B205.   Tischler, Barbara L.   An American Music: The Search for an American Musical Identity.   New York: Oxford University Press, 1986.

Reference to Thompson's study College Music for the Association of American Colleges in 1935 with regard to the changing role of music in American life. Music had become a part of the university curriculum.

B206.   [Unsigned]   "2 Premieres at Eastman."   The New York Times (3 May 1952), 18.

Brief notice of the Eastman School's presentation of Thompson's Testament of Freedom and Weldon Hart's Concerto for Violin and Orchestra.

B207.   [Unsigned]   "U. C. Symphony, Chorus to Give Joint Concert."   Berkeley Gazette (6 April 1938).

Announcement of upcoming concert at the end of Thompson's first academic year at Berkeley where he directed the University Chorus. On the program were The Piper at the Gates of Dawn, and Americana. Albert I. Elkus led the University Symphony.

B208.   Urrows, David Francis.   "Choral Performances--
            Emory, Virginia."   American Choral Review
            XXVI/1 (January 1984), 29.

Review of premiere of Thompson's Twelve Canticles by the
choir of Emory and Henry College under the direction of
Charles R. Davis.   Thompson received "an overwhelming
ovation."   The origin of the work is outlined here, and noted
are "God is a Spirit," "When Thou Liest Down," "I call to
Remembrance," and "Face Answereth Face."   Thompson was
interviewed by National Public Radio during his visit in
Emory, Virginia.

B209.   --------.   "Five Love Songs: Reflections on a
            Recent Work."   American Choral Review XXII/2
            (April 1980), 28-38.

As Thompson's amanuensis, Urrows helped the composer in
1978 and 1979 to write down "The Happy Shore," the last piece
in his Five Love Songs.   In interview, Urrows discusses with
Thompson the emergence and musically-connected threads found
in the Five Love Songs.   The musical thread that runs through
The Passenger (1957), part of the Requiem (1958), and finally
"The Happy Shore," is illustrated here with musical examples.
    Discussion of the meaning of its two themes, love and
death, and Thompson's view of himself as a Classicist.
Thompson sides with the craftsmanship of the classicist over
the romanticist's reliance on inspiration.
    This entry also appears in B133.

B210.   --------.   "A 'Lost' Choral Masterwork of Randall
            Thompson."   American Choral Review XXXII/1-2
            (Winter/Spring 1990), 8-16.

In the fall of 1925 before Thompson's return to America
from his study at the American Academy in Rome, he sketched
and partly orchestrated settings of two odes of the Roman
poet Horace.   In these settings for chorus, baritone solo and
orchestra, "Poscimur" and "Vides ut alta" were not brought to
fruition.   When Howard Hanson came to Thompson in the fall of
1929 with an "informal" commission for a symphony, Thompson
used these works as the basis for his First Symphony.
Thompson's own assessment of his original ideas (an
assessment with which Urrows takes exception), the details of
the reworking of these pieces into the First Symphony
(written with organ and perhaps under the influence of Aaron
Copland's 1924 Organ Symphony), along with glimpses of
Thompson's contacts and influences during his Roman studies
are chronicled in detail for the first time.

B211.   --------. "Randall Thompson and the Organ." The
            American Organist 22/10 (October 1988), 72-77.

Some of Thompson's earliest musical instruction took place
in Vienna, Maine during summers spent with his "Aunt"
Marietta Eaton on her "vestry organ." The photo of this
still-extant instrument shows it to be a curious instrument
indeed. Urrows gives an account of Thompson's study with F.
C. van Dyck, Jr., his earliest recital program, and his post
at Wellesley College where he was college organist as well as
conductor of the college choir. This post prompted his
writing for the organ. The place of the organ in Thompson's
oeuvre is given a careful account: from the First Symphony
(1929) with its "concertante organ part," the Nativity
According to St. Luke (1960-1961), A Psalm of Thanksgiving
(1967), The Mirror of St. Anne (1972), A Hymn for Scholars
and Pupils (1973), to the largest contribution he made to the
organ's repertory, the Twenty Chorale Preludes, Four
Inventions and a Fugue (1947-1959). This latter is a
collection of works accumulated from his counterpoint classes
at Harvard.

B212.   --------, compiler. Randall Thompson: On Choral
            Composition, Essays and Reflections. Special
            issue of American Choral Review XXII/2 (April
            1980).

Contains Thompson's "Writing for the Amateur Chorus, A
Chance and a Challenge," (See T19), "On Contrapuntal
Technique," (See T12, "Model Counterpoint . . . "), "The
Story of an Alleluia," (See T17), and Urrows's "Five Love
Songs: Reflections on a Recent Work" (See B209). Preface by
Alfred Mann. Frontispiece: photograph of the composer
working at a table in front of his piano.

B213.   [Unsigned] "U. Va. Singers to Take Part in RM
            Festival." Lynchburg [Va.] Advance (13 April
            1946).

Randolph Macon's music department's annual spring
festival, held on the 22nd and 23rd of April, featured
Thompson's music in Smith Memorial Auditorium. Thompson was
on the campus with the University of Virginia Glee Club and
its director Stephen D. Tuttle. Photo of Thompson.

B214.   Walz, Jay. "Meet the Composer: (II) Randall
            Thompson." Musical America LXIV/14 (10
            November 1944), 8; 23.

One of the earliest personal profiles of Thompson for the general American public. Walz talked with Thompson during his time at the University of Virginia, where after only three years Thompson "hero-worshipp[ed] the guy [Jefferson] like a native." Thompson explains his philosophy of composition, which was established during his three years in Rome. He points to the fact that he feels his compositions are successful if they are performed enthusiastically by, for example, a Baptist church in the panhandle country, rather than by their acceptance by an audience at Carnegie Hall. And his music is more widely performed than that of many of his fellow colleagues whose names "create sensations" when they appear on programs. The Guggenheim Memorial Foundation report for 1941 and 1942 showed that "17 Thompson works received a total of 106 performances, not including inumerable repetitions of solo pices, notably songs, presented by artists on tour." Photos of the composer accompany this profile which finds Thompson in that period in which he was composing his Third Symphony.

B215.   --------. "Virginia Festival; Jamestown Celebrates the 1607 Landing." The New York Times (7 April 1957), Sect. 2, 9.

Thompson's Ode to the Virginian Voyage was premiered at the first of a series of concerts celebrating the 350th anniversary of the landing of the first English-speaking settlers in America. The work was performed before British and American notables in the new Phi Beta Kappa Memorial Hall on the campus of William and Mary in Willamsburg. 120 singers of the Norfolk Civic Chorus and the William and Mary Choir, and the Norfolk Symphony Orchestra were led by Edgar Schenkman. After the performance there was a shouting ovation in which the "composer joined."

Thompson had been approached one year earlier about a commission, which was to be a setting of Drayton's text. Thompson read the poem a number of times and had to consider the problems of several lines, such as "And useful sassafras," "In kenning of the shore," and "industrious Hakluyt," a reference to the geographer Hakluyt who gave Drayton his view of the New World. Thompson finally decided the text was worth the trouble in tackling these problems. "Industrious Hakluyt" became a four-voice fugue that brings the work to its climax.

Thompson turned some of the lyrical lines about Virginia's natural beauties into the ballad, "Virginia, Earth's Only Paradise."

B216.   Watanabe, Ruth.   "Autograph Scores from the
             American Composers' Concerts, 1925-1930."
             University of Rochester Library Bulletin 17
             (Spring 1962), 58-62.

    Howard Hanson, Director of the Eastman School of Music,
began the American Composers' Concerts in 1925 with the
distinct idea of promoting the music of American composers.
This particular series of concerts was succeeded by the
Annual Festivals of American music, begun in 1931, and the
two annual Symposia of American Music, begun in 1935.   By
1962 the series of Festivals of American music was in its
32nd year.   The Sibley Music Library of the University of
Rochester became the repository for the "collection of
compositions representing the best of American creative
effort.   By the end of the 1959 season over a thousand pieces
had been performed at [these series], out of which 489
compositions by 355 writers were given their world premieres,
and some fifteen others were given their first American
performance."   Watanabe lists the works performed by the
Rochester Philharmonic Orchestra during the American
Composers' Concerts; Thompson is represented by his Pierrot
and Cothurnus, The Piper at the Gates of Dawn, and the First
Symphony.

B217.   --------.   "The Sibley Music Library of The Eastman
             School of Music, University of Rochester." MLA
             Notes 33/4 (June 1977), 783-802.

    "Between 1925 and 1940 autograph scores by American
composers Chadwick, Foote, Hill, MacDowell, Mason, Porter,
Rogers, Thompson, White, Harris, Copland, Bacon, Antheil, and
Diamond were added [to the Sibley Music library]; some were
obtained through purchase, while others were presented to the
library through the American Composers' Concerts and the
annual Festivals of American Music, instituted at the Eastman
School of Music by Director Howard Hanson in 1925 and 1930,
respectively, and featuring performances by the Rochester
Philharmonic Orchestra of compositions by young native
writers."

B218.   Watkins, Glenn.   Soundings: Music in the 20th
             Century. New York: Schirmer Books, 1988.

    Thompson appears with "Other Americans," those born from
about 1910 to 1950 and who "came to maturity during that time
and period and who helped secure the notion of an American
school."   He lists Thompson's Jazz Poem under jazz-
influenced works by Americans, c. 1915-1930.

B219.   Webster, Daniel. "A Composer who was distinctly American." The Philadelphia Inquirer (11 July 1984), 1-G; 3.

Obituary. "His career peaked in the 1940s and he lived to see his music overshadowed by that of a generation enthralled by the model of Arnold Schoenberg. . . . His work affirmed the structural power of tonality and took on its probity through his unfailing sense of melody. The shapes of his melodies remain in mind after the performance; audiences could sing his music on the way home from the concerts.

"Such immediacy went out of style in the 1960s, and Thompson's own productivity declined in the '70s." While Thompson may have outlived his music, "audiences surely will hear that American freshness again when Thompson's symphonies and chamber music are taken up in the future."

B220.   White, J. Perry. Twentieth Century Choral Music: An Annotated Bibliography of Music Suitable for Use by High School Choirs. Metuchen, New Jersey: The Scarecrow Press, 1982.

A useful guide with comments on the style, degree of difficulty, usage, and range of those choral compositions that White feels high school choirs are capable of performing, including Alleluia (a "'classic' often performed but still a marvelous work. Extremely difficult to maintain intonation and intensity throughout the work. Not for the beginning choir.") Also here: The Best of Rooms, and The Last Words of David.

B221.   Widder, Milton. "Ringwall Program at Hall Varied Entertaining Bill." Cleveland Press (22 February 1946).

Brief mention of performance of Thompson's Second Symphony in performance by the Cleveland Orchestra under Rudolph Ringwall. "The Thompson, in spite of its shortcomings, is a catchy piece with spirit; . . . ."

B222.   Wienandt, Elwyn A. "Choral Music." MLA Notes 24/2 (December 1967), 357.

Review of the piano/vocal score of Thompson's oratorio The Passion According to Saint Luke. Wienandt finds fault with the fact that Thompson did not have a narrator for his work. Thompson chose to let the chorus identify for the audience the characters and provide "a rapid thrust of expository

material." Wienandt finds it "difficult to speak of the
music of this setting. Much of its difficulty arises from
the lengthy text and Thompson's allocation of material to the
chorus and soloists. His decision to deal only with the
biblical material . . . and to avoid the insertion of poetic
segments for solos or chorus robs the piece of any moments of
lyrical interest."

B223.   Williams, Alexander. "Music."   Boston Herald (7
            October 1939).

   Review of second concert of American composers's music
conducted by Koussevitsky at Symphony Hall in Boston.
Thompson's Second Symphony was on the program. Williams
found it "something of a disappointment, for we recall having
liked it very much some years ago. It now appears as a very
much too conventional work, with a good deal that is merely
competent padding. The slow movement, however, is a charming
piece of writing."

B224.   Woodworth, G. Wallace.   Boston Symphony Program
            Notes, 1947-1948. Tuesday Evening Series, No.
            5.

   Notes for performances of Thompson's Alleluia and The
Peaceable Kingdom.

B225.   [Unsigned] "World Premiere to be Today at Emory &
            Henry College."   Bristol Virginia-Tennessean
            (30 October 1983).

   Article in Bristol, Virginia's evening paper on the
premiere of Thompson's Twelve Canticles dedicated to the
Concert Choir of Emory and Henry College of Emory, Virginia.
"At age 84, Thompson admits that the Canticles may be his
last composition, and he shyly says they may be his best. The
work is "based on 12 of his favorite Biblical passages or
phrases."
   David Francis Urrows, Thompson's "musical colleague, accompanied him on this trip. Urrows actually set much of the
work on paper as Thompson dictated it to him."

B226.   [Unsigned] "Yaddo Group Gives Annual Concerts."
            The New York Times (19 September 1937), Sect.
            N, 8.

   Twenty-three Americans were among the thirty composers
represented on the four public programs at the Yaddo Festival

of American Music at Saratoga Springs, New York.   "The composers are only in part familiar names—Porter, Richard Donovan of Yale (who conducts the orchestra here), Randall Thompson, Arthur Shepherd (long Cleveland's favorite native son) and Otto Luening of Bennington College."   These composers and others were mixed with older music, Mozart, Handel, and Bach.

B227.   Zuck, Barbara.   A History of Musical Americanism.
            Studies in Musicology, No. 19.   Ann Arbor,
            Michigan: UMI Research Press, 1980.

   Zuck mentions Thompson's Testament of Freedom as a work representing the way composers related their fundamental beliefs to American heroes or historical figures.   This was part of the musical Americanism of the Second World War. Zuck mistakenly places Thompson in the Boulangerie.
   She quotes from Thompson's 1932 article in which he pointed to the "use of jazz and Negro spirituals as manifestations of the nationalist trend. . . ."   It was rare in 1932 but it became commonplace in the 1940s.
   Americana "represents a general nostalgia for America's rural and small-town past" and as well is representative of the trend to be "non controversial."

B228.   "To the Editor of the New York Times."   The New
            York Times (17 April 1932), Sect. 8, 6.

   "A New Symphony of Randall Thompson's was performed in Rochester for the first time on March 24, at one of the American Composers' Concerts, under the direction of Dr. Howard Hanson.   Important for the American composer as these concerts are, they should be, as well, opportunities for the public to discover outstanding works which deserve repeated performances.
   Feeling that this Second Symphony of Thompson's is a work of vitality and beauty, and one which is outstanding among the works of our country, we earnestly hope that it will find a place on regular symphonic programs, ..."
   Emanuel Balaban, Leopold Mannes, Bernard Rogers, Edward Royce, Sandor Vas; Rochester, April 12, 1932

Dictionary, Encyclopedia, And Brief Citations

Ammer, Christine. The Harper Dictionary of Music, 2nd edition. New York: Harper & Row Publishers, 1987, p. 440.

Anderson, E. Ruth. Contemporary American Composers: A Biographical Dictionary, 2nd edition. Boston: G. K. Hall, 1982, p. 517.

Arnold, Corliss. Organ Literature: A Comprehensive Survey, 2nd edition, 2 vols. Metuchen, New Jersey: Scarecrow Press, Inc., 1984. Vol. II, p. 492.

The ASCAP Biographical Dictionary, 4th edition, compiled for the American Society of Composers, Authors and Publishers by the Jacques Cattell Press. New York: R. R. Bowker Co., 1980, p. 505.

Åstrand, Hans, editor-in-chief. Sohlmans Musiklexikon, rev. and engl. edition. Stockholm: Sohlmans Förlag, 1975-1978. Vol. V, p. 614.

Berman, Laurence, editor. Words and Music: The Composer's View; A Medley of Problems and Solutions Compiled in Honor of G. Wallace Woodworth by Sundry Hands. Department of Music: Harvard University, 1972, p. 1; p. 6. Thompson's The Eternal Dove (SATB) is printed here pp. 123-32.

Blom, Eric, compiler. Everyman's Dictionary of Music. London: J. M. Dent & Sons, 1954, p. 604.

Broder, Nathan. "Thompson, Randall." Grove's Dictionary of Music and Musicians, 5th edition, 10 volumes, edited by Eric Blom. London: Macmillan, 1954. Vol. VIII, pp. 429-30. Peggy Glanville-Hicks prepared the catalog of works.

--------. "Thompson, Randall." Die Musik in Geschichte und Gegenwart, 16 vols., edited by Friedrich Blume. Kassel and Basel: Bärenreiter-Verlag, 1949-1979. Vol. XIII (1960), cols. 366-67.

Bull, Storm. Index to Biographies of Contemporary Composers. New York: Scarecrow Press, 1964. Vol. I, p. 367.

--------. Index to Biographies of Contemporary Composers. Metuchen, New Jersey: Scarecrow Press, 1974. Vol. II, p. 504.

--------. Index to Biographies of Contemporary Composers. Metuchen, New Jersey: Scarecrow Press, 1987. Vol. III, p. 764.

Butterworth, Neil. A Dictionary of American Composers. New York: Garland Publishing Co., 1984, pp. 466-68.

Chase, Gilbert. America's Music: From the Pilgrims to the Present. New York: McGraw-Hill Book Company, Inc. 1955, pp. 538-40.
Thompson does not appear in Chase's 1987 third edition.

Claghorn, Charles Eugene. Biographical Dictionary of American Music. West Nyack, New York: Parker Publishing Co., 1973, p. 437.

Deri, Otto. Exploring Twentieth-Century Music. New York: Holt, Rinehart and Winston, Inc., 1968, p. 474.

Dougherty, F. Mark, and Susan H. Simon, editors. Secular Choral Music in Print, 2nd edition, 2 vols. Philadelphia: Musicdata, Inc., 1987. Vol. 2, p. 1003.

Downes, Irene, editor. Olin Downes on Music: A Selection from his Writings During the Half-Century 1906 to 1955. New York: Simon and Schuster, 1957. Reprint. New York: Greenwood Press, 1968, p. 281; 283.

Ellinwood, Leonard. The History of American Church Music. New York: Morehouse-Gorham Company, 1953, p. 143; 165.

Eslinger, Gary S. and F. Mark Dougherty, editors, Sacred Choral Music in Print, 2nd edition, 2 vols. Philadelphia: Musicdata, 1985. Vol. 1b, pp. 1139-40.

Espina, Noni.   Repertoire for the Solo Voice: a fully
annotated Guide to works for the solo voice published in
modern editions and covering material from the 13th century
to the present, 2 vols.   Metuchen, New Jersey: Scarecrow
Press, Inc. 1977, Vol. II, p. 207.
The particulars given on "My Master Hath a Garden," "The
Passenger," and "Velvet Shoes."

--------.   Vocal Solos for Prostestant Services.   New
York: Vita 'Arte, 1974, pp. 125-26.
Three entries: "Lullaby" and "My Soul doth magnify the
Lord," from The Nativity According to St. Luke, and "My
Master Hath a Garden."

--------.   Vocal Solos for Christian Churches,   3rd
edition.   Metuchen, New Jersey: Scarecrow Press, 1984, p.
140; 163.
Three entries: "Lullaby" and "My Soul doth magnify the
Lord," from The Nativity According to St. Luke, and "My
Master Hath a Garden." Choral Music: two entries.

Evans, Margaret R.   Sacred Cantatas: An Annotated
Bibliography, 1960-1979.   Jefferson & London: McFarland,
1982, p. 186.

Ewen, David, editor.   The New Book of Modern Composers,
3rd edition, revised and enlarged.   New York: Alfred A.
Knopf, 1961, p. 40.

--------, compiler and editor.   American Composers Today:
A Biographical and Critical Guide.   New York: The H. W.
Wilson Co., 1949, pp. 242-43.

Forbes, Elliot.   "Thompson, Randall."   The New Grove
Dictionary of American Music, 4 vols.,   edited by H. Wiley
Hitchcock and Stanley Sadie.   London: Macmillan, 1986.   Vol.
IV, pp. 383-85.
Much of the same material found in the 1980 New Grove
Dictionary of Music and Musicians.

Gaster, Adrian, editor.   International Who's Who in Music
and Musicians's Directory,   9th ed.   Cambridge, England:
International Who's Who in Music, 1980, p. 726.

Gatti, Guido, editor. La Musica: Dizionario. Turin: Unione Tipografico-Editrice Torinese, 1968-1971. Vol. II, p. 1305-06.

Gradenwitz, Peter. Leonard Bernstein: The Infinite Variety of a Musician. New York: Oswald Wolff Books, 1987, p. 3; 9; 16; 29; 30; 31.

Gray, Michael, compiler. Classical Music Discographies, 1976-1988: A Bibliography. Westport, CT.: Greenwood Press, 1989, p. 263.

Greene, David Mason. Green's Biographical Encyclopedia of Composers. New York, New York: Doubleday and Co., 1985, p. 1138.

Greene, Frank, compiler. Composers on Record; An Index to Biographical Information on 14,000 Composers Whose Music Has Been Recorded. Metuchen, New Jersey: Scarecrow Press, 1985, p. 523.

Griffiths, Paul. The Thames and Hudson Encyclopedia of 20th-Century Music. London: Thames and Hudson, 1986, p. 181.

Gurlitt, Wilibald, editor. Riemann Musik Lexikon, 12th enlarged and newly-edited edition, 3 vols. Mainz: B. Schott's Söhne, 1961. Personenteil, Vol II, 792.

Hadley, Benjamin, ed. Britannica Book of Music. Garden City, New York: Doubleday/Britannica Books, 1980, p. 808.

Hitchcock, H. Wiley. Music in the United States: A Historical Introduction, 3rd edition. Englewood Cliffs, New Jersey: Prentice Hall, 1988, p. 190.

Honegger, Marc, editor. Dictionnaire de la Musique, 2 vols. Paris: Bordas, 1970. Vol. II, p. 1093.

Hovland, Michael, compiler. Musical Settings of American Poetry. Music Reference Collection # 8. Westport, Ct.: Greenwood Press, 1986.

Hovland lists poets set by Thompson: Stephen Vincent Benét,
Robert Frost and Elinor Wylie.

Howe, Mark Anthony DeWolfe. The Boston Symphony Orchestra,
1881-1931.   Boston: Houghton Mifflin, 1931.   Reprint.
Semicentennial edition, revised and extended in collaboration
with John N. Burk.   New York: Da Capo Press, 1978, p. 225.

Hutcheson, Ernest.   The Literature of the Piano, 3rd
edition, revised and brought up to date by Rudolph Ganz.   New
York: Alfred A. Knopf, 1972, p. 402.

The Institute of American Music of the University of
Rochester; American Composers' Concerts and Festivals of
American Music, 1925-1971 Cumulative Report.   Rochester, New
York, 1972,   p. 39; 69.

Jablonski, Edward.   The Encyclopedia of American Music.
Garden City, New York: Doubleday & Co., 1981, pp. 299-300.

Kennedy, Michael.   The Concise Oxford Dictionary of Music,
3rd edition.   Based on the original publication by Percy
Scholes.   London: Oxford University Press, 1980, p. 655.

--------.   The Oxford Dictionary of Music.   New York:
Oxford University Press, 1985, pp. 729-30.

Leinsdorf, Erich.   Cadenza: A Musical Career.   Boston:
Houghton Mifflin Co., 1976, p. 145.

Meckna, Michael.   Virgil Thomson: A Bio-Bibliography.
Westport, CT.:   Greenwood Press, 1986, p. 4.
Thompson was a Harvard classmate of Virgil Thomson.

Michel, Francois, editor.   Encyclopédie de la Musique, 3
vols.   Paris: Fasquelle editeurs, 1958-1961.   Vol. III L-Z,
1961,   pp. 793-94.

Nardone, Thomas R., James H. Nye, and Mark Resnick,
editors.   Choral Music in Print.   Vol. I: Sacred Choral
Music; Vol. II: Secular Choral Music.   Philadelphia,
Musicdata, 1974, Vol. I, p. 577-78; Vol. II, p. 532-33.

Vol. II: Secular Choral Music mistakenly lists Randall
Thompson as the composer of "Cousin Jedediah" (by H. S.
Thompson), "Easy Songs For Boys" and "Echo Carol" (both
probably also by H. S. Thompson), and "Softly and Tenderly"
(by Will Lamartine Thompson).

Nardone, Thomas R., editor. Choral Music in Print. 1976
Supplement. Philadelphia: Musicdata, 1976, p. 205 (Sacred);
p. 386 (Secular).

Pavlakis, Christopher. The American Music Handbook.   New
York: The Free Press, 1974, p. 4; 183; 356; 577.

Peyser, Joan. Bernstein: A Biography. New York: Beech
Tree Books, 1987, p. 70; 80; 81.

--------. The New Music: The Sense behind the Sound.
New York: Delacorte Press, 1971, p. 163.

Pirrotta, Nino. "The Eda Kuhn Loeb Music Library."
Harvard Library Bulletin XII/3 (Autumn 1958), p. 410.

Sartori, Claudio, editor-in-chief. Enciclopedia della
Musica, 4 vols. Milan: G. Ricordi, 1963-1964. Vol. IV, p.
1049.

Scholes, Percy A. The Oxford Companion to Music, 9th
edition. New York: Oxford University Press, 1955, p. 1026.

Simon, Susan H., editor. Sacred Choral Music in Print.
1988 Supplement. Philadelphia: Musicdata, Inc., 1988, p.
187.

Slonimsky, Nicolas, editor. Baker's Biographical
Dictionary of Musicians, 7th edition. New York: Schirmer
Books, 1984, pp.2304-05.

Stebbins, Lucy Poate and Richard Poate Stebbins. Frank
Damrosch: Let the People Sing. Durham, N. C.:   Duke
University Press, 1945, p. 223; 262.

Stoddard, Hope. _Symphony Conductors of the U. S. A._ New York: Thomas Y. Crowell Co., 1957, p. 30.

Thompson, Oscar, editor-in-chief. _The International Cyclopedia of Music and Musicians,_ 11th edition, edited by Bruce Bohle. New York: Dodd, Mead & Company, 1985, p. 2270.

Tortolano, William. _Original Music for Men's Voices: A Selected Bibliography,_ 2nd edition. Metuchen, New Jersey: Scarecrow Press, Inc., 1981, pp. 98-99.
Seven entries

Ulrich, Homer. _A Survey of Choral Music._ New York: Harcourt Brace Jovanovich, Inc., 1973, p. 188; 211. _Mass of the Holy Spirit, Americana, The Peaceable Kingdom,_ and _The Testament of Freedom._

Westrup, Jack and Frank Lloyd Harrison, editors. _The New College Encyclopedia of Music,_ revised by Conrad Wilson. New York: W. W. Norton, 1976, p. 547.

Who's Who in America, 43rd edition, 2 vols. Chicago: Marquis Who's Who, Inc., 1984. Vol. II, p. 3255.

Woodworth, G. Wallace. _The World of Music._ Cambridge, Mass.: The Belknap Press of Harvard University Press, 1964, p. 42.

Oral History Collections

Oral History Research Office. Butler Library. Columbia University in the City of New York. Interviewer in each case is unknown.

1. Interview with Robert Lester: comments on Thompson's _College Music._

2. From interview with Otto Luening: remembrances of Howard Hanson and his American Composers Concerts. On Thompson: "He was an extremely conservative guy who actually wrote I would say very much by ear. Also in the Second Symphony he first got into jazz--putting jazz in the orchestra--with great success. I found some of his works--a

string quartet and also choral music--deceptively simple, but very clearly heard, which explains why they are very successful. . . . They are unpretentious in a way. He himself--I had a lot of dealings with him in various committees and so on--was always very much the academic, the Harvard professor in his tastes and everything. [He] sort of made great predictions and so on, [was] a fairly knowledgeable man, and in his music rather simple and direct, which I respected."

Oral History Collection (#9800-OH-12), Manuscripts Division, Special Collections Department, University of Virginia Library. Charlottesville, Virginia. Interview with Thompson by Jean Bonin made 18 October 1973.

Thompson recalls the genesis of The Testament of Freedom, written in 1942 for the University of Virginia. After taking on his teaching post at the University, Thompson discovered he was surrounded by the likes of Dumas Malone, Bernie Mayo, and Helen Bullock who were all interested in aspects of the study of Thomas Jefferson. Professor Harry Pratt first approached Thompson about writing a piece on a Jeffersonian topic. For Founder's Day, 1943 Thompson also made an arrangement of "Hail Liberty the Sweetest Bliss--A Quick Step to the New President's March" for a small band. Thompson recalled a moving performance of Testament at service for F. D. Roosevelt, and Koussevitsky's intuition. Thompson remembers friends from his Charlottesville years: John and Louise Powell, Agnes and Harry Pratt, and the University's President: [John Lloyd] Newcomb, A. K. Davis, Arthur Kyle, Winston and Marie Wilkinson, Ernest and Sally Mead, Robert and Blanche Webb, Charles and Rosalie Henderson, Stephen D. Tuttle and many others, including the students he taught. On John Powell: ". . . an important influence on my own thinking and feeling about music." Thompson felt that he owed a great deal to the University of Virginia for all that he gained from his five years there.

National Public Radio. Morning Edition with Bob Edwards. ME 831028. Interview with Thompson occassioned by the premiere of his Twelve Canticles in Emory, Virginia. Interview was broadcast 28 October 1983.

Vienna Historical Society. Vienna, Maine. Thompson gave the Society in 1983 a dictated "report" about his early associations with Vienna, Maine. See B108 and B211.

Discography

Between 1979 and 1983 there appeared four discographies, two exclusively and two partially, devoted to Thompson's recorded works. They are listed here chronologically.
D=Discography
R=Recording

Discography

D1.   Skinner, Robert, compiler. A Randall Thompson Discography: Preliminary Edition. Issued by the Eda Kuhn Loeb Music Library, Harvard University on the occasion of the composer's 80th birthday, 21 April 1979.

This was a preliminary discography that covered the commerical recordings of Thompson's music. The few "semi-private" recordings included were those in which Thompson took part. The recording (Yaddo 8A) of "Velvet Shoes" made at the 1937 Yaddo Festival, probably the first recording made of Thompson's music, is not included here. Performer index.

D2.   --------. "A Randall Thompson Discography." Journal of the Association for Recorded Sound XII/3 (1980), 184-95.

This list is a revision of the 1979 work above; it covers only commercial recordings. "'Semi-private' recordings (which included most church, school and choral festival discs) and non-commercial and non-processed materials are excluded, except for a few discs in which the composer took part."

D3.   Oja, Carol J., editor. <u>American Music Recordings. A Discography of 20th-Century U. S. Composers.</u> New York: Institute for Studies in American Music; Conservatory of Music, Brooklyn College of the City University of New York, 1982, 293-95.

Robert Skinner contributed to the Thompson list which is a supplement to his 1980 list. This list covers commercial recordings and is the most complete listing of recordings made of Thompson's work. Of the 72 items found here, only 16 were labled "currently in print" in 1982.
Benjamin DeLoach, baritone, is listed on the Yaddo 8A recording, Thompson's first, made at the 1937 Yaddo Festival.

D4.   Solow, Linda I., editor. Mary Wallace Davidson, Brenda Chasen Goldman, Geraldine E. Ostrove, associated editors. <u>The Boston Composers Project: A Bibliography of Contemporary Music/Boston Area Music Libraries.</u> Cambridge, Mass.: MIT Press, 1983.

Works are listed alphabetically under composer. The editors list discs (including commercial recordings), as well as reels and cassette tapes; many of these are non-commercial "recordings," of which many are now long out of print. This is a valuable guide to the recorded holdings of Thompson's music found at both the Houghton Library and the Eda Kuhn Loeb Music Library at Harvard University as well as other libraries in the Boston area. Many of these "recordings," a number of which are first performances in which Thompson himself took part, were made at churches, colleges and universities throughout the United States.

Recordings

The following list of recordings focuses on available LPs, CDs, cassette tapes. Although some items have been deleted, they were widely available upon their release, reached a classic status, and thus today may sometimes be found in shops that specialize in older, out-of-print recordings, especially LPs.

R1. <u>Alleluia</u> (1940)

Roberts Wesleyan College Chorale
Robert Shewan, conductor
Bay Cities; CD <u>American Voices:</u> # BCD-1011 (1990)

R2.   Americana (1932)

     University of Michigan Chamber Choir
     Thomas Hilbish, conductor
     Recorded: 1977
     New World Recordings 219 (1978)

R3.   The Best of Rooms (1963)

     Roberts Wesleyan College Chorale
     Robert Shewan, conductor
     Bay Cities; CD American Voices: # BCD-1011 (1990)

R4.   A Feast of Praise (1963)

     Roberts Wesleyan College Chorale and Brass Ensemble
     Barbara Dechario, harp
     Robert Shewan, conductor
     Bay Cities; CD American Voices: # BCD-1011 (1990)

R5.   Frostiana (1959)

     University of Houston Symphonic Chorus
     University of Houston Orchestra
     Charles Hausmann, director
     Bay Cities; CD   (1991)

R6.   The Last Words of David (1949)

     Roberts Wesleyan College Chorale and Brass Ensemble
     Robert Shewan, conductor
     Barbara Harbach, organ
     Bay Cities; CD American Voices: # BCD-1011 (1990)

R7.   The Peaceable Kingdom (1936)

     -Pepperdine University Chorus
     Lawrence McCommas, conductor
     Recorded: May 1976
     Orion ORS-76228 (1977)

     -The Whikehart Chorale
     Lewis E. Whikehart, conductor
     Recorded: January 1964
     Lyrichord Stereo LLST 7124 (1964)

R8. First String Quartet in D Minor (1941)

Lyric Art String Quartet
Kenneth Goldsmith, violin
David Halen, violin
Lawrence Wheeler, viola
Kevin Dvorak, cello
Recorded: 1990
Bay Cities; CD (1991)

R9. Suite for Oboe, Clarinet and Viola (1940)

Crystal Chamber Soloists
Peter Christ, oboe
David Atkins, clarinet
Alan de Veritch, viola
Recorded: November 1978
Crystal S-321 (Stereo LP); (1979)
Crystal C-321 (cassette tape)
Crystal CD-321 (CD)

R10. First Symphony (1929)

Utah Symphony Orchestra; Maurice Abravanel
Alexander Schreiner, organ
Recorded: May 1978; Mormon Tabernacle, Salt Lake City
Angel S-37315 (1978); deleted

R11. Second Symphony (1931)

Vienna Symphony Orchestra; Dean Dixon, conductor
American Recording Society; ARS-4 (1951)

-Desto; D-406/DST-6404 (1964)

-Bay Cities; CD # BC1007 (1989)

New York Philharmonic; Leonard Bernstein, conductor
Recorded: 22 October 1968
Columbia MS-7392 (1970); deleted in 1973

R12. Third Symphony (1949)

Bakersfield Symphony Orchestra
John Farrer, conductor
Recorded: November 1990
Bay Cities; CD (1991)

R13. The Testament of Freedom (1943)

    Utah Symphony; Maurice Abravanel, conductor
    Utah Chorale; Newell B. Weight, director
    Recorded: May 1978; Mormon Tabernacle, Salt Lake City
    Angel S-37315 (1978); deleted

    Eastman-Rochester Orchestra and Chorus
    Howard Hanson, conductor
    Recorded: 1952; originally for Mercury MG-40000
    Eastman Rochester Archives- ERA 1007
    Pheiffer College Concert Choir
    Richard H. Brewer, conductor
    Recorded as part of the Pheiffer College Bicentennial
        Celebration in 1976
    Pheiffer 8777 (1976)

R14. Velvet Shoes (1927)

    Povla Frijsh, soprano
    Celius Dougherty, piano
    Recorded 12 April 1940
    Victor 2157B, included in set M-789

    -RCA Victor LCT-1158 Red Seal Collectors Issue (1955)
    "Critic's Choice," Chosen by Paul Hume (Music Editor of
        The Washington Post-Times Herald)

    -New World Records 247 (1976): "When I have Sung My
        Songs: The American Art Song 1900-1940

Appendix I:
Chronological
List of Compositions

1915 Anniversary (Hymn tune for Lawrenceville School
  Hymnal)
As of Old
Sonata for piano

1916 In Memoriam, F. C. van Dyck, Jr. for organ

1917 Septette for flute, clarinet, string quartet

1918 Allegro in D major for piano
Four Waltzes for Two Violins and Piano
Indianola Variations for piano
The Light of Stars

1919 All on a Summer Eve

1920 Mariner's Song
Night
Serenade in Seville
Scherzino for flageolet, violin, viola
Spring
Torches
Quintet for flute, clarinet, viola, cello, piano

1921 Scherzo in G minor for piano
Scherzo in F major for piano
Varied Air for piano

1922 A Book of Songs by Erskine Wood with
  Accompaniments for Piano by Randall
  Thompson
The Last Invocation
Piano Sonata in G Minor
Pierrot and Cothurnus: Prelude for Orchestra
The Ship Starting
Suite for Violin and Piano

1923   Piano Sonata in C minor

1924   Five Odes of Horace
                The Piper at the Gates of Dawn: Symphonic
                    Prelude
                Suite for piano
                The Wind in the Willows for string quartet

1925   The Boats were Talking for piano
                Tapestry

1926   A Ballad
                Doubts
                Five Songs for Low Voice
                The Grand Street Follies; Musical Revue
                Mazurka for piano
                Southwind
                The Straw Hat for piano; incidental music

1927   Canons
                Jazz Poem
                New Songs for New Voices: Five Songs
                    The Wild Home Pussy
                    The Echo Child
                    My Master Hath a Garden
                    Velvet Shoes
                    Some One
                Two Amens for SATB

1928   Larghetto for organ
                Pueri Hebraeorum

1929   Rosemary
                First Symphony

1931   Second Symphony

1932   Americana

1935   Little Prelude for piano
                Song after Sundown for piano

1936   The Peaceable Kingdom
                    Say ye to the righteous
                    Woe unto them
                    The noise of the multitude
                    Howl ye
                    The paper reeds by the brooks
                    But these are they that forsake the Lord;
                        For ye shall go out with joy

1937   Tarantella

1938   The Lark in the Morn (arrangement)

1940   Alleluia
            Suite for oboe, clarinet, and viola

1941   First String Quartet

1942   Solomon and Balkis

1943   Hail, Liberty, the Sweetest Bliss! (arrangement)
            Hail, Tuttle! Round for three equal voices
            Jefferson's March (arrangement)
            Lovely Peggy (arrangement)
            Tacite ombre orrende larve (arrangement)
            The Testament of Freedom

1947   Nowell
            Now I Lay Me Down to Sleep

1949   The Last Words of David
            Third Symphony
            Trio for three double basses

1951   Aria Pensée (from Tavern Club play: The
                Millionaire)
            The Jabberwocky for piano
            Prairie Home (from Tavern Club play: The
                Millionaire)

1952   Cold on the Mountain (arrangement)
            Siciliano, Love is like the wind upon the water
                (from Tavern Club play: The Gorgonzola)

1953   The Battle of Dunster Street for piano
            Felices ter (Sixth Horace Ode)

1954   A Trip to Nahant, Symphonic Fantasy
            Veritas

1955   Mass of the Holy Spirit

1956   Ode to the Virginian Voyage

1957   The Passenger

1958   Glory to God in the Highest
            Requiem

1959   Frostiana
                The Road not taken
                The Pasture
                Come in

                        The Telephone
                        A Girl's Garden
                        Stopping by Woods on a Snowy Evening
                        Choose Something like a Star
                        The Gate of Heaven

1961   The Nativity According to Saint Luke

1962   The Lord is My Shepherd

1963   The Best of Rooms
                A Feast of Praise

1964   The Passion According to Saint Luke
                Hymn: Thy Book Falls Open Lord

1966   Solstice (from Tavern Club play: Fearful
                    Symmetry)
                Chanson gourmand (from Tavern Club play:
                    Fearful Symmetry)

1967   A Psalm of Thanksgiving
                Second String Quartet

1968   The Eternal Dove

1969   Katie's Dance
                The Place of the Blest
                    The Carol of the Rose
                    The Pelican
                    The Place of the Blest
                    Alleluia, Amen

1970   Bitter-Sweet
                Twenty Chorale Preludes, Four Inventions and a
                    Fugue for Organ

1971   Antiphon
                Two Amens for string quartet
                Wedding Music

1972   A Mirror of St. Anne

1973   Fare Well
                A Hymn for Scholars and Pupils

1975   A Concord Canata
                Music for Promotion, Oh, Promotion (Tavern Club
                    play)

1977   Fuga a tre
                Two Worlds

1978   Five Love Songs
                 The Light of Stars
                 The Passenger
                 Two Worlds
                 Siciliano
                 The Happy Shore

            The Morning Stars

1983   Twelve Canticles

Appendix II:
Alphabetical
List of Compositions

Thompson's compositions as they appear in dictionary and encyclopedia entries have not been noted here. See pp. 188-94.
n=Note. For example: 52-n62. A Concord Cantata is cited on page 52 in note # 62.

Adoration, The (from The Nativity According to St. Luke) W58
Agony in the Garden, The (from The Passion According to St. Luke) W41
All on a Summer Eve W68
Allegro in D major (Piano) W80
Alleluia ix; 1; 26; 28; 30; 37; 39; 50-n43; W29; T11; T17; B3; B10; B20; B41; B51; B96; B98; B101; B119; B133; B154; B155; B166; B172; B195; B198; B212; B220; B224; R1; 217
Alleluia (from The Place of the Blest) 39; W44
Amen (# 12 of Twelve Canticles) W50
Amen and amen, alleluia (from The Leave-Taking in Requiem) W35; T15
Amens (Two) (a. SATB-1927; b. String Quartet-1971) a. 15; 42; W26a; 217 b. W26b; 54-n74
Americana (movements listed separately) 20; 26; W8; B22; B35; B41; B96; B101; B136; B159; B197; B198; B207; B227; R2
Anniversary 5; W24
Annunciation, The (from The Nativity According to St. Luke) W58
Antiphon 40; W45
Apprition, The (from The Nativity According to St. Luke) W58
Aria pensée (from The Millionaire; Tavern Club play) W113
Ariel's Fairy Song (A Book of Songs by Erskine Wood with Accompaniments for Piano by Randall Thompson) W111
Ariel's Sea Dirge (A Book of Songs by Erskine Wood with Accompaniments for Piano by Randall Thompson) W111
Arise, Shine (from Twelve Canticles) W50
As of Old 5; W25
Ave Caelorum Domina (Josquin des Prez) W113

Ballad, A W99; 217
Ballad of the Bridge, The (from A Concord Cantata) W20
Ballade des dames des temps jadis (A Book of Songs by Erskine
    Wood with Accompaniments for Piano By Randall Thompson)
    W111
Battle of Dunster Street, The W57
Be filled with the spirit (from The Call to Song in Requiem)
    W35
Best of Rooms, The W38; B220; R3
Boats were Talking, The 42; W88
Book of Songs by Erskine Wood with Accompaniments for Piano
    By Randall Thompson, A W111
Bitter-sweet 40; W45
But these are they that forsake the Lord (from The Peaceable
    Kingdom) W28

Call to Song, The (from Requiem) W35
Canon a three for equal voices, I will lift up mine eyes W110
Canons W6
Carol of the Rose, The (from The Place of the Blest) W44
Chanson gourmand (from Fearful Symmetry; Tavern Club)
    W120; 217
Choose Something Like a Star (from Frostiana) 35; W16; W17
Cold on the Mountain W117
Come in (from Frostiana) W16; W17
Concord Cantata, A (movements listed separately) 40; 52-n62;
    W20; B31
Crucifixion, The (from The Passion According St. Luke) W41

Doubts W100; 217

Echo Child, The (from New Songs for New Voices) W103
Entombment, The (from The Passion According to St. Luke) W41
Entry into Jerusalem, The (from The Passion According to St.
    Luke) W41
Eternal Dove, The 39; W43

Face answereth to face (from Twelve Canticles) W50
Fare Well 40; W19
Fearful Symmetry (Tavern Club play; incidental music) W120
Fear Thou Not (from Twelve Canticles) W50
Feast of Praise, A 37; W39; B19; B28; B41; B54; B64; B147;
    B148; B192; B193; B201; R4
Felices ter 32; 51-n51; W14; B166
Finally, Bretheren, Farewell (from Twelve Canticles) W50
Five Love Songs (movements listed separately) 40-41; 52-n59;
    W23; B209; B212
Five Odes of Horace (listed separately) 13; 32; 38; 47-n24;

51-n51; W5; B22; B41; B74; B91; B166
Five Songs for Low Voice W101; 217
Foolish men are plagued (from A Psalm of Thanksgiving) W42
For ye shall go out with joy (from The Peaceable Kingdom) W28
Four Waltzes for Two Violins and Piano W67
Frostiana (movements listed separately) 35; 38; W16; W17;
    B56; B115; B128; B137; R5
Fuga a tre W108

Garment of Praise, The (from Requiem) 35; W35
Gate of Heaven, The W36; B10; B41
Gift Outright, The (from A Concord Cantata) 52-n62; W20; B31
Girl's Garden, A (from Frostiana) W16; W17
Glory to God in the Highest 37-38; W34; B166
God Is a Spirit (from Twelve Canticles) W50
God's Bottles (from Americana) W8
God Who Gave Us Life, The (from The Testament of Freedom)
    W10; W11; W12
Good tidings to the meek (from The Triumph of Faith in
    Requiem) W35
Gorgonzola, The (Tavern Club play; incidental music) W119
Gourmet Song (originally Chanson gourmand from Fearful
    Symmetry; Tavern Club play) W120; 217
Grand Street Follies of 1926, The (incidental music) 15; W54
Gunga Din (A Book of Songs by Erskine Wood with
    Accompaniments by Randall Thompson) W111

Hail, Liberty, the Sweetest Bliss! W115; 195
Hail, Tuttle! Round for three equal voices W13
Happy Shore, The (from Five Love Songs) 41; W22; W23; B209;
    B212
Have ye not known? (from The Peaceable Kingdom) W28
He turneth the wilderness (from A Psalm of Thanksgiving) W42
Howl ye (from The Peaceable Kingdom) W28
Hymn: Thy Book Falls Open Lord W40
Hymn for Scholars and Pupils, A W47; W48; B211

I am their music (from The Garment of Praise in Requiem) W35
I Call to Remembrance (from Twelve Canticles) W50
Indian Lullaby, An (A Book of Songs by Erskine Wood with
    Accompaniments by Randall Thompson) W111
Indianola Variations 7; W81
In Memoriam, F. C. van Dyck, Jr. 5; W79
Inscription (from A Concord Cantata) W20
I shall not die without a hope (from The Testament of
    Freedom) W10; W11; W12
Institution of the Lord's Supper, The (from The Passion
    According to St. Luke) W41

Sonata in C Minor for Piano 45-n16; W86; B73
Sonata in G Minor for Piano W85
Song after Sundown (Piano) 53-n68; W91; B175
Song of Simeon (from The Nativity According to St. Luke) W58
Southwind W102
Spring W96
Staff Necromancer, The (from Americana) W8
Stopping by Woods on a Snowy Evening (from Frostiana) W16;
    W17
Straw Hat, The (incidental music) 15; W55; B111
String Quartet No. 1 in D minor 27; 28; 53-n68; W74; B20;
    B126; B198; B202; B203; R8
String Quartet No. 2 in G major 2; 38; W76
Sublime Process of Law Enforcement, The (from Americana) W8
Such as sit in darkness (from A Psalm of Thanksgiving) W42
Suite for oboe, clarinet, and viola 2; 26; W73; B159; B196;
    R9
Suite for Piano (1924) 13; 42; 46-n21; W87; B70; B134; 217
Suite for Violin and Piano W71
Summer Lullaby, A (A Book of Songs by Erskine Wood with
    Accompaniments by Randall Thompson) W111
Symphony No. One 2; 13; 18; 24; 40; 46-n19, n20; 48-n30;
    49-n35; 53-n68; W62; B49; B88; B113; B173; B198; B210;
    B211; B216; R10
Symphony No. Two in E minor 2; 18-19; 20; 24; 27; 47-n28;
    48-n30; 53-n68; W63; B6; B8; B9; B14; B16; B17; B29; B37;
    B48; B53; B60; B61; B62; B67; B69; B73; B82; B85; B92;
    B95; B104; B122; B135; B150; B158; B159; B177; B198; B202;
    B221; B223; B228; R11
Symphony No. Three in A minor 2; 29; 30; 31; 53-n68; W64; B7;
    B40; B63; B123; B198; B204; B214; R12

Tacite ombre orrende larve (Maria Cosway) W115
Tapestry W98
Tarantella 24; W9; B22
Telephone, The (from Frostiana) W16; W17
Testament of Freedom, The (movements listed separately) 28-
    29; 30; 52-n64; W10; W11; W12; B22; B51; B57; B67; B80;
    B83; B94; B113; B114; B118; B119; B156; B163; B171; B182;
    B188; B198; B206; B227; R13; 195
They that go down to the sea in ships (from A Psalm of
    Thanksgiving) W42
They wandered in the wilderness (from A Psalm of
    Thanksgiving) W42
Thou hast given him (from The Leave-Taking in Requiem) W35
Tiger Joy (from Rosemary) W7; B52
Torches (incidental music) 9; 43; W53
Trial, The (from The Passion According to St. Luke) W41
Trio for Three Double Basses W75
Trip to Nahant, Symphonic Fantasy, A 32-33; 42; W65; B50;
    B120; B184

Appendix III:
Forthcoming Publications
from E. C. Schirmer

<u>Alleluia</u> (W29) arranged for string quartet/string orchestra
by Daniel Pinkham # 4589 (1991)

Ballad (W99) # 4491 (1991)

Doubts (W100) # 4490 (1991)

Five Songs (W101) # 4494 (1991)

Gourmet Song (W120) # 4492 (1991)

<u>The Morning Stars</u> (W49) for SATB and keyboard # 4359 (1991)

Nun danket alle Gott (W52) arranged for organ solo by
Jonathan Barnhart # 4495 (1990)

The Ship Starting (W97) # 4493 (1991)

Suite (W87) (1991)

<u>Two Amens</u> (W26a) # 3078 (1992)

<u>Wedding Music</u> (W77) # 263 (1991)

Index

Persons are indexed as subject, not author, of entries.
n=Note. For example 44-n10: American Academy in Rome
appears on page 44 in note # 10.

About the Authors

CAROLINE CEPIN BENSER lives in Tuscaloosa, Alabama. She is the author of *Egon Wellesz (1885-1974): Chronicle of a Twentieth-Century Musician* and has contributed to *Alabama Heritage*.

DAVID FRANCIS URROWS, a lecturer in the Department of Music and Fine Arts at Hong Kong Baptist College, has the distinction of being Randall Thompson's final student.